TEACHING
1 KINGS

From text to message

BOB FYALL

SERIES EDITORS: DAVID JACKMAN & ADRIAN REYNOLDS

Reading Bob Fyall's *Teaching 1 Kings* is like walking into a hermeneutical candy store! He is a master at condensing the flow of a narrative, all the while keeping his finger on the jugular vein of the text. He is guilty of biblical over-stimulation. If you're planning on preaching First Kings (or preaching in it), get this book; if you're not planning to preach First Kings, get this book and you'll want to preach First Kings.

Dale Ralph Davis
Minister in Residence, First Presbyterian Church,
Columbia, South Carolina

The Teaching series is a great resource for Bible study leaders and pastors, indeed for any Christian who wants to understand their Bible better.

Mark Dever
Senior Pastor of Capitol Hill Baptist Church and
President of 9Marks, Washington, DC

North India desperately needs men and women who will preach and teach the Bible faithfully and PT's Teaching series is of great value in encouraging them to do just that. They are just what we need. We have found the books of great help in English and eagerly anticipate the day when they will be available in Hindi also.

Isaac Shaw
Executive Director,
Delhi Bible Institute, Delhi, India

This teaching series, written by skilled and trustworthy students of God's Word, helps us to understand the Bible, believe it and obey it. I commend it to all Bible readers, but especially those whose task it is to teach the inspired Word of God.

Peter Jensen
Former Archbishop of Sydney, Sydney, Australia

TEACHING
I KINGS

From text to message

BOB FYALL

SERIES EDITORS: DAVID JACKMAN & ADRIAN REYNOLDS

PT RESOURCES

CHRISTIAN
FOCUS

Copyright © Proclamation Trust Media 2015

ISBN: 978-1-78191-605-6

10 9 8 7 6 5 4 3 2 1

Published in 2015
by
Christian Focus Publications Ltd.,
Geanies House, Fearn, Ross-shire,
IV20 1TW, Scotland, Great Britain
with
Proclamation Trust Resources,
Willcox House, 140-148 Borough High Street,
London, SE1 1LB, England, Great Britain.
www.proctrust.org.uk

www.christianfocus.com

Cover design by DUFI-art.com

Printed and bound by Nørhaven, Denmark

Contents

SERIES PREFACE

Like many other books containing Old Testament story, 1 and 2 Kings are both well known and obscure. Certain stories are remarkably familiar and part of regular Sunday school curriculum material. Others are hardly ever preached or taught and contain gems of familiarity only because they pop up from time to time in reading plans.

This mix is to be lamented as God has divinely inspired the whole Bible, including books within it. The books of 1 and 2 Kings stand as a whole and whilst providing fertile passages for family services, it is good for the preacher or teacher to consider them in their unity, rather than as a collection of stories from which we selectively pick and mix.

Teaching 1 and 2 Kings (of which this is the first of two volumes) is, therefore, an important contribution to our series. We need help getting the familiar parts right and tackling the less well-known stories. Bob's volume does both of these things, appropriately pointing us to the King who would one day come in David's line.

The volumes are purposely practical, seeking to offer real help for those involved in teaching the Bible to others. The preacher or teacher, the sermon or talk, and the listener are the key 'drivers' in this series. The Introductory Section contains basic 'navigation' material to get you into the text of Kings, covering aspects like structure and planning a preaching series. The 'meat' of the book then works systematically through the major sections of Kings, suggesting preaching or teaching units, including sermon outlines and questions for Bible studies. These are not there to take the hard work out of preparation, but as a starting point to get you thinking about how to preach the material or prepare a Bible study.

Teaching 1 Kings brings the number of published volumes in the series to fourteen. We are encouraged at how the series is developing and the positive comments from the people that really matter – those at the chalkface of Christian ministry, working hard at the Word, week in week out, to proclaim the unsearchable riches of Christ.

Our thanks must go to Celia Reynolds for help with proofreading and checking references. As ever, our warm gratitude goes to the team at Christian Focus for their committed partnership in this project.

David Jackman & Adrian Reynolds
Series Editors
London 2014

Author's Preface

Three outstanding history teachers in my school days gave me an abiding love for the subject and showed how the past could live in the hands of gifted and imaginative communicators. This easily transferred to a love of biblical history and narrative. The books of 1 and 2 Kings have therefore been a part of Scripture I have long enjoyed, and when I started to study the Old Testament seriously I returned to them with renewed interest and with a growing appreciation of their great importance in the big story and their powerful message for today.

Probably like most preachers who tackle these books, I turned first to the Elijah/Elisha stories with their compelling characters and strong narrative drive. However, it soon became apparent that these stories were even more compelling when seen in the overall flow of the books.

Over the years I have preached both longer and shorter series on the books. In my first ministry in Bannockburn, Scotland, I did a series of moderate length on Elijah and

Elisha. In my years in Durham, England, in the congregation now known as Christchurch (then Claypath) a number of series were preached and, I trust, a growing understanding of the overall message emerged. A longer series, covering much of both books, was preached in the Tron Church, Glasgow, over the period 2008-10.

I have also had the privilege of teaching large sections of the book in other contexts. In 2002-05 I taught a module on 'Preaching OT narrative' in Cranmer Hall, St John's College, Durham where I was once on the staff. That module was repeated at the International Christian College, Glasgow in 2007. At Cornhill Scotland, I often use material from Kings, especially when teaching how to preach biblical narrative.

Plainly I have gained a great deal from those who have commented on the sermons and lectures and I am most grateful for that. I have also learned much from commentators, and mention that in the 'Further Reading' section. As always, I have learned from those I disagree with and am thankful for all whose work has fed into mine.

This *Teaching* book has also given me the opportunity to engage with parts of the books I have passed over lightly in the past. I trust it will encourage others to study Kings as a whole and not simply pick out the purple passages. The length can be daunting, but when we consider that the time covered is some five hundred years we see that the author has been ruthlessly selective in including what carries on his theme.

Like the other *Teaching* volumes this is not a commentary, although it engages closely with the text, nor simply a collection of sermons although there are suggested sermons and Bible study questions. Thus it will be most useful if the reader does some detailed exegetical work on the text first. Often there is more than one suggested sermon outline to emphasize that once you really get into what the passage says there are many ways of expressing and applying the message.

It is my prayer that this book will help many to explore the books of Kings and be captured by their riches, and preach and teach their God-honouring and Christ-anticipating message.

Bob Fyall
Glasgow 2014

How to use this Book

This book aims to help the preacher or teacher understand the central aim and purpose of the text, in order to preach or teach it to others. Unlike a commentary, therefore, it does not go into great exegetical detail. Instead it helps us to engage with the themes of Kings, to keep the big picture in mind, and to think about how to present it to our hearers.

'Part 1: Introducing Kings' examines the book's themes and structure as well as seeing why it is considered a difficult book to preach. This material is crucial to our understanding of the whole book, which will shape the way we preach each section to our congregations. As a preliminary to the rest of the book, it divides the two Bible books up into manageable units. This preliminary work leaves us with three major sections: 1 Kings 1–11, 1 Kings 12–2 Kings 17 and 2 Kings 18–25. These will be covered over two volumes with, for ease of use, 1 Kings being considered in volume 1 and 2 Kings in volume 2.

The remainder of the two volumes contains separate chapters on each preaching unit considered in Part One. The structure of each chapter is the same: it begins with a brief introduction to the unit followed by a section headed 'Listening to the text.' This section outlines the structure and context of the unit and takes the reader through a section-by-section analysis of the text. All good biblical preaching begins with careful, detailed listening to the text, and this is true for Kings as much as any other book.

Each chapter then continues with a section called 'From text to message.' This suggests a main theme and aim for each preaching unit (including how the unit relates to the overall theme of the book) and then some possible sermon outlines. These suggestions are nothing more than that – suggestions designed to help the preacher think about his own division of the text and the structure of the sermon. We are great believers in every preacher constructing his own outlines, because they need to flow from our personal encounter with God in the text. Downloading other people's sermons or trying to breathe life into someone else's outlines are strategies doomed to failure. They may produce a reasonable talk, but in the long term, they are disastrous to the preacher himself since he needs to live in the Word and the Word to live in him, if he is to speak from the heart of God to the hearts of his congregation. However, these sections provide a few very basic ideas about how an outline on some of these passages might shape up. There are also some helpful bullet points on possible lines of application with particular focus on how lines to Christ may be drawn.

Each chapter concludes with some suggested questions for a group Bible study split into two types: questions to help *understand* the passage and questions to help *apply* the passage. Not all the questions would be needed for a study, but they give some ideas for those who are planning a study series.

The aim of good questions is always to drive the group into the text, to explore and understand its meaning more fully. This keeps the focus on Scripture and reduces speculation and the mere exchange of opinions. Remember the key issues are always, 'What does the text say?' and then 'What does it mean'? Avoid the 'What does it mean to you?' type of question. It is much better to discuss the application more generally and personally after everyone understands the intended meaning, so that the Bible really is in the driving-seat of the study, not the participants' opinions, prejudices or experiences! These studies will be especially useful in those churches where Bible-study groups are able to study the book at the same time as it is preached, a practice we warmly commend. This allows small groups to drive home understanding, and especially application, in the week after the sermon has been preached, ensuring it is applied to the daily lives of the congregation.

Part I
Introducing Kings

I

Getting our Bearings in Kings

Introduction

For many, tackling the books of Kings is like embarking on a rather unfamiliar sea with just a few well-known islands, such as some of the stories of Elisha and Elijah. We reach these with relief and see the rest of the voyage as rather tedious and uninspiring. The brief notes on individual kings in passages such as 1 Kings 15 and 16 or 2 Kings 13–15, not to say the long details of temple building in 1 Kings 6 and 7, seem dull and lacking in either narrative drive or spiritual nourishment. Faced with this, many preachers focus on the purple passages and neglect the rest of the books.

This is a great loss because, as I hope to show, the books are a unified and powerful narrative with a coherent message, and both strong narrative interest and relevant theology. There is a lot of hard work to be done, but this will be wonderfully rewarding as we see God working His purpose out with flawed people, bringing His kingdom nearer, and pointing to the day when the true King will come. Our horizons will be expanded and our faith quickened as we look beyond our own little sphere and see God in the sweep of history. Our confidence in His Word will grow as we see that Word raise up and depose kings and empires; we will be able to read this as part of God's story about God, where the best of His servants only make it by grace and where human leadership depends on faithfulness to the Lord.

There are important issues of background to be covered as we approach these books, and we will need to look at such matters as place in the Bible, historical situation, genre and particular problems such as idolatry and judgment. Much of the terrain will be unfamiliar, but if we study diligently under the guidance of the Spirit we shall hear the Master's voice and see His face.

Kings in its setting
The place of Kings in the Bible

Kings is one book and the division is because of the amount of material which can usefully be included in one scroll (if we may compare the sublime to the ridiculous, this is also why the present guide is also coming out in two volumes!). Thus we will refer to Kings as 'the book' rather than 'the books'. Its place in the Bible is first of all as a significant part of the Big Story which runs from creation to new creation and, more specifically along with 1 and 2 Samuel, a history first of the united monarchy and then the divided kingdoms: the northern kingdom of Israel which fell to Assyria in 722 B.C. and the southern kingdom of Judah which was taken into exile in Babylon in 587 B.C. But the first hint of the story of the monarchy comes much earlier when God promises to Abraham (Gen. 17:6) and repeats to Jacob (Gen. 35:11) that kings would come from them. So this story is part of the promises to the patriarchs and points forward to the King who is to come (more of this later).

One other point to notice is that while we call Kings a history book (and it is not less than that), in the Hebrew Bible, the books of Joshua to 2 Kings (except for Ruth) are called 'the former prophets'. This is an important clue as to how we are to look at these books. We will consider this in more detail later, but this emphasis is seen in the large amount of space given to prophets, especially Elijah and Elisha, and the way history is seen as God unfolding His purpose.

Kings and history

One of the things which daunts preachers is the length of the book. That, however, should not be exaggerated. The book of Kings in Eugene Peterson's *The Message*[1] runs to only 105 pages. That is not a lot in which to cover nearly 500 years. Imagine compressing the history of Britain from the reign of Elizabeth I to the reign of Elizabeth II into a book as short as that! So the first point to make is that the history is ruthlessly selective, and we shall see examples as we work our way through the book (for example, Omri, Ahab's father is dismissed in six verses, 1 Kings 16:23-28, although we know that he was a big player on the international stage and impressed the Assyrians).

We also need to note that the book is no mere chronicle of events, but a record of the living God active in history. This is important as we try to apply the book. We ourselves are not David (Solomon, Josiah, and so on), but we have David's God. What God writes large on the pages of history reveals the kind of God He is, and thus how He is to be worshipped and obeyed. What

1. E. Peterson, *The Message* (Carol Stream, U.S.: NavPress, 1993)

Paul says, speaking specifically of Numbers, 'these things occurred as examples to keep us from setting our hearts on evil things as they did' (1 Cor. 10:6), applies to the rest of the Old Testament. Indeed, since Paul goes on to speak particularly about idolatry, the relevance to Kings is obvious. Thus, while in Kings we are meeting people who actually lived and reading about events which actually happened, we are not taking an antiquarian interest in the book. We are seeing windows into God's purposes and learning how to live lives which honour Him in the present world as we wait for the kingdom.

Thus we shall look at each section in its context , but link these with the wider picture as it points to Christ, and more will be said of this later in the Introduction. This is a book which will lead us to pray 'your kingdom come, your will be done on earth as it is in heaven'.

The book begins with David at the end of his life and continues with a glimpse of glory days under Solomon, but this glory fades rapidly before the end of his reign and the kingdom is soon split under his foolish son Rehoboam. The northern kingdom lapses entirely into idolatry and much of the southern kingdom's story is similar, punctuated by a number of relatively good kings such as Asa and Jehoshaphat and two notable Davidic kings, Hezekiah and Josiah, but exile in Babylon looms and Zion mourns. Both kings are talked about in terms which specifically recall David. Hezekiah 'did what was right in the eyes of the LORD just as David his father had done' (2 Kings 18:3). Josiah 'did what was right in the eyes of the LORD and walked in all the ways of his father David' (2 Kings 22:2).

So what is the book about? Can we find a theme which unites the disparate material and which helps us to set about teaching it?

The theme of Kings

Early in the book (1 Kings 2:2-4) we find, I believe, the key which will unlock the riches of the book.

> 'I am about to go the way of all the earth,' he said. 'So be strong, show yourself a man, and observe what the LORD your God requires: Walk in his ways, and keep his decrees and commands, his laws and requirements, as written in the Law of Moses, so that you may prosper in all you do and wherever you go, and that the LORD may keep his promise to me: "If your descendants watch how they live, and if they walk faithfully before me with all their heart and soul, you will never fail to have a man on the throne of Israel."'

These are David's words to Solomon as David bows out. The supreme authority of the words of Moses, which are the words of God, is to be the charter of the kingdom for both king and subjects. We might suggest that the book's theme could be expressed as 'ruling justly and wisely depends on obeying God's Word and this is not only true of the kings, but of the people; disobedience is deadly'. The people cannot lead, but they can choose to follow or not follow the Word of God. Both Hezekiah and Josiah were faithful to the Word of God, but their reformations were dismantled after their deaths and the whole nation reverted to paganism.

This emphasis is underlined throughout the book, with the Word of God coming through many named and unnamed prophets. The great central section of the book (1 Kings 17–2 Kings 13) is dominated by the ministries of Elijah and Elisha. Jonah is mentioned in 2 Kings 14:25. Isaiah plays a prominent role in 2 Kings 19 and 20. The great reforms of Josiah are given new impetus by the discovery of the Book of the Law (2 Kings 22:8). The exile is attributed to disobeying the prophetic word (2 Kings 24:3).

Unpacking this a bit more, we can see how the Word of promise and rebuke binds the book together. The Word of God covers the whole of life, but there are particular ways in which this theme is specifically treated in Kings. Three issues in particular deserve to be mentioned.

The Davidic King

The bookends of Kings draw attention to both the vulnerability of David's house and the enduring promise which sustains it. At the beginning of the book, David lies weak and decrepit, but with the help of Nathan and Bathsheba, rallies and secures the succession of Solomon and speaks to him the words already noted (2:2-4) about the future of the kingdom depending on obedience. At the end of the book (2 Kings 24:27), the Davidic king Jehoiachin is raised from prison to sit in a seat of honour at the table of the Babylonian king. That may be a long way from the kings of the earth honouring the Son of David, but it is a light in a dark place. Zion is down, but not out.

Throughout the book there is constant reference to the promise to David: the covenant with David of 2 Samuel 7 and Psalm 89. The references are multiple: 1 Kings 11:32; 15:4; 2 Kings 8:19; 20:6 are examples. These, coupled with the frequent references to the city of David and the commendation of Hezekiah (2 Kings 18:30) and Josiah (2 Kings 22:2) for walking in the ways of David, show Yahweh's continuing favour to David's house. Also they point to his Greater Son (a subject we will return to shortly).

The Prophetic Word

As already mentioned, the story is punctuated by frequent references to the prophetic Word, both in judgment and salvation. It would be tedious simply to give a list of references and a couple of examples will suffice. Six chapters (1 Kings 17–22) are given to Ahab and the prophetic Word to him from Elijah, Micaiah and an unnamed prophet. These are words of judgment on Ahab and his house for idolatry, but all through the section there is the call to repent. Indeed when Ahab partially responds after his murder of Naboth and the grabbing of his vineyard (1 Kings 21:28-29), Yahweh delays the judgment. In chapter 22:19-23, the false words of the court prophets are attributed to a lying spirit, but it is the words of the true prophet Micaiah which show reality.

Another example of the power of the prophetic Word to save the godly and overthrow kingdoms occurs in 2 Kings 19. The Assyrian spokesman has boasted of the power of Sennacherib. His words are defied by Isaiah, who retorts with the Word of Yahweh (vv. 21-29) and the great Assyrian army is destroyed. Plainly the power of the Word is at the heart of the story.

God's providence and human responsibility

In the unfolding drama of Kings, the responsibility to respond to the Word is central. The Word cannot be broken, but human beings are not puppets, as we have already seen in the case of Ahab. The preaching of judgment is in fact a sign of God's grace because it calls for repentance and faith. A clear example of this is 1 Kings 11:29-39, where the prophet Ahijah speaks to Jeroboam, using an acted parable of tearing his cloak into twelve pieces and giving ten of these to Jeroboam to symbolize the ten northern tribes of whom he is shortly to become king. Two tribes remain to the royal house of Judah because of the promise to David. Ahijah promises Jeroboam an enduring royal house as well (v. 38), but that promise depends on Jeroboam's obedience. Jeroboam is hardly crowned when he shows his faithlessness (12:28ff) and judgment is announced (14:6-12).

This emphasis of the challenge of the prophetic Word continues, and even good kings like Hezekiah are judged if they turn to expediency and dangerous alliances rather than follow the path of simple obedience (2 Kings 20:16-18). This pattern of God speaking and humans responsible for hearing and acting is part of the great value of the book. It is of immense practical significance and we shall look at this further as we explore the possibilities of teaching and preaching the book. The important thing is that the Word is living and we cannot simply treat it with indifference.

Structure

Taking it as a unified work one possible approach would be to see six main sections with further subdivisions:

1. Solomon's glory and disgrace (1 Kings 1:1–11:43). Solomon is an ambiguous figure and we shall explore this in the commentary.
   a. David bows out and Solomon succeeds to the throne (1:1–2:46). Here we see human vulnerability and divine promise.

   b. Wisdom in wise government (3:1–4:34). Solomon at his best gives us a glimpse of the kingdom to come.

   c. Building projects (5:1–9:9): temple, palace and cities. The high-water mark comes at 8:27-30.

    d. National and international activities (9:10 –10:29), including the memorable visit of the Queen of Sheba.

    e. Ending badly (11:1-43). Solomon displays the tragedy of a divided heart.

2. A dismal bunch of kings (1 Kings 12:1–16-34)

    a. Bad in both north and south (12:1–14:31). There is a lot of prophetic activity, especially in chapter 13.

    b. Decline in Israel; better things in Judah (15:1 –16:20), especially seen in the reign of Asa.

    c. Worse still (16:21-34). The house of Omri leads Israel to new depths.

3. Bringing God's Word in dangerous times (1 Kings 17:1 –2 Kings 13:21); the stories of Elijah and Elisha. There is more in this long central section than the ministry of the two prophets, but they dominate this part of the book.

    a. Elijah and Yahweh's powerful protection (17:1 –19:21). God protects Elijah and shows the power of His Word.

    b. Ahab confronted by the prophetic Word (20:1 –22:41). Ahab is given chance after chance.

    c. Elijah's continuing ministry and his ascension to heaven, and Elisha comes into prominence (2 Kings 1:1–2:25).

    d. Elisha's words and actions (2 Kings 3:1–9:13). These are both on the political stage and in private.

> e. More politics (2 Kings 9:14–13:13). Jehu destroys house of Ahab; Athaliah tries to destroy house of David; Joash half-heartedly repairs the temple.
>
> f. Elisha dies, but brings life (2 Kings 13:14-21).

4. More bad kings (2 Kings 13:22–17:41)

> a. Little to choose between Israel and Judah (13:22 –15:38). Israel continues its downward spiral – things are only slightly better in Judah.
>
> b. Goodbye Israel (16:1–17:41). The northern kingdom is exiled to Assyria and we see why this happened.

5. Reformers and wreckers (18:1–23:30). We see the two best kings since David, but also the worst.

> a. David comes again (18:1–20:21). Hezekiah stands up to the Assyrian Goliath, but succumbs to flattery – like David he is flawed, but faithful.
>
> b. Judah's Ahab (21:1-18). Manasseh is the worst of all the kings. His behaviour makes exile inevitable; a footnote (vv. 19-26) talks of his equally godless son, Amon.
>
> c. The Word of Yahweh honoured (22:1–23:30). Josiah's great reformation comes too late to save the nation and he loses his life in an unwise battle with the Pharaoh.

6. Zion down, but not out (23:31–25:30). These are the last dismal days of Judah leading to inevitable exile – but there is a hint of hope for David's line (25:27-30).

A much simpler outline would be to see three main sections:

1.   The glimpse of glory (1 Kings 1–11)
2.   The divided kingdom (1 Kings 12–2 Kings 17)
3.   The closing years of Judah (2 Kings 18–25)

It is important that we do not impose a straightjacket on such diverse material, but, as we shall explore further in the section on planning a series, it is important to divide the book into manageable chunks for teaching and preaching. The weakness yet divine protection of the Davidic house with which the book begins and ends give the guiding thread of promise and fulfilment.

It is also important with narrative to read large enough chunks to get the flow of the story as a whole, as well as to see how the smaller units fit into the larger narrative. We will explore the teaching of narrative further in the section on planning a series, but it is important to remember that genre is vitally important.

Context

The place of Kings in the Big Story, beginning with the promise of kings to Abraham (Gen. 17:6) and Jacob (Gen. 35:11), has already been noted, as has the significance of David and his sons. The apparent eclipse of that promise at the Exile is gloriously transformed with the words of Gabriel announcing the birth of great David's Greater Son, 'the Lord God will give him the throne of his father David, and he will reign over the house of Jacob for ever' (Luke 1:33). Paul, in Romans 15:12, speaks of the Davidic King reigning over the nations as the Gentiles gather to Christ. In Revelation, the 'Lion of the tribe of Judah, the root of David' opens the scroll of history (5:5). In Revelation 22:16 He is the origin and also the offspring of David.

However, there is one book which invites specific comparison with Kings and that is Chronicles (like Kings, one book, but divided for convenience into two scrolls). Both cover similar ground, but with different emphases. Kings shows why the exile happened, whereas Chronicles is written to encourage the remnant who returned from exile to see themselves in direct continuity with Moses and David as the covenant people whom God would continue to bless.

Thus many of David and Solomon's failures are omitted in order to emphasize their positive achievements as the foundation of Israel's hopes. The Chronicler particularly emphasises the extensive role of David in planning and providing for the work of the temple (1 Chron. 22–27) as well as the orderly transfer of power from David to Solomon (1 Chron. 28–29). Also, there is far more extensive coverage of many of the kings of Judah: e.g. Jehoshaphat, the weak man who nevertheless trusted God in a crisis (2 Chron. 20); Uzziah the strong man discredited because of his pride (2 Chron. 26); the religious reforms of Hezekiah (2 Chron. 30–31); the belated repentance of Manasseh which failed to avert the Exile (2 Chron. 33).

The books of Kings and Chronicles complement each other, but their theology of a God who saves and judges is common to both. The genealogies which open Chronicles are a reminder of God's care for all His people and their personal importance to Him. Likewise the glories of David and Solomon anticipate the greater glory of the King who is to come.

It is important when we are preaching on Kings not to import too much material from Chronicles, but to focus on the particular emphases of the author. Otherwise we shall end up by preaching a mishmash which does not do justice to either book, rather like some sermons on the Gospels which takes an incident such as the Feeding of the Five Thousand and preach something which does not do justice to the emphases of any of the particular Gospels.

An example of this would be the treatment of Jehoshaphat. In 1 Kings 22–2 Kings 3 he appears as an associate of Ahab and then Jehoram. His reforms are not ignored (1 Kings 22:41-50), but the author's emphasis is on his unwise cosying up to Ahab's house. Kings does not deny that he was a good man, but shows how he failed to realize his potential. Chronicles, while recognizing his weakness, contains more detailed treatment of his reforms and especially his faith (in 2 Chron. 20) when he is faced with a vast army. Each book is contributing to the total picture, but we need to stick to the text in front of us. We can mention the differences, but not major on them.

Authorship

The book itself gives no hint about who wrote it; the evidence of unified themes and careful planning suggests a single author. It was long believed that this was Jeremiah, not just because of the identical endings of the books (2 Kings 25 and Jeremiah 52), but because of a similarity in outlook and theology, not least the extensive treatment of the Word of Yahweh. Clearly it cannot have been earlier than about 560 B.C., given the reference to Jehoiachin at the end of the book.

Obviously the author used sources such as royal annals, temple records and stories passed down in prophetic circles. The important thing is that this book is part of Scripture and is profitable whosoever the human author may have been.

2

WHY SHOULD WE PREACH AND TEACH KINGS?

We can dodge this important issue and say, in effect, we have to preach it because is there. Naturally, if we are committed to preaching the whole Bible we will preach on Kings as well as every other part. But more specifically, what is there about the book that makes its own unique contribution to the canon and makes it profitable as we follow the Lord? Four reasons can be given to help us to unpack the riches of this book.

1. Kings is God's story about God

One of the ways in which narrative works (see section on preaching narrative) is by presenting truth indirectly as well as directly. What I mean is that in the narrative, without specific comment, the author shows us the nature, activities and ways of God by the flow of the story itself. Thus the cluster of Elijah stories in chapters 17–19 of 1 Kings, apart from the specific attack on idolatry, shows us important truths about God in the way the narrative progresses. Thus we learn that He cares about physical needs and can supply these in unexpected ways (ravens and a widow in 17:6, 14; an angel in 19:5-7). He answers not fanatical ravings and hype, but simple, heartfelt prayer (18:27-29; 36-7). He does not dump His faithful servants on the scrap heap but allows them to rest and then gives them new tasks to do (19:5-8; 15-18).

Also, God's care for ordinary, often nameless, people is powerfully brought out in a chapter such as 2 Kings 4. There, those who receive the Lord's blessing through Elisha are otherwise unknown. That is not, of course, confined to this chapter: the wise treatment of the prostitutes by Solomon (1 Kings 3:16-28); the lepers in 2 Kings 7:9; the concern of Hezekiah for the ordinary citizens as they hear the Assyrian boasts (2 Kings 18:36) show similar emphasis.

There is also the activity of God in the events of history. He raises up kings against Solomon (1 Kings 11:23); controls events (1 Kings 12:15); removes His people to exile when they rebel against Him (2 Kings 17:20-23; 23:27). He acts in judgment: death by fire (2 Kings 1:12). He acts in mercy as the One who hears and answers prayer (for Elijah in 1 Kings 18:36-38; for Hezekiah in 2 Kings 19:14-19). Many similar examples could be cited, but these will suffice to show how awesome and gracious is the God of Kings.

In today's world these are truths which need to be preached over and over again. Too often in pursuit of trying to deal with felt needs, we strive for a superficial relevance rather than allowing these great truths about God to fill our hearts and stretch our minds. Often, we offer a tame domesticated God whose main function is to make us feel comfortable and offer quick fixes to deep-rooted problems. We need a God who can handle the giant evils of the world to all who repent.

This book will point to God-centred preaching which is vital in the building of God-centred congregations and which will encourage faith in God's promises and obedience to God's Word. Since this is narrative these great truths about God are embodied in real people and situations, and this brings us to our next reason for preaching Kings.

2. Kings tells us about the kingdom of God

When we pray 'your kingdom come, your will be done on earth as it is in heaven', we know that prayer will only ultimately be fulfilled when the King returns and ushers in the new heaven and the new earth. However, it is also a prayer for that kingdom to be anticipated in our lives, both communal and personal. We also know only too well that values which are not kingdom values often predominate. Here in Kings (as in Samuel) we have a visual aid of an earthly kingdom which points to the future. This is an important point: at various times this small earthly kingdom was a genuine anticipation of the kingdom of our God and His Christ.

Unsurprisingly, the clearest glimpses of the kingdom come from the early and middle years of Solomon when the nation was united. The unity of God's people remains an important biblical truth (John 17:22). But there are other important glimpses of how, even on earth, the kingdom is anticipated. In 1 Kings 3:7-15, the kingdom is strongest when the king rules with God-given wisdom. We are not Solomon, but those in pastoral oversight need wisdom and the mind of Christ through listening to Him in His Word, and by His Spirit applying that Word both to ourselves and then others. The story of the two prostitutes (3:16-28) shows that such rule is marked by compassion and a shrewd understanding of human nature.

First Kings 4 also shows wise administration of the kingdom and the fulfilment of the prophecy to Abraham in Genesis 15:18 that the kingdom would stretch from the Nile to the Euphrates. These territories had been conquered by David (see 2 Sam. 8). Further wisdom involves intellectual, imaginative and aesthetic pleasure in God's creation. These emphases give a rich and rounded picture of human life, partial here but fully realized in the new creation. Teaching such truths will help to avoid super-spirituality which denies the good gifts God has given us in this present life and has an unattractive and disembodied view of the new creation.

The next few chapters (5–8) show the genuine worship of the kingdom in the loving care lavished on the building of the temple. This is not to be pressed into service to prop up an ailing fabric fund. This is ultimately about building living stones in the Temple of God's people: God's people in the OT were an anticipation of the new creation. The high-water mark is 8:27-30 where Solomon worships the Lord who is both enthroned in the highest heaven but condescends to come into time and space. As any serious Bible student will be able to tell you, the key to biblical theology is God up there (Gen. 1) who comes down here (Gen. 2) , pointing to the perfect union of the new heaven and earth (Rev. 21:1-4).

There are other glimpses of the kingdom later in the book, not least in the goodly fellowship of the prophets (I will come to this shortly). However, even in days of decline, good things happen. Asa of Judah removes idolatrous practices in face of strong family opposition (1 Kings 16:11-14), a policy followed by his son Jehoshaphat (1 Kings 22:43). Jehosheba hides the young Joash, thereby saving the Davidic line (2 Kings 11:1-3). Hezekiah gives a glimpse of the Davidic kingdom, including defying the Assyrian Goliath (2 Kings 18–19). Josiah makes a valiant effort to reinstate the Word of God at the centre of national life (2 Kings 22–23).

The kingdom is under persistent attack and this is the other side of the same coin: there is much to learn about this from Kings. We do not have to choose between focusing on the big picture of the kingdom and the ethical imperatives of that kingdom. To preserve the sheep we have to fight the wolf; to live according to kingdom principles we have to fight the enemies of the kingdom.

So, as we teach Kings we will need to present the negatives as well as the positives. At the heart of Kings is the warning expressed by John at the end of his first letter 'Dear children, keep yourselves from idols' (1 John 5:21). This perpetual temptation to build a visible kingdom which ultimately we can manipulate is first disastrously seen in the great Solomon himself (1 Kings 11:1-8). The whole sorry story continues to exile because once Yahweh becomes simply another godlet, the distinctive kingdom lifestyle disappears. As we preach and teach this we need to examine our own idolatries, not least our evangelical ones: the celebrity culture; the obsession with numbers; the excessive busyness, and the like. Each of us is in different situations with different idolatries. We also need to deal with the idols in our own hearts and it is surely significant that Solomon's idolatry was traced to his heart (1 Kings 11:4, 9).

3. Kings tells us about the Word of God

The book is dominated by the centrality of the Word of God which saves and judges. This is established by David's last words to Solomon (1 Kings 2:2-4) and continued in the prophetic ministries of the great and the unknown; it culminates in the great reforms of Josiah (2 Kings 22 and 23). One thing this does is help to create and sustain confidence in the Word of God to do its work. This is a Word which 'will not return empty ... but achieve the purpose for which I sent it' (Isa. 55:11). We see this over and over again in the narrative of Kings.

We are not prophets, but we have been given the prophetic Word which as Peter says is 'a light shining in a dark place' (2 Pet. 1:19). At significant crisis points, prophets are involved bringing the Word of God into the situation: Nathan in the accession of Solomon (1 Kings 1:22); Ahijah announcing the divided kingdom (1 Kings 11:29-39; 14:1-18); Elijah to the house of Omri (1 Kings 17–2 Kings 1), and Isaiah to Hezekiah (2 Kings 19:20-34). That does not mean that we can look at the politics of today and give authoritative messages to prime ministers and presidents as if we had God-given authority to pronounce on government policies. Rather, the general principles of a worldview flowing from a God of justice and mercy are the foundation of truly biblical living and God-fearing community.

The Word of God is more important than the messenger who brings it and it is a Word of challenge in the present which shapes the future. It is encouraging to see how the Word is not bound by time; a striking example of this is when the man of God from Judah prophesies to Jeroboam about how one day a Davidic king called Josiah will cleanse the land from idolatry (1 Kings 13:2-3). As we preach and teach we understandably like to see fruit from our labours and often God generously gives that. However, that Word spoken and apparently opposed or ignored may bear a harvest long after we have gone.

4. Kings points to Christ

Preachers are often uneasy about how to see appropriate lines to Christ, and one reason for the neglect of much of the Old Testament is that many find it hard to see Christ in the text. Thus there may be a sermon on Esther which could have been preached in the synagogue, followed by some lame statement like 'it's really all about Jesus'. At this point the hearers may legitimately scratch their heads and think 'Did I miss something?' Or else the OT passage may simply be used as a springboard to jump into the New Testament. Thus a sermon, allegedly on Isaiah 53 is in effect a sermon on Acts 8. However, we need to remember that the apostles and other preachers in the early decades preached from the 'Scriptures' by which, like the risen Lord on the way to Emmaus (Luke 24:27), they meant what we call the Old Testament.

At first sight Kings does not seem to be the most promising book from which to proclaim Christ, but if we take seriously the points already made about the nature of God and the kingdom, quite a different picture begins to emerge. The starting point is the emphasis on David and the Davidic dynasty. Neither David himself, nor even the most deserving of his sons, truly ruled over a kingdom whose throne was established for ever (see 2 Sam. 7:13). Yet, as already noticed, there are tantalizing glimpses of that kingdom and, while in the northern kingdom four dynasties rise and fall, the house of David persists to the Exile and beyond. Even in human terms, five hundred years is a long time for a royal house to survive.

Thus, in spite of the failures of the human kings, the hope still burns that one day there will be a son of David who will embody the covenant and fulfil all its promises. This is already implied in the words of Ahijah to Jeroboam that David's descendants would be humbled but not for ever (1 Kings 11:39). Even Exile did not break the line of promise. The Davidic king, Jehoiachin, in exile in Babylon is raised to the highest place at the king of Babylon's table (2 Kings 25:27-30). This points to the day when the King reigns on the holy hill of Zion.

The reigns of the better kings, as already noticed, point to the time when David's Greater Son will reign over the whole of creation. But on the other hand the reigns of the bad kings point to the need for the true King who will reign in righteousness and peace. Idolatry and apostasy brought nothing but misery, tyranny and endless wars, and showed starkly the need for a different kind of kingdom. The words of David to Solomon (2:2-4) not only emphasize the centrality of the words of Moses, but the vital importance of a son of the Davidic line who would embody their truth.

Kings is a vital stage in the journey which is to lead to the announcement to Mary by Gabriel that the Saviour to be born was the one to whom 'the Lord God will give the throne of his father David, and he will reign over the house of Jacob for ever; his kingdom will never end' (Luke 1:32-33). The phrase 'house of Jacob' neatly sums up the book of Kings, as that name reminds us of all the waywardness and sinfulness of the people as God's abundant grace transforms Jacob into Israel.

Similarly, Jesus is the true Prophet to whom all the prophetic figures in Kings point. But He is also the true Word, not simply the one who brings that Word. It was from the book of Kings that He spoke in his first synagogue sermon, speaking of the grace of God to Gentile widows and lepers (Luke 4:24-27). And there He was the object of hatred that is so often the lot of the true prophet.

Preaching Christ from Kings is not an alien construct imposed on the text but rises naturally and inevitably from it. Different preachers will tackle these issues in different ways and we need to be sensitive and not over-allegorize, for example, the details of the temple furnishings, but our task is faithfully to proclaim the living Word as He appears in the pages of the written Word. As we preach Christ it is not so much having a checklist imposed on every passage as developing an ear to hear the Master's voice.

At various points in the commentary, I will pause to consider the question of how we preach Christ faithfully from the text. The aim of these sections attached to clusters of chapters, rather than individual ones, is to underline that our purpose in preaching is never simply to 'explain the passage' as if it were a mere exercise in comprehension, but to proclaim Christ who is the great centre of the Bible. This is not simply in terms of His earthly life, but His eternal being and activity throughout history and the eternal kingdom. Not every passage or even every book will focus on all these aspects and in Kings especially His kingship and His role as the great Prophet and occasionally the Priest will be emphasized.

3

PREACHING OLD TESTAMENT NARRATIVE

Kings is part of the great narrative of the Bible which begins with creation and culminates in the new creation and, as we preach it, we need to consider how we can handle narrative effectively. This is worth some brief consideration before we get to the text itself. The first thing that needs to be said is that, if we believe that God gave us the Bible, then *how* He says something will be a vital part of *what* He says. Thus we will not preach narrative as if it were a doctrinal passage. We will be primarily interested in how God's story about God embodies the gospel.

So what are the characteristics of narrative and how can we avoid moralizing platitudes which is a constant danger in preaching a story? First, we must remember these are, in many cases, exciting and gripping stories, and we need to enjoy reading them as we would any other good story. Not all of Kings is narrative of that kind and, as we go through the exposition, we will consider the place and value of such passages as the long temple-building section (1 Kings 5–7) and the brief notes on the inglorious reigns of insignificant kings (e.g. 1 Kings 15 and 16). However, we need to be absorbed in the flow of the story and the place of individual episodes in the great narrative.

OT narrative, like any other story, has a number of components which together create the text. It is not a case of simply isolating these elements so much as seeing how together they create the story as we have it.

Plot is the first major part of story: the sequence of events, including principles of selection and the silences of the text. For example, in Kings, the author gives a brief summary of the sequence of kings in 1 Kings 15 and 16, concluding with Ahab and we expect he will be dismissed in a few verses like his predecessors. However, the account of his reign spans chapters 17–22 because it is to be the backdrop to the ministry of Elijah and others, and to underline the supreme importance of the prophetic Word. Hezekiah's religious reforms are given one verse (2 Kings 18:4) because again the emphasis is on the prophetic word brought by Isaiah. As we preach the individual stories we will also notice the structure of the narrative and how the author's emphases are shown within episodes as well as the wider balance in the book as a whole.

Characterization is another important element in story. God is the main actor but the part played by humans matters, hence the frequent references to David. Sometimes these characters will be developed at some length, notably Solomon. If the interpretation of Solomon in this book is accepted, then we have a more convincing human being than if we see him as virtually flawless from 1 Kings 2–10 and then suddenly and without warning falling from grace in chapter 11. However, it is not just the big players, but the 'little' people who are vital in God's purpose, for example, the little girl who told Naaman's wife about Elisha in 2 Kings 5:3 and the unnamed prophet who anointed Jehu in 2 Kings 9:6. Very often dialogue develops characterization as in 1 Kings 1 and 2 where Solomon emerges as king.

Setting is important and often draws attention to deeper elements in the story. Warning bells ring in 1 Kings 10 at the elaborate luxury and extravagance of Solomon's court (compare a similar technique in Esther 1 regarding the Persian court). Also the significance of Mount Carmel in 1 Kings 18 which emphasizes that this contest of Yahweh and Baal is happening on Baal's home ground; if he cannot win here he cannot win anywhere.

Application needs to be considered carefully. Narrative is not normative: for example, 'David did well, so imitate him'; 'David did badly, so don't imitate him'. However, in a legitimate desire to avoid this kind of moralizing, there has developed a tendency to flatten out every narrative in terms of the big picture. This results in very repetitive preaching where virtually the same thing is said every week. Also, a commendable desire to avoid moralizing has led to a neglecting of the 'so what?' There are implications for our lives and Paul sets this out clearly in 1 Corinthians 10:1ff. These will follow from close exegesis of the text and showing not only the big picture but showing how particular passages bring their own contribution to it.

Above all, we are not following a formula, we are developing an instinct for seeing each part of the Bible and each genre making their own unique contributions to the developing story. Kings speaks of a vital time in the history of God's people when they declined from the glory days of David and Solomon to bitter exile. Along the route prophets warned them, and some good kings tried to stop the rot, but the dream ended in apparent failure. Yet, as we shall see at the end of the book in 2 Kings 25:27-30, there is hope beyond despair. We are part of that story and so the story speaks to us.

List of Kings of Israel

(Dates of reigns are B.C. and all approximate)

THE UNITED KINGDOM		
Saul	1050-1010	-
David	1010-970	1 Kings 1:1
Solomon	970-930	1 Kings 1:30

THE DIVIDED KINGDOM					
Kings of Judah			Kings of Israel		
Rehoboam	930-913	1 Kings 11:43	Jeroboam I	930-910	1 Kings 11:31
Abijah	913-911	1 Kings 14:31	Nadab	910-909	1 Kings 14:20
Asa	911-870	1 Kings 15:8	Baasha	909-886	1 Kings 15:16
Jehoshaphat	870-848	1 Kings 15:24	Elah	886-885	1 Kings 16:8
J[eh]oram	848-841	2 Kings 8:16	Zimri	885	1 Kings 16:15
Ahaziah	841	2 Kings 8:25	Omri	885-874	1 Kings 16:16
Qu. Athaliah	841-835	2 Kings 8:26	Ahab	874-853	1 Kings 16:29
J[eh]oash	835-796	2 Kings 11:2	Ahaziah	853-852	1 Kings 22:40
Amaziah	796-767	2 Kings 14:1	J[eh]oram	852-841	2 Kings 1:17
Azariah	767-740	2 Kings 14:21	Jehu	841-814	2 Kings 9:1
Jotham	740-732	2 Kings 15:5	Jehoahaz	814-798	2 Kings 10:35
Ahaz	732-716	2 Kings 15:38	Jehoash	798-782	2 Kings 13:10
Hezekiah	716-687	2 Kings 16:20	Jeroboam II	782-753	2 Kings 14:23
Manasseh	687-642	2 Kings 21:1	Zechariah	753-752	2 Kings 14:29
Amon	642-640	2 Kings 21:19	Shallum	752	2 Kings 15:10
Josiah	640-608	2 Kings 22:1	Menahem	752-742	2 Kings 15:14
Jehoahaz	608	2 Kings 23:30	Pekahiah	742-740	2 Kings 15:23
Jehoiakim	608-597	2 Kings 23:34	Pekah	740-732	2 Kings 15:25
Jehoiachin	597	2 Kings 24:6	Hoshea	732-722	2 Kings 15:30
Zedekiah	597-586	2 Kings 24:17	*Fall of Samaria 722 B.C.*		
Fall of Jerusalem 586 B.C.					

Part 2

THE GLIMPSE OF GLORY
(1 KINGS 1-11)

I

THE KINGDOM IN DANGER
(1 KINGS 1)

Introduction

Some U.K. readers may recall the television programme 'After They Were Famous' which tells the story of people who briefly were stars of stage, screen or sports. Many simply returned to ordinary life, but there were also sad stories of early promise snuffed out by addictions and character flaws. As the book of 1 Kings opens, we have the melancholy feeling that here is David 'after he was famous'. The mighty warrior and great lover lies helpless in bed and the beautiful Abishag completely fails to arouse any response in him.

It seems all over, and God's promises to David seem to have become empty words at the mercy of political manoeuvring. We feel a sense of panic as the kingdom is in peril and, far from being the head of a dynasty (as Nathan the prophet had promised back in 2 Sam. 7:1-17), he looks like a tired old man in charge of nothing. So as we start work on the chapter we fear that God's kingdom has run into the sand.

Listening to the text
Context and structure
The books of Kings form part of a much larger narrative and have an important place in the great story itself which runs from creation to new creation. More particularly it flows from the promise to Abraham that kings would come from his line (Gen. 17:16 and repeated to Jacob in 35:11). In the immediate context the story continues from 1 and 2 Samuel with the closing days of David and the rise of Solomon. The books cover more than 400 years from Solomon through to the divided kingdom and eventual exile of the northern kingdom to Assyria and the southern to Babylon.

The bulk of this long chapter deals with intrigues which are to result in the emergence of Solomon. We shall divide it into sections, following the flow of the narrative:

+ The end of an era (1:1-4)

+ Is David outwitted? (1:5-10)

+ David's friends strike back (1:11-27)

+ Don't underestimate David (1:28-40)

+ Long live King Solomon (1:41-53)

Notice two general points: the first is that much of the story is advanced by dialogue which gives insight into the leading characters. The second is the idea of 'ruling' or 'sitting on the throne' (1:13, 17, 20, 24, 27, 30, 35, 46, 48). This is to be about who is reigning and whether, behind all human manoeuvring, Yahweh[1] is in control.

---

1. Throughout, I have used 'Yahweh' to represent the divine name, often identified in our Bibles using small capitals: 'LORD'.

Working through the text
The end of an era (1:1-4)

This is the end of the story which began long before in 1 Samuel 16 when the young David was anointed and had eventually come to the throne. This chapter is one of the transition points where the leadership is about to be passed on. A good parallel is Joshua 23:1 where Joshua is also described as 'old and well advanced in years', and his death was shortly followed by apostasy and rebellion. This is a situation God's people often find themselves in: a leader influential in many churches and many lives passes away; a minister who has led wisely and well dies; a mentor is no longer there. What will happen now? In such circumstances we need to recall the words of Jacob to his sons: 'I am about to die, but God will be with you' (Gen. 48:21). God is in control; as Charles Wesley said, 'God buries His workmen, and carries on His work'.

Yet the emphasis on the helplessness of David and the lack of his old vigour and shrewdness casts a deep unease over the chapter and a real fear for what is to happen. This is a crisis and a wrong move could mean disaster, not least the apparent failure of God's purposes. We are going to have to get used to that as we work through 1 and 2 Kings. This is not just the history of the kingdom of God then, it is the experience of that kingdom now.

Is David outwitted? (1:5-10)

At first sight it does indeed seem that the kingdom is in real danger of bad leadership, with the emergence of Adonijah who seizes the chance and 'puts himself forward'. This suggests a lust for power rather than a desire to serve, emphasized by his statement 'I will be king'. Here we have

someone who is big on posturing and has an ego the size
of a planet. It is important to see what the author is doing
here. This is not a simple description of Adonijah's activities;
rather he is giving us hints as to how to read the story.

True, he has a good conceit of himself and a big
mouth, but there is more than that. The mention of
Adonijah's handsome appearance recalls that of Absalom
(2 Sam. 14:25-27), and earlier, Eliab (1 Sam. 16:6-7)
and Saul (1 Sam. 9:2; 10:23-24). All these men, royal
or potentially so, had looked impressive, but had been
rejected. The author wants to set Adonijah in that same
line. There is also the problem that David had been too
doting a father to him, as he had been to Absalom (compare
v. 6 with 2 Sam. 14:1). Who can say this is a merely ancient
problem, a wholly unsuitable man setting himself in a place
of leadership to which he has not been called and for which
he is not qualified?

However, also like Absalom, Adonijah is not just a
handsome playboy, but shows skill in building up support.
He enlists the support of the wily Joab, commander of the
army, someone whose ambiguous relationship with David
is a recurring motif in 2 Samuel. Sadly, Abiathar the priest,
who had been a crucial support for David at many points
(1 Sam. 22:20-23; 23:9; 30:7) also joins the conspiracy.
Adonijah cements this conspiracy by offering sacrifices
at Enrogel, just south of Jerusalem; the pieties must be
observed! Then a party is under way and the conspirators
are riding high.

Adonijah is alive and well today. We meet him in
the New Testament in 3 John 9-10 where he is called
Diotrephes 'who loves to be the first', and who treats the
church as his own private fiefdom where he can bully and

lord it over God's people. We meet him in the church leader who cannot tell the difference between godly authority and bullying domination. We meet him in powerful cliques who try to push their own agenda and make life impossible for godly leaders. We meet him in our own hearts when the desire to be prominent at all costs is continually looking for an outlet.

David's friends strike back (1:11-27)
Adonijah, however, has overreached himself. One of those he failed to invite to his party was Nathan, and it is on Nathan that the spotlight now falls. The narrative here is gripping and exciting and makes much of its impact by direct speech. Repetition is cleverly used: verses 18 and 25 showing how advanced and formidable Adonijah's preparations are; verses 19 and 26 underlining who has been excluded, especially Solomon. Nathan goes first to Bathsheba (1:11-14) and reminds her of David's oath that Solomon would be king, and how this explains Adonijah's exclusion of Solomon from the feast (vv. 10, 19, 26). The stakes are raised as Nathan and Bathsheba both infer that once Adonijah reigned, Solomon and probably themselves would be eliminated (vv. 12, 21).

Bathsheba then reminds David of his responsibilities. He may be old and decrepit, but 'the eyes of all Israel' (v. 20) are looking to him and expecting a statement on the succession. This is followed by Nathan himself visiting David and by actions (bowing) as well as words reminding him he is still king and has the power if he is willing to exercise it.

Three particular features of the story invite comment. The first is the circumstantial detail and the dialogue which draws us into the world of the story and helps us to see the characters as real flesh-and-blood people. These are real people facing a situation of tension and peril and not certain if they are going to succeed or even survive. This is what the life of faith looks like so often and one of the important themes in the historical narratives is to show how God's people often operate in a world where He appears to be absent. The most striking example of this is the book of Esther, but we shall find many such passages in Kings (as there are in Samuel as well).

Second is the emphasis on human activity and decision-making. The account of David's last days in 1 Chronicles 28 and 29 emphasizes God's overruling and is silent about these intrigues and conspiracies. These accounts are not contradictory, but complementary. Chronicles underlines God's providence and the very secondary nature of human involvement. Here our author emphasizes the very human and imperfect nature of the people through whom these purposes were to be fulfilled. Both these emphases are at the heart of the life of faith. If we do not have a firm belief in God's providence we will quickly become discouraged. If we do not have a realistic view of human nature, including our own, we will soon become disillusioned.

Third is the key role of Nathan. This is not the first time his intervention has been crucial. After the dark story of David's adultery with Bathsheba and murder by proxy of Uriah (2 Sam. 11) which could easily have ended the story, the words of 2 Samuel 12:1 – 'The Lord sent Nathan to David' – open the way for repentance and grace. Here again, although no explicit mention is made of the Lord sending him, Nathan exercises a crucial service for the kingdom. We are not Nathan, but we have Nathan's God and we need to be alert for opportunities, however small, to advance that kingdom.

Don't underestimate David (1:28-40)

We are quickly disabused here of any idea that David is 'past it' as, with his old vigour, he acts decisively and immediately sets in motion the process of Solomon's accession to the throne. Technically what happens here is that he appoints Solomon as co-regent with the promise that he will succeed him on the throne. This is underlined in the most binding way by linking it with his own experience of God's deliverance. And so, for the first time in this chapter, specific mention is made of how the Lord has been at work in this story which so far seemed only to be about human activity. The promise of 2 Samuel 7:12-16 about David's heirs will be fulfilled after all because God is on the throne. It is this kingdom which will come and last for ever.

Once again the true David is revealed, the one who was fully devoted to the LORD his God (11:4). He cared passionately for God's honour and that roused him from somnolence; we glimpse briefly the young man who defended that honour in the Valley of Elah so long before. This is his first concern and we cannot write him off as a spent force (1 Sam. 17).

Yet this is not simply a pious hope because words are followed by vigorous action. David calls Zadok and Nathan, representing the priests and prophets who had so much helped him both in his rise to power and his reign. They are joined by Benaiah, the captain of his guard, who had also been sidelined by Adonijah, as public support begins to rally behind Solomon. The words 'Long live King Solomon'

are the public declaration of the new regime and again the
Lord's blessing is called on (1:36-37).

The loyalty of the army has been ensured by Benaiah,
and the presence of the Kerethites and Pelethites (v. 38),
mentioned in 2 Samuel 8:18 as part of David's bodyguard,
has underlined this. The anointing of Solomon (v. 39) by
Zadok recalls that of his father by Samuel (1 Sam. 16), 'All
the people' (v. 39) probably is a contrast to the select group
of followers clustering around Adonijah.

As we look beyond this to the bigger picture we should
not ignore the detail in verse 37 – 'make his throne even
greater than the throne of my lord King David'. To some
extent this did happen – see chapters 3 and following –
but it is ultimately to be fulfilled in 'Great David's Greater
Son'. As we read Luke 1:32 ('The Lord God will give him
the throne of his father David') we see this being fulfilled
beyond our wildest dreams. But just as Nathan played a
vital role earlier, so here the role of the rejuvenated David
is vital and must contribute to the final assessment of this
truly remarkable man.

Long live King Solomon (1:41-53)

Adonijah's conspiracy collapses as suddenly as it began.
Jonathan, Abiathar's son (not the more famous Jonathan,
David's friend in 1 Samuel) must have witnessed Solomon's
coronation. He gives the main point first: 'Our lord King
David has made Solomon king' (v. 43). Just to underline
this he describes those who have now come out publicly
for Solomon and the popular support they have received.
Those around Adonijah see quickly the way the wind is
blowing and make themselves scarce (v. 49). Adonijah
himself flees for sanctuary and grasps the horns of the altar;

Solomon strikes a bargain with him which falls short of a total amnesty shown by the absence of the words 'in peace' at the end of verse 53. It is hard to believe (and chapter 2 will demonstrate this) that Adonijah's 'loyalty' was more than skin deep: further problems lie ahead.

From text to message

As we begin preaching on historical narrative, especially a long and complicated one like 1 and 2 Kings, we will need to remember that many people subconsciously hold to Henry Ford's dictum that 'history is mainly bunk'. We ourselves need to work carefully at understanding the text, including its historical details, but we will not serve these neat. Sometimes these historical details matter, but we need to show their relevance to the exposition and blend them into the complete meal rather than show them off as ingredients.

On the other hand we need to avoid the kind of devotional application which is tenuously related to the text. What we are aiming at is responsible exegesis where we have done our homework on the historical background, examined theology and literary art, and used these to expound and teach Kings as the Word of God for today.

Getting the message clear: the theme

The theme of the chapter is that the kingdom of God is often in danger and although the Lord is in control, people are responsible for their attitudes and actions.

Getting the message clear: the aim

The aim of the message is to show how God reigns, but our part in the kingdom matters.

Ideas for application

Perhaps nowhere more than in biblical narrative do we need to be sensitive and careful in our application. We will go wildly astray if we try the moralizing approach: e.g. we need to be careful we don't become cold and apathetic like David, but we need to have renewed spiritual energy (also like David); we must not arrange parties like Adonijah when we ought to be getting on with our business. Like all platitudes, these comments contain truths, but truths that have become soporific rather than life-changing and have led essentially to a 'good-works' gospel which is no gospel at all. We are not David, Solomon, Hezekiah, Josiah; but we have the same God as they did and that needs to be our starting point.

+ The Bible is God's story about God and therefore we need to ask first what this chapter is saying about Him. We must see first of all His guiding hand behind these very political and 'unspiritual' events. God is in charge of His kingdom even when events conspire against. The kingdom, at this point of transition, looks very fragile and that is a stark reminder of how only the Lord can keep that kingdom safe and make it prosper.

+ The other side of that coin is that even the best of God's servants only make it by grace. There is a constant temptation to exaggerate our importance in the kingdom and imagine our own right hand has saved us. Our evangelical celebrity culture, aided by the Internet, has hugely overplayed our 'successes'. We need to be careful what we put on our websites and other publicity material. The truth is that none of our ministries, this side of glory, are all that impressive.

Realizing this, will help us to avoid two pitfalls: one is despair as we feel our efforts are so futile; the other is conceit as we imagine our exploits are so magnificent. Rather we need to rejoice in the grace that saved us, wrote our names in heaven and now allows us to play our little part.

+ We also see here the need for the life of faith to be lived in the messiness of human circumstances. The overruling hand of God does not mean that we 'let go and let God', but that we need to make choices, do what is right, and not simply become puppets.

+ Here we have – as in all of 1 Samuel through to the end of 2 Kings – studies of leadership where we are given glimpses of both effective and ineffective kinds of rule. Adonijah is the self-promoting, self-appointed leader who imagines that the qualification for leadership is simply to say 'I am a leader'. We have the spiritual leadership of Nathan which is vital in the crisis. We have David who, all through his story, has shown a remarkable ability to 'come back' and a remarkable sense of God's deliverance which had kept him throughout his turbulent and eventful life.

+ We must see this fragment of story as part of the Big Story. Indeed 1 and 2 Kings show their incompleteness by beginning with the close of David's reign and ending with the Exile already many years old. This is part of the same story of faith as Abraham, particularly that part in Genesis 17:6 where, to promises of descendants and land, God had added; 'I will make you into nations and kings shall come from you.'

+ The place of faith is vitally important, but even more so is God's faithfulness. A working title for a series on Kings could be 'Faithful God, Fickle People'. This is part of the covenant (more in later chapters) by which God pledges Himself to His people, yet for that covenant to be effective in our lives there needs to be a loving response.

+ Above all we need to find Christ in the text because the kingdom of David and sons is to be an acted parable on earth of the kingdom of his Greater Son. That kingdom now often looks feeble and threatened; yet it will one day fill the earth.

Many of these points will come up again as we work through Kings and we shall look at the many different contrasts and settings to find applications for our own day.

Suggestions for preaching
Sermon 1: The Kingdom in Danger
As a first sermon in a series, it is important to set the scene. For an introduction, the preacher could briefly fit the beginning of 1 Kings into the overall story of David and of David's Greater Son – 'we are not David, but we have David's God'.

+ **The kingdom often seems weak** (1:1-11). David seems inactive and his story is petering out whilst an impressive-looking rival king emerges. The preacher would need to expound the detail of the text, but continually apply it to the way the kingdom seems so weak now.

+ **The kingdom always has resourceful servants** (1:11-27). The text underlines the significance of

Nathan who has intervened at other critical points (especially 2 Sam. 11 and 12). There is always a need to be alert and watchful.

+ **The kingdom will certainly come** (1:28-40). There is a new energy in the cause of the kingdom – David shows his passion for the LORD: not that David is to bring in the kingdom, but that his renewed energy is a sign that God is at work.

+ **The kingdom's enemies are conquered** (1:41-53) – temporarily then and now, but completely when Christ returns.

The preacher needs to make sure he emphasizes that this is God's story about God's kingdom and that the human agents, good and bad, operate under His will. This sermon is one of encouragement when the kingdom seems weak, but also contains a challenge to be ready for the Master's use.

Sermon 2
In the next chapter, I shall suggest a sermon outline for dealing with chapters 1 and 2 together.

Suggestions for teaching
Likewise, I shall reserve comments on Bible studies until the end of chapter 2 and deal with the two chapters together.

2

THE KINGDOM SAVED
(1 KINGS 2)

Introduction

In a large book like 1 and 2 Kings it is not altogether easy to get our bearings or to find the underlying theme and that is why this chapter is so important. The first few verses (2:1-4) seem to be the key which unlocks the treasures of the book. The twin themes of ruling justly (see 2 Sam. 23:1-7) and obeying the Word of God are linked inextricably. Thus as a working concept we can see the theme of the entire book as 'ruling justly when obeying God's Word'. This can be traced throughout the book in the following way: in chapters 1–16, there is the role of Nathan and various named and unnamed 'men of God' who speak to those in the seats of power; there are the great prophetic ministries of Elijah and Elisha which dominate the major middle section (1 Kings 17–2 Kings 13) and the great reformation of Josiah (2 Kings 23). Indeed we can see this pattern in 1 and 2 Samuel with Samuel himself and

Nathan and Gad. Obeying the covenant is the only way to peace and prosperity for king and people.

The rise of Solomon has not in itself resolved the tensions of chapter 1. We have yet to discover what kind of a king he will be and not least what are to be his guiding principles. That is the importance of verses 1-4, already identified in the Introduction as the key to the book. If Solomon is to be a godly king and not simply a competent one, he must rule justly while obeying God's Word: thus the emphasis on Moses the supreme prophet (Deut. 34:10-12) and the continuing emphasis throughout the book on the words of prophets. God will remain faithful, but His covenant people and especially their kings need to walk in His ways. This is a major concern in the chapters which follow.

Listening to the text
Context and structure

The context is the death of David; not just the close of a reign, but the end of an era and the firm establishing of Solomon's reign.

There are three main divisions which form the structure of the chapter:

+ The obedience of faith (2:1-4)

+ The danger from enemies (2:5-12)

+ The overthrow of enemies (2:13-46)

The repetition of the word 'established' (vv. 12 and 46) underlines that the main concern of this chapter is to show that after the intrigues of chapter 1 the kingdom is now secure and the promises of 2 Samuel 7 are being fulfilled.

Working through the text
The obedience of faith (2:1-4)

As David approaches death he gives a charge to Solomon about what matters most. David turns to the fountain from which the life of the kingdom flows, which is faithfulness to the LORD's commands. The fact that this is the end of an era is underlined by the echo of words used by Joshua – 'I am about to go the way of all the earth' (Josh. 23:14), a phrase reminding us of human frailty and transience. There is a call for courage and stamina and a total lifestyle. This will be both in conduct – 'walk in his ways' – and in detailed obedience – 'keep his decrees and commands, his laws and requirements'. These are not arbitrary ideas dreamed up by David, but faithfulness to the Torah; the words of Moses which are the words of God. It is important to remember that there is no authority in the Old Testament which supersedes or bypasses that of Moses. Here the Torah is explicitly linked with the covenant with David; 2 Samuel 7:14-15 shows that God will fulfil His covenant promises in spite of the disobedience of any Davidic king, but there will be no enjoyment of the blessings of that covenant without obedience. Indeed we can go back further to the promise to Abraham in Genesis 17:6 – 'I will make nations of you and kings will come from you'. The story of God's covenant faithfulness is the story of Scripture.

But these words are not only for the Davidic kings; these are words for all who by grace belong to that kingdom. Jesus speaks of the wise as those who hear His words and do them (Matt. 7:24-25). Like the Davidic king, they will also be established. It is a reminder of how the kingdom comes. We rate obedience fairly insignificantly in our priorities and place more emphasis on programmes, personalities and politics. This chapter and the following ones will deal with all these latter matters, but we need to establish our priorities and remember the earlier prophetic Word 'to obey is better than sacrifice' (1 Sam. 15:22). Such obedience in heart and action builds for eternity.

The danger from enemies (2:5-12)

However, there is unfinished business to be dealt with. Enemies remain and it is unlikely that they will disappear quietly. These verses and the rest of the chapter have sometimes been seen as showing a callous and calculating side of both David and Solomon. We need to remember that ancient Israel was a political state as well as God's people and had to operate in the world of war and politics. David is concerned about the continuing threat to his kingdom. We are not being asked to admire or imitate this advice and Solomon's subsequent actions. 'Narrative is not normative' (see Introduction on Preaching Narrative).

The Torah is the authoritative message and requires complete obedience. Here in the messiness of life (read again 1/2 Samuel!) and in the ambiguities of difficult situations, these principles are to be worked out. The question is whether Solomon will show the same alacrity in obeying the Torah as he does in eliminating the enemies. I think it is fair to see Solomon as an astute politician here rather than callous and vindictive. Also, and significantly, we need to recognize the importance of verse 7 about Barzillai of whom we read in 2 Samuel 17–19. He had been loyal and generous to David as he fled from Absalom and now David characteristically (remember Mephibosheth in 2 Sam. 9?) provides for his family.

This section ends with the passing of the kingdom from David to Solomon (vv. 10 and 11) and this passing establishes the pattern for the death announcements of the kings of Judah and Israel. 'Rested with his fathers' not only means buried in the family vault, but the continuity of the dynasty and indeed the continuing story of all God's people. The 'City of David' is to be of great significance throughout the story (for example, 2 Kings 19:34 when the LORD rescues Jerusalem from the Assyrians). In Acts 2:29ff, Peter, in his Pentecost sermon, speaks of David's tomb. He also uses Psalm 16 showing that David's destiny is finally fulfilled when his Greater Son defeated death and brought in a kingdom which would never end.

In the meantime the throne is secure – 'firmly established' (v. 12); a phrase echoed in verses 24 and 46. God is at work and the kingdom will come in spite of the weakness of His servants and the attacks of His enemies.

The overthrow of enemies (2:13-46)
This introductory narrative of chapters 1 and 2 ends with an account of the ways in which Solomon acted decisively and rid himself of four main enemies. The first to go is Adonijah who provides the occasion for his own removal (vv. 13-25). This is a fascinating paragraph full of cross-currents and questions. Is Adonijah simply being naive (he had overestimated his support in chapter 1)? Here he shows he has learned nothing – 'All Israel looked to me as their king'. Now he wants Abishag as a consolation prize. Again it is not clear whether Bathsheba is being naive or making a shrewd calculation. Adonijah's motives are obscure and even if he was not actively seeking the throne he was being foolish. A wiser man would have sat tight and been careful not to draw himself to Solomon's attention. Also Solomon is concerned with the future of

the dynasty and its connection with Yahweh's promise to David (v. 24).

Similarly the removal of Abiathar from the priesthood (vv. 26 and 27) is seen as a fulfilment of the prophecy of the demise of Eli's house (1 Sam. 2:31-33). God who ensures the continuance of David's house carries out His just judgment on the faithless family of priests.

The axe now falls on Joab (vv. 28-35) and we are reminded of the story of Joab's ruthlessness in 2 Samuel. We are also reminded that Joab was a political schemer and that he 'had conspired with Adonijah though not with Absalom'. The reason for this is that he thought Adonijah would win, but that Absalom would not; although he advanced the cause of Absalom when it suited him (2 Sam. 14). Again we are reminded that God had chosen the house of David (v. 33) and that Joab had ultimately chosen another way. When it suited him, Joab had been loyal to David, but he had never loved David's God.

One figure remains, and now Solomon turns his attention to Shimei who had cursed and stoned David during Absalom's rebellion (2 Sam. 16:5-13) and had subsequently made a grovelling peace (2 Sam. 19:18-23). Presumably the command to stay in Jerusalem was to cut him off from his power base in Bahurim. With seeming inevitability Shimei breaks his parole and is executed. Yet again the promise and covenant with David is emphasized and the reign of Solomon is now firmly established.

From text to message
Getting the message clear: the theme
The theme of the text is how to balance faithfulness to God's Word with the complicated realities of living

in the world; difficulties which are especially acute for leaders.

Getting the message right: the aim
The aim is to show that while the Word of God must determine all we do, there are often difficulties, especially in situations of leadership, in applying it.

A way in
Leadership is very much the flavour of our time. Conferences, courses, books and DVDs all give guidance on this matter. There is no doubt much to learn and many of the techniques suggested can be helpful. There is a danger, though, that leadership is seen mainly as a mastering of certain ways of operating and finding a winning formula. But what really matters, not least to the Christian leader, is humble listening to the Word of God and behaving as a servant rather than a manipulator. This chapter, springing from David's words to Solomon, emphasizes the character of the leader as it is shaped by that Word.

Ideas for application
Bearing in mind the comments made in Part 1 about not treating narrative as moralizing anecdote, some further comments can be made:

+ The text teaches the importance of God's providence. At first that might seem more theoretical than practical, but failure to grasp this will mean either we will resort to moralizing or to delivering historical lectures. Providence is essentially a doctrine which encourages perseverance; God is working out His purpose with indifferent human material and that is

writ large in 1/2 Kings. The book was written to those
who knew the bitterness of exile (see Part 1) and had
to be reassured that, while God's just anger had led to
this, His covenant love endures forever. This remains
as true today as at every stage of the history of God's
people. Thus we are both challenged and encouraged.

+   Humans are responsible for their actions. Providence
    does not reduce people to puppets. The four characters
    here whom Solomon judged were responsible for
    their past actions and for how they would now react
    to Solomon's rule. This is the same for us: the life of
    faith is not lived in a vacuum and every circumstance,
    however major or trivial, ultimately reveals where our
    loyalties lie. Far from being a denial of providence and
    grace, this is a sign that grace is at work.

+   The centrality of Scripture in the lives of God's people
    is underlined. Chapter 2:1-4 is the peak from which
    we survey the surrounding landscape and gives us the
    authoritative view on the personalities and events.
    Scripture will give us the way to live in changing
    circumstances. At the time of writing, the author of
    Kings did not have the complete canon, but certainly
    had the authoritative Torah of Moses, the Word
    which was to be taught to children, to be the subject
    of conversation and the rule of life (Deut. 6:4-9). That
    this is no mere head knowledge is shown by the words
    of response to the Torah: 'be strong' indicates that
    these words will give courage; 'walk' means they will
    determine lifestyle; 'keep' shows they are authoritative
    and mandatory. 'You may prosper' (v. 3) is not the
    prosperity gospel. They are in context a promise of

God's blessing to the covenant king. The application is not that the Lord will give us a Mercedes-Benz, but that the character of the kingdom will be shown in the midst of hostility; we will be building for eternity.

+ These stories are a warning that we must not be super-spiritual and sentimental. The narrative as it continues from 1 and 2 Samuel is a reminder that David is flawed and the mention of Bathsheba is a continual reminder of this. Read the sordid story of the complete breakdown of anything resembling godliness in David's family in 2 Samuel 13ff. Yet read these also as a story of 'where sin increased grace increased all the more' (Rom. 5:20). All of us are only going to make it by grace. Yet these stories also show that while it is not possible to serve God perfectly, it is possible to serve Him faithfully. David may have been flawed, but David was faithful.

Preaching Christ faithfully (chapters 1 and 2)

Long ago God had promised Abraham (and repeated the promise to Jacob) that 'kings will come from you' (Gen. 17:6; 35:11). Second Samuel 7:8-16 had seen that promise given not only to David, but to his descendants. However, the story of Kings raises huge question marks which can only be resolved when the true King comes: the Davidic kingdom genuinely pointed to Christ and as we preach the story of the earthly kingdom we need to show that.

Here two particular points can be made. The first is the inadequacy of the Davidic king who, like other sinners, is only going to make it by grace. The other is the genuine link of the king with his Greater Son. There we have true gospel, not moralizing platitudes about being or not being like David.

Suggestions for preaching

It is important to do justice to the twin themes of providence and human responsibility in the text and to show the broad sweep without ignoring the detail. As we saw the kingdom in danger in chapter 1 we might use the heading:

Sermon 1: The Kingdom established

It will be useful for the preacher to point out the importance of the verb 'established' (vv. 12, 24, 45, 46) and show how this links the two parts of the chapter: the divine promise and the human actions.

Two main points would reflect the text:

+ **The kingdom established by obedience** (2:1-12).
    + Covenant theme of Scripture. Throughout the Bible, obedience is a strong theme of response to the sovereign Lord. Here David refers back to the law of Moses and how it should be a characteristic of Solomon's reign.

    + Comprehensive obedience (v. 3). It is important to take seriously the whole Word of God.

    + Continuity of dynasty. The Greater Son will one day rule the world – in the shorter term David's dynasty is to last over 400 years.

    + Completion of task left unfinished by David (5-12). No leader, however effective, can complete all the tasks and solve all the problems.

+ **The kingdom established by overthrowing enemies** (2:13-46).
    + Messy work of eliminating the four enemies. As already seen, these are ambivalent actions.

+ Messianic theme. Christ will reign until all His
enemies are eliminated. In times of effective
leadership we see partial glimpses of the final
victory Christ will achieve.

Sermon 2: The Kingdom disputed

The first two chapters are an introduction to Kings as a whole
and more specifically to the reign of Solomon which is to occupy
almost half of 1 Kings. At the end of chapter 1 we looked at the
canonical significance of Solomon. These have established the
main themes of God's providence; the centrality of covenant;
the overriding authority of Torah; the anointed king and the
human circumstances in which these all unfold.

However, there is merit in taking these two chapters
together. I want to suggest how we might preach and teach
on the two chapters as a whole to reflect the importance of
them as an introduction to the bulk of 1 Kings. The title
'The Kingdom disputed' combines the sense of vulnerability
and yet suggests that there is a certainty about its arrival.

By way of introduction, the preacher would need to:

+ fit the first two chapters into the big picture,
especially emphasizing the covenant promises,
and glance at 2 Samuel 7.

+ give some indication of how this is about an
unchanging God in changing circumstances –
i.e., show it is God's story rather than the story of
David or Solomon.

A possible outline could be:
+ **The endangered kingdom** (Chapter 1)
    + The crisis of leadership. This is a danger point
    because of the possibility of a power vacuum,

exactly what happened at the end of Joshua and led to the chaos of Judges. The preacher could also refer to Paul's letters to Timothy and Titus and the necessity of godly leadership after the apostles had passed on.

+ The emergence of bad leadership. Adonijah has echoes of both Absalom and Saul.

+ **The obedient kingdom** (2:1-4)

  + Obedience is the key to unlock the book: faithfulness to the words of Moses which are the words of God Himself. This is integral to God's covenant with David (2 Sam. 7).

  + Obedience is comprehensive: whole Torah for whole lifestyle.

  + Obedience is practical: building to last for eternity.

+ **The established kingdom** (2:5-46)

  + Defeat and removal of enemies.

  + Emphasis on the line of David – to be fulfilled in his Greater Son.

Suggestions for teaching
Questions to help understand the passage

1. How do David's words (2:2-4) link effective leadership with obedience and set the pattern for future kings?

2. David's second instructions (2:5-9) speak of unfinished business from his reign. What aspects of David's character do they reveal?

3. How does 2:11-12 show the importance of David in the story?

4. Do you think Solomon overreacted in his treatment of Adonijah? (2:13-25) Why, or why not?

5. Why was Abiathar removed from the priesthood? (2:26-27)

6. Why do you think the death of Absalom (2 Sam. 18:9-14) is not mentioned in 2:32 as a reason for killing Joab?

7. Why does Solomon link the killing of Shimei (2:44-45) with the blessing on David's throne.

8. What does 2:46b suggest about the author's attitude to the events of the chapter?

Questions to help apply the passage

1. What do we learn about the importance of obeying the Word of God (2:2-4) and how would that help in recognizing true leaders?

2. How do we avoid dealing with enemies from becoming mere personal vindictiveness? (Reading 2 and 3 John may be helpful as, in 2 John, the apostle shows us how to recognize the fake, and, in 3 John, how to appreciate the genuine).

3. What qualities of Barzillai and his sons (see 2 Sam. 19:31-39) are commended (2:7) and how might we recognize these today?

4. There are several references to the throne of David (2:12, 24, 33, 45). As we think through these, how can we show that in the middle of what seems a catalogue of violence the story is pointing to Christ.

5. It is always easier to follow specific instructions, as
    Solomon does here in the eliminating of trouble-
    makers, than the daily obedience to the Word of God
    (2:2-4). How do we practise this daily obedience?

3

Solomon's Springtime
(1 Kings 3)

Introduction

In *The Lion, The Witch and The Wardrobe*, as the White Witch drives her sledge through the wintry landscape, the severe weather begins to change and the snow starts to melt. She is forced to abandon the sledge and, dragging the hapless Edmund along at a fast walk, finds that the green patches are growing and the sky is turning blue. She is furious, but her attendant, the dwarf, makes it worse by saying: 'This is no thaw ... This is spring ... This is Aslan's doing'. C.S. Lewis is depicting the dying of the winter power of the White Witch as spring comes on, a sign of King Aslan's coming. The retreat of winter and the transformed landscape is a trailer of the new creation.

A similar atmosphere is almost palpable in this chapter. After the intrigues and violence of the previous chapters, we breathe freer air; there is a youthful vitality here and a sense of enormous promise. David had compared the rule of the just king to morning sunlight and fresh, springing

grass (2 Sam. 23:4) and here and in the following chapters
we sense that this might just be happening. Here begins the
focus on wisdom which is to dominate the Solomon story
and to be explored in a number of spheres.

Listening to the text

Context and structure

Solomon is now king and, as 2:46 says 'the kingdom was
now firmly established in Solomon's hands'. This chapter
is a series of snapshots of the early years of his reign and
presents an attractive picture of his rule beginning wisely
and compassionately.

The chapter has three main movements which form the
basis for the teaching points.

+ An ambiguous start (3:1-3)

+ A faithful prayer (3:4-15)

+ A wise act (3:16-28)

The theme of wisdom binds the chapter together and
provides the standpoint from which to view the events.

Working through the text

An ambiguous start (3:1-3)

How are we to read Solomon's story? A common way is to
see it in two distinct parts. The first part up to chapter 10 is
a record of consistent faithfulness and conspicuous success
both for the king and the nation. The second (ch. 11) is
unmitigated disaster and leads to the break-up of the
kingdom. That is far too neat a division however, and,
I believe, ignores the hints of ambiguity in the text. Another
view is far more critical and sees him as severely flawed
from the start and on a fairly steady downward course. My

own reading is that it is too severe to see Solomon that way and thus I want to suggest that there is an ambivalence in Solomon's character which I think is faithful to the text and is pastorally helpful.

Two things call for comment in 3:1-3. The first is Solomon's marriage to the Pharaoh's daughter. Doubtless both sides would see great diplomatic advantages in this. For Solomon there would be great prestige and for the Pharaoh a means of keeping an eye on this often troublesome nation just to the north of his borders. However, warning bells begin to ring as we remember David's instruction to keep all the commands of Moses. Deuteronomy warns against a king making the people return to Egypt (Deut. 17:16). Solomon was doing something at least as dangerous, bringing Egypt into Jerusalem. We can see this as the beginning of the large numbers of foreign wives (11:1) where we learn that the only difference between this princess and the others was the eminence of her dad.

The other is the mention of the 'high places' which we will meet often in our journey through Kings and it is worth saying something about their significance. They were local sacred sites, often on high ground, and may originally have been places of Canaanite worship. Moses had specifically forbidden the use of such centres in the worship of Yahweh (Deut. 7:5; 12:3). They remained as a temptation and only in the reigns of the great reforming kings Hezekiah (2 Kings 18:4) and Josiah (2 Kings 23:5) were they removed. The key question here is what we make of the phrase 'a temple had not yet been built'. That is a simple enough phrase and clearly a building project like the temple could not be completed overnight. Is there, however, a hint of delay on the part of Solomon?

There is potential for disaster here, then, but that is as yet far away, and verse 3 speaks of Solomon's love for the Lord and his taking seriously his father's words in 2:1-4. There is no suggestion of hypocrisy; Solomon's love for Yahweh was genuine, but it was fitful and we will see the result of this in chapter 11. I think this assessment of Solomon is also pastorally helpful. The view that he was wonderful and then with startling suddenness apostatized is a counsel of despair. The idea that we can go to bed one night loving the Lord and get up the next morning having completely fallen away is totally untrue to life as we live it. On the other hand, the view which sees him as unsatisfactory from the start is too cynical. He is an ambiguous figure and most of his story is inspiring, but the small compromises gradually erode his first love and lead to disaster.

A faithful prayer (3:4-15)

Gibeon housed the tabernacle after the destruction of Shiloh (1 Chron. 21:29) and it is here that Yahweh appears to Solomon in a dream. Thus the initiative is wholly God's and that truth sits right at the heart of covenant. The verb 'ask' dominates this section (vv. 5, 10, 11, 13). When human weakness meets divine grace, then God is pleased (v. 10a). Like other prayers in Scripture this one is specific to the person and unique to the situation, but since prayer is about the nature of God we learn a lot about what true prayer is. God appears here in a dream, but that is a common biblical way of revelation, as with Jacob at Bethel (Gen. 28).

God is amazingly generous: this is a blank cheque, an open-ended offer: 'Ask for whatever you want me to give you' (v. 5). Now, we are not Solomon, but James 1:5 echoes the same generosity: 'If any of you lacks wisdom he should ask God who gives generously to all'. Prayer is not forcing concessions from a niggardly God. The poet John Newton writes: 'You are coming to a King; large petitions with you bring'. We often limit the Lord by forgetting His amazing generosity. This *does not* mean as in the silly TV commercial – 'Oh Lord, won't you buy me a Mercedes-Benz', but *does* mean that He will use all the resources of the Godhead to bring us to glory and to guard us on the way, and more particularly to give us the wisdom for faithful and consistent living.

God is consistently faithful: Solomon's prayer focuses on who God is and what He has done before the king requests anything. He uses the language of covenant, here specifically relating to the covenant with David (2 Sam. 7). He himself is living proof that the first part of that promise has been fulfilled – 'When your days are over ... I will raise up your offspring to succeed you ... and I will establish his kingdom' (2 Sam. 7:12). But the promise goes far back beyond David to Abraham for verse 8 is an echo of the promise that Abraham's descendants are too numerous to be counted.

God is faithful; that is an absolute truth; not that God is *sometimes* faithful; not even that He is *mostly* faithful; but that, at all times and in all places, He is *always* faithful. This is what Paul emphasizes to the Corinthians (1 Cor. 1:9). It is what brings confidence in praying. There is a saying which is often misused – 'Prayer changes things'. We know what that means, but it places the emphasis on the intensity and frequency of the praying rather than on the faithfulness of God, and leads either to triumphalism or despondency. Prayer puts us in touch with God who does change things and people.

God also cares for His people. The people are at the heart of Solomon's concern and this leads to his request for wisdom. He is a 'little child' and totally inexperienced in governing. His modesty might not have impressed U.K. business guru Lord Sugar and won him a place as an apprentice, but it certainly shows his sense of the enormous responsibility. So he asks for 'a discerning heart'. 'Heart' in Hebrew is a bigger thing than it is in English and includes the intellect as well as the emotions. The heart is essentially who we are; Solomon asks for spiritual, intellectual and emotional understanding to govern all he does and is. Verse 9 needs to be pondered deeply by all in leadership. Of course we are not kings, even if we are senior pastors of large and flourishing churches, but we need to pray this prayer if we have any responsibility at all as leaders among the Lord's people.

We can also see how God's pleasure is the true aim of prayer. 'The Lord was pleased that Solomon had asked him for this' (v. 10). Yahweh now gives Solomon not only what he asks, but many things for which he did not ask. These other things God grants must be good things, otherwise they would not have been granted. Wealth and long life are generous gifts of God and should be received with thankfulness. Likewise, honour, if it is received humbly, is a blessing. But surely the point is that prayer is more about relationship than request. So often we lapse into shopping lists which show little sense of the majesty of God or even of His capacity to do immeasurably more than we can ask or imagine. The reminder of the need of obedience (v. 14) is not the gospel of good works smuggled in the back door, but rather the reality that, while the covenant expresses the unconditional love of the Lord, for its blessings to be enjoyed there needs to be obedience.

It is interesting that Solomon's first action is to offer covenant sacrifices and give a feast. The earlier feast in this book was Adonijah's party (see 1:9-10) as he made his abortive bid for the throne, but this feast is a sign of a harmonious and united court ready to obey the rule of the wise king.

A wise act (3:16-28)

This story is a practical example of the wisdom for which Solomon had asked and an early answer to his prayer. It is a classic example of biblical narrative with a brilliant use of suspense, characterization advanced by dialogue and effective use of circumstantial detail (vv. 16-28). The narrative has an eyewitness feel and a clear sense of authenticity. It is an illustration of Proverbs 16:10 – 'The lips of a king speak as an oracle'. We have our first glimpse of the wise king administering justice and ruling in the fear of God (see 2 Sam. 23:3). In chapters 4 and 5 we will see this principle illustrated far more widely. The fact that these women are prostitutes is very significant because this shows that everyone, however despised or on the margins, will receive justice from the wise king.

The evidence is presented by the accuser and the absence of any witnesses makes confirmation or denial impossible, and therefore makes severe demands on the king's wisdom. We might well wonder how the woman knew what happened in the night when she was asleep, but her reconstruction of events is probable since obviously she knew her own child. Solomon's decision is well known. He gives instructions to cut the child in two; the true mother is willing to give up her child alive, but the other, who appears to be heartless, is willing that this child should die as well. This shows that people have genuine choices. Both women were rejects and had no place in society except at the bottom. Yet while one chooses the path of self-interest that is the essence of sin, the other shows a capacity for unselfish love which is a response to the grace of God.

However the main focus of the story is the wisdom of Solomon and the deep impression it made on the kingdom. This is important because without justice the other kinds of wisdom outlined in the next two chapters would evaporate. The kingdom of Yahweh on earth anticipates that of heaven when justice is enthroned and partiality expelled.

From text to message
Getting the message clear: the theme
Wisdom is a God-given gift and thus only dependence on God and prayer can ensure the gift is used properly.

Getting the message clear: the aim
The aim of the passage is to show that when God calls someone to a position, He will provide the necessary resources and those so called need to remain in humble dependence on Him.

A way in
When we read the biography of a significant person it is often fascinating to read about their early days: the people who influenced them and the circumstances which shaped them. In the biographies of Churchill, for example, we read of the determination to succeed and compensate for his father's lack of belief in him, and of the early experiences of journalism, war and politics.

While 1 Kings 1–11 is not a biography of Solomon, yet here we see some of the early influences in his reign which shape the mature person and which underlie the rest of the story. The ambiguities of his marriage to the Pharaoh's daughter, and the keeping of the high places alongside his love for Yahweh and his wisdom are all depicted here.

Ideas for application

We have already noticed the ambiguities in the text which make this more interesting than a simplistic 'Solomon is good here; follow Solomon'. Indeed we can only make proper application once we see that this is God's story about God. With that in mind we can consider the following points.

+ Wisdom is clearly at the heart of this chapter and is already seen to be much more than intelligence, and that theme will be developed in the following chapters. Here it includes government in its broadest sense ('to govern this great people of yours') and in the affairs of individuals. Careful administration (as we will see in chapter 4) is a vital part of this, but on its own could be carried out in a soulless manner which sees individuals as merely units. Similarly, the 'pastoral' case of the two prostitutes shows that insight into human nature is indispensable. If wisdom were a human aptitude, then indeed we would be perpetually condemned to frustration as we try in our churches both to be caring and efficient. The trouble is that so often this is exactly how we operate, trusting in our organizational skills or our charismatic personalities. We need to learn and keep on learning that we have nothing which we did not receive.

+ We need to be careful about compromise, illustrated here by Pharaoh's daughter and the non-removal of the high places. Both these arise, as we have seen, from imperfect obedience and at root believing we know better than the Lord. Both can be justified in terms of expediency and sensible policy, but both produce a string of consequences. The romantic one in the multiple idolatries of chapter 11; and the worship one in the continuing fascination with Canaanite religion seen throughout 1 Kings. Both are symptoms of a divided heart and an early suggestion of fickleness.

- The nature of God is revealed here and we are shown how this relates to effective prayer. It begins with the overflowing mercy and faithfulness of God which is the basis of bold asking. Government and policy are wrapped in prayer here and thus in the next few chapters we are going to see a king and nation who have been marvellously blessed. Great thoughts of God will lead to effective praying and will save from pride. The generosity of God will prevent our prayers being self-centred, as will our understanding of his prayer for his people. Solomon recognizes his inadequacy and thus is open to receive the gifts of God. The echo of the promise to Abraham reminds us that these promises are to the whole family of faith generally as well as to the royal line specifically. The prayer of faith is also the prayer of obedience which draws on the character of God and what He is able to do.

- Revelation by a dream is worth considering; many biblical examples can be given, such as (notably) Joseph and Daniel and also the dreams in the New Testament to Joseph and the wise men in Matthew 1 and 2, and to Paul in Acts 16. This reminds us of the mystery of

God's ways and that He works independently of the control of humans and can in His wisdom bypass the normal means of communication. In our desire to explain everything we often forget this. Obviously we have the complete canon of Scripture and look to that as a light in the darkness and as the supreme authority, but we need to avoid rationalism and not to impose on God false limits of our own. A good example would be the many who have been converted from Muslim backgrounds by an appearance of Christ in a dream.

+ Above all we need to see how Solomon points beyond himself to the King who is to come. The gifts of wisdom, discernment and wise judgment are only to be fully realized in the Davidic King of the future: 'The Spirit of the LORD will rest on him – the Spirit of wisdom and understanding ... with righteousness he will judge the needy and with justice he will give decisions for the poor of the earth' (Isa. 11:2-4).

+ At this particular time in his life Solomon points to the king who will rule in righteousness (Isa. 32:1). In his springtime we catch a glimpse of what British poet Matthew Arnold calls 'the high midsummer pomps' when the Son of Man comes into His kingdom. This will be explored further in chapter 4. Solomon points to the One who is not simply a Wisdom Teacher, but One in whom 'are hidden all the treasures of wisdom and knowledge' (Col. 2:3).

Suggestions for preaching

If you follow my suggested interpretation of Solomon you will want the overall picture to be positive, but point out the warning signs and probably concentrate on the heart or the deep wells of Solomon's character – always remembering this is not a series of character studies of Solomon, but a picture of how God is bringing His kingdom.

Sermon: God's King starts to reign

There is a clear set of bookends in this chapter 'Solomon made an alliance' (v. 1) and 'he had wisdom from God' (v. 28). This suggests that these first two actions, i.e., marrying the Pharaoh's daughter and the use of the high places, were taken at his own initiative rather than in the light of the wisdom God gave him.

+ **A heart for God** (3:1-3). Solomon's love for God is genuine, but fickle, as seen in his links to Egypt and failure to deal with the high places.

+ **An open heart** (3:4-15). There is much that we can learn about God from Solomon's prayer:

    + God is amazingly generous.

    + God is consistently faithful.

    + God cares for His people.

    + God's pleasure is the aim of prayer.

+ **A wise heart** (3:16-28). The preacher needs to make sure he conveys the narrative brilliance of this section where everyone receives justice; and people have genuine choices. Above all, Solomon points to the King who is to come.

Suggestions for teaching
Questions to help understand the passage

1. Why does the author place the marriage of Pharaoh's daughter alongside the mention of the City of David (v. 1)?

2. What were the 'high places' (v. 3) and why were they dangerous?

3. Why does God sometimes use dreams to communicate? (vv. 4-5).

4. What qualities of Solomon are shown in verses 7-9?

5. Why does Yahweh give Solomon exceptional wisdom (v. 12)?

6. What does the fact that the prostitutes (v. 16) appear to have access to the king show about Solomon's style of government?

7. What does Solomon's judgment (v. 27) show about his understanding of human nature?

Questions to help apply the text

1. The passage is positive about Solomon, but his marriage and the high places (vv. 1-3) ring warning bells. What areas of compromise are we prone to in individual and corporate life?

2. Verses 7-9 show Solomon's sense of inadequacy and the need for help. Are we inclined often to think we can get by without God's help and what are the consequences?

3. Yahweh clearly knew what Solomon would ask (v. 10), but He still responded in grace to Solomon's request. What light does this throw on guidance?

4. We now have the full revelation and thus would not expect God to speak through dreams unless in exceptional circumstances, for example, stories of Muslims to whom Jesus has appeared in a dream. Do we sometimes, in a commendable desire to avoid sensationalism, too readily dismiss the ways in which the Lord might speak to us? Why?

5. What does the incident of the prostitutes teach us about true pastoral care to those at the bottom of society? As individuals and churches how can we show care to such people?

4

REIGNING AND BUILDING
(1 KINGS 4–5)

Introduction

'What I like about the New Testament,' said the man, 'is that it doesn't have these long lists of names that the Old Testament does.' In fact, the New Testament begins with such a list and there are others such as Romans 16. Yet it must be said that the list of names in 1 Kings 4:1-19 is unlikely to fill readers with wonder, love and praise. Long-dead officials and details of administration can have little interest for anyone. Similarly, in chapter 5, logs floating on rafts and the cutting of stones can hardly cause our hearts to burn. But that is fundamentally to misunderstand why these chapters are here and how they flow from chapter 3 and show how Solomon's God-given wisdom extended to the details of daily life – just such details which are vital at home and work and which we take for granted until they fail to be present.

Listening to the text
Context and structure
These chapters show Solomon's wisdom working out both in the administration of the country and the building of the Temple. The chapters can be looked at in the following sections:

+ All the king's men (4:1-6)

+ All the king's lands (4:7-19)

+ All the king's wealth (4:20-28)

+ All the king's admirers (4:29-34)

+ All the king's friends (5:1-7).

+ All the king's plans (5:8-18)

We shall look at some points of detail as well as exploring the chapter as a whole.

All the king's men (4:1-6)
This list of officials recalls similar ones from David's reign (2 Sam. 8:16-18 and 2 Sam. 20:23-26) and reveals evidence both of continuity and new blood. Presumably Azariah (v. 2) is the priest, i.e., the High Priest, as opposed to the ordinary priests (v. 4); thus Zadok and Abiathar have gone to make way for Zadok's sons; new days, new faces. The reference to 'forced labour' (v. 6) will remind the alert reader of Samuel's warning of a king lording it over the people (1 Sam. 8:10-18).

This list is another evidence of God's concern for individuals, the forgotten as well as the famous. There is also the evidence of Solomon's practical wisdom in the balancing of old and new appointments.

All the king's lands (4:7-19)

This is a list of administrative districts and their officials whose purpose was to provide taxation and revenue. Some commentators take the phrase 'all Israel' (v. 7) to mean that Judah is excluded from these arrangements because it had a privileged place in the tax system, but rather it seems to draw attention to the unity of the people which is one of the blessings of Solomon's wisdom.

The purpose of 4:1-19 is to remind us that the people of God do not exist in a rarefied spiritual vacuum. Good administration, attention to detail and accountability are necessary for the community to flourish. There is a kind of super-spirituality which despises practicality and thinks that sloppiness and lack of organization is more glorifying to God. The land promised to the patriarchs must be properly cared for and its resources used wisely.

All the king's wealth (4:20-28)

However, the real point of this detail comes in the sparkling words of verses 20 and 21. Here the promises to Abraham are being fulfilled as Solomon reigns over the lands between the Nile and the Euphrates (Gen. 15:18-21); those lands which his father had conquered (see 2 Sam. 8). This is much more than competent administration; this is a fulfilment of covenant promises. The people are rejoicing and it is a time of plenty and party which anticipates the new creation. It is the promises of Yahweh rather than the prudence of Solomon which this text emphasizes. So this apparently dull passage bursts into life and points beyond itself to the time when the true King will reign and creation will wear the new clothes of its joyous liberation from the curse.

The details of the daily consumption of Solomon's court also underline the generosity of God, the gracious Giver who delights to bless His people. Perhaps a warning note may sound in verse 26 where the reference to horses recalls the warning that the king is not to multiply horses and chariots and thus rely on military hardware (Deut. 17:16). Like the earlier warning bells, they are just that; the emphasis is still very positive.

All the king's admirers (4:29-34)

Here we move to Solomon's international prestige and the astonishing depth and range of his wisdom. Yet this wisdom is a gift and as long as Solomon remains humble and teachable, this will prevent pride. This is almost a hymn to wisdom and the excitement of the author is unmistakable. The first emphasis is the quality of Solomon's wisdom: it is 'very great insight'; a phrase also used of Joseph in Genesis 41:33, 39. 'Breadth of understanding' shows that his was no narrow ability, but a generous range of talent. This led to his acquiring an international reputation and this will be illustrated in the visit of the Queen of Sheba (10:1-13). His wisdom exceeded that of the centres of wisdom in the ancient world in the Tigris/Euphrates valley and along the Nile, famous for their wisdom long before Solomon's time. The names in verse 31 are long forgotten, but at the time were bywords for wisdom, as we might say someone has the brains of Einstein.

This wisdom is further specified as being in the realm of observation, speaking and writing. We think of the book of Proverbs, but beyond that the word 'wisdom' also includes parables, similes, metaphors and other literary forms. All creatures great and small, all things bright and beautiful and all life from earth, sky and sea came under Solomon's probing and observant eye. But he did not, at this stage, worship the creation rather than the Creator.

All the king's friends (5:1-7)

Here we are reminded of the significant covenant chapter, 2 Samuel 7, where Nathan says that, while David will not build the temple, his son 'will build a house for my Name and I will establish the throne of his kingdom for ever' (2 Sam. 7:13). Here Solomon is starting to carry out that task. The language is of diplomatic courtesies, but behind that it is the language of covenant: 'friendly terms' (v. 1) means more than pleasantries; there is commitment. The emphasis is on the Name of Yahweh which evokes Exodus 3 and the revelation to Moses. Thus Solomon is not only being faithful to his father, but remembering and honouring the words of Moses as David had urged him to in 1 Kings 2:3.

Again the practicalities are taken care of in verse 6 as the felling of trees is to start immediately, and the section ends with a reminder that the building of the temple, like the administration of the kingdom, is further evidence of the wisdom God has given to Solomon. Here Hiram is one of 'the kings of the earth' (4:34) who honour David and Solomon. Here we have a true, if faint, glimpse of the time when all the lands will worship and the kings of the earth bring their treasures into the city.

All the king's plans (5:8-18)

The key verse in this section is verse 12 'Yahweh gave Solomon wisdom as he had promised him'; Yahweh is emphatic in the sentence and it could be paraphrased 'It was Yahweh who gave Solomon wisdom'. This summarizes in effect chapters 3, 4 and the part of chapter 5 up to here.

It points to the whole process of temple-building and dedication which is to begin in the rest of chapter 5 and occupy the whole of chapters 6, 7 and 8. This is helpful in our assessment of the verses on forced labour (5:13-18), which can be seen as harsh and oppressive and recall the words of Samuel, warning of the consequences of having a king, one of which will be 'you yourselves will become his slaves'(1 Sam. 8:17). There may be something in this, but the provision of one month in Lebanon and two months at home seem more humane than mere slavery (v. 14). We need to remember this conscription was for a specific project rather than a permanent arrangement and that the summary of Solomon's building activities (9:20-22) speaks of some of the labour force being drawn from the pagan enclaves still in the land. There is also a reminder that this is not simply manual labour, but that great skill and expertise went into the enterprise as the chapter ends with the craftsmen and their specialized work of cutting and preparing the materials.

From text to message

Getting the message clear: the theme

These chapters show the importance of good and faithful stewardship of the resources God has given.

Getting the message clear: the aim

The aim of the sermon will be to convey the need to be practical and faithful in the business of ordinary living and relationships.

A way in

We are often inclined to compartmentalize our lives into 'sacred' and 'secular' to the detriment of both. Sundays, especially, become divorced from the rest of the week, and we increasingly live in a rarified super-spiritual atmosphere and fail to enjoy the rich gifts God has given us in the created order. We very narrowly define what is right and are suspicious of art, music and literature and other gifts which, even in this fallen world, are part of the good Creator's provision for us to develop as humans.

In these two chapters the vine and fig tree are as much part of God's good provision as the temple. Wise administration is a blessing, and good government anticipates very partially, but genuinely the blessings of the kingdom to come. All this comes under the umbrella of wisdom, itself the supreme gift which Yahweh gave to Solomon and from which flowed all the other blessings.

Ideas for application

As always we need to remind ourselves that narrative is not normative. We must, therefore, avoid the inbred tendency to moralize, which in the case of these chapters would be to say that we need to work hard at administration, be carefully organized, and if we are building we need to ensure we get good materials. All these are true enough, but we hardly need to expound 1 Kings 4 and 5 to discover them. We need to see these chapters as part of the story of the kingdom and rejoice in Yahweh's faithfulness as well as respond to His grace by transformed living. Notice the following points:

+ These are chapters which show part of the slow mustard seed-like growth of the kingdom. Underneath the detail and sometimes coming up to the light, like snowdrops in February, the green shoots of the kingdom are there if we have eyes to see. We need in our day to look for such shoots – often frail and in unexpected places: the addict who not only goes to rehab, but finds Christ; the shy student who finds unexpected courage in sharing her faith; the unsung servants who are faithful away from the limelight and do not brag about it on Facebook and Twitter; the couple who faithfully keep their vows to the Lord and to each other. Readers will think of numerous other examples. These are not great manifestations of the Spirit, but of the silent work of that same Spirit as He brings people to glory.

+ The magnificence and range of the wisdom God gives is evident here. That wisdom cares about the details of people's lives and the happiness of their living. It creates order and safety and enables ordinary activities to flourish. Common grace is very evident here and is a reflection of the principles God has built into the universe and which we ignore at our peril.

+ The importance of the covenant promises is underlined. The promises to Abraham, as we have noticed, are at least partially fulfilled here in a specific location. These are real fulfilments; they are not the new creation, but they are accurate visual aids and show the kingdom of God at least partially and temporarily being manifested. Kings is to explore later the theme of exile from the land and how that does not ultimately set aside the covenant. We need to explore this theme of the faithful God, the guarantor of the covenant who is committed to His people by promises that He cannot and will not break.

+ There is a powerful creation current flowing here.
  The land flowing with milk and honey recalls Eden
  and is an anticipation of the new creation. Solomon's
  reign reminds us of the original destiny of humans to
  'Edenise' the world and be God's vicegerents for His
  glory. But even more it is an anticipation of the King
  who is to come who 'will be like rain falling on a mown
  field, like showers watering the earth' (Ps. 72:6).

+ Above all we find Christ in these chapters, the Christ
  whose reign will fill the earth with blessings. Although
  this is low-key and lacking high drama, something of
  the multifaceted splendour of the King shines through.
  He is not only wise, but the One in whom are all the
  treasures of wisdom and knowledge, and His universal
  reign will bring true and eternal joy. Only in Him will
  there be no unhappy ending and mourning over what
  might have been.

Preaching Christ faithfully (chapters 3 and 4)

Christ is 'the power of God and the wisdom of God'
(1 Cor. 1:24). These chapters point to that kingdom in which
wisdom will reign and humans will flourish. The wisdom
shown by Solomon in the incident of the baby (3:16-28) is
a wonderful illustration of the 'throne of grace' (Heb. 4:16)
where the humblest find mercy. The wise administration
of 4:1-19 points to the King who will reign in justice and
righteousness. The peace and prosperity of 4:20-28 points
to the new creation. In that new creation all that has been
worthy in this world in learning, beauty and imagination
will flourish (4:29-34). We need to show that Christ is lord
of all life and without Him nothing flourishes.

Suggestions for preaching

We need to be careful not to give the idea that these chapters can be sidelined and have nothing really significant to say. These are about how wisdom is no mere abstract quality of the mind, but the driving force of a godly lifestyle. Thus a possible title could be:

Sermon: Wisdom reigns at home and at work

As an introduction, the preacher needs to highlight the significance of the fulfilment of the promises of Abraham and thus the place of these chapters in the great story of God's purposes; it is useful to mention – without labouring the point – the historical accuracy of this account because 'the Great Power vacuum' leaves room for a mini-empire between the Nile and the Euphrates.

But what happens when wisdom reigns at home and work?

+ **Ordinary life flourishes** (4:1-19). This is the gift of wisdom in everyday details of work and administration. We see both Solomon's shrewdness in balancing old and new appointments and Solomon giving a strong lead.

+ **Joy and peace are experienced** (4:20-28). The final aim of God is for His people to enjoy permanent happiness.

+ **Minds and hearts are satisfied** (4:29-34). Note the importance of verse 29 – 'God gave Solomon wisdom' – this is a gift of grace. This wisdom is greater than the wisdom of the world although it drew the good things from it; it ranges over the whole of God's creation and is wisdom for teaching others.

+ **Wisdom wants to build the house of the Lord** (5:1-18). This is a reminder of David's place in the story. Here we see kings of the earth bringing their treasures to the city as the anointed king prepares wisely.

Suggestions for teaching
Questions to help understand the passage

1. How does the list of Solomon's officials (4:1-6) flow naturally from 3:28?

2. What is the significance of 4:20-21, not just in Solomon's story, but in the bigger story? (See Gen. 15:18-21)

3. Why is Solomon's wealth emphasized in 4:26-27?

4. What does 4:29-30 add to the picture of Solomon's and, indeed, biblical wisdom?

5. How is temple-building linked with wisdom (5:3-5)?

6. What does 5:12 show about the relationship between Solomon's wisdom and his international policies?

7. Why do you think 'forced labour' (5:14) is mentioned?

Questions to help apply the passage

1. These chapters show us how God's wisdom covers the whole of life, including administration as well as temple building. How does that affect the way we live and work for God?

2. In what ways does Solomon's kingdom anticipate the kingdom to come and how does that teach us something about how we can anticipate that kingdom (4:20-28)?

3. How can 4:29-34 help us to avoid a rarified and super-spiritual view of the life of faith?

4. Solomon's politics, at this stage, were guided by God-
   given wisdom (5:1-12). How can we live as faithful
   Christians and good citizens?

5

Unless the Lord Builds the House (1 Kings 6–7)

Introduction

It is often astonishing that the present age, while often ruthlessly brushing the past aside, also wallows in nostalgia and loves the ancient, the quaint and the picturesque. Other enterprises may be failing, but the heritage industry is alive and well. Therein lies the temptation to treat these chapters as antiquarian and miss their contemporary message. It is particularly easy to dismiss their importance because we know that the true Temple is the Lord Jesus Christ Himself and we are the living stones who form His body.

None of our buildings are temples and we are all too aware of how buildings can become idolatrous (see Jeremiah 7). But that is too narrow a view of the importance of the temple as the place where the Lord meets His people and, as we shall see, this is not a guidebook to Solomon's temple, but a visual aid of the presence of the living God. We shall take chapters 6 and 7 together as this will show us an overview of Solomon's building projects.

Firstly, a word about the significance of the temple. Until Jesus pronounces the end of the temple (Matt. 24:2; Mark 13:2; Luke 21:6), it remains the sacrament of God's presence among His people, echoing Exodus 25:8 'Make a sanctuary for me, and I will dwell among them'. This is the emphasis of the message of Haggai – 'If you don't build the temple, you are virtually saying you don't care whether God is among you or not'. Building the temple was a response to God's gracious promise that He would live among them. Thus it was not primarily a cultic centre, but a place to meet God (as Eden had been and the new creation will fully be). Indeed the tabernacle was also sometimes called 'the tent of meeting'. We need to be alert to this as we explore chapters 6–8, which stand at the centre of Solomon's story and at the heart of his reign.

Listening to the text
Context and structure
We shall try to identify the flow of the text and concentrate on its highlights and in 'Ideas for application' say something more on the significance of the detail. A way of dividing the text could be:

+ A date to celebrate (6:1; underlined in 6:37-38)

+ A solid structure (6:2-10)

+ Conditions for God's presence (6:11-13)

+ The heart of the building (6:14-36)

+ Another building project (7:1-12)

+ Temple furnishings (7:13-51)

Working through the text
A date to celebrate (6:1; 37-38)
All too often commentators spend their time wrangling over the details of chronology here and miss their theological significance. Some see the 480 years as a round rather than a precise figure, i.e. twelve generations of forty years, but it could equally be a precise figure because of the precision of the other date 'the month of Ziv'. Either view can legitimately be held. What is of far greater significance is the linking of the temple building with the Exodus. The Exodus marked the end of 430 years in Egypt (Exod. 12:40-41) and here now the 480 years since the Exodus marked God's giving rest to His people and thus allowing this temple to be built. It is also the midpoint between Exodus and Exile.

The author writes from the perspective of the Exile having already happened with its destruction of the temple. He realizes this building is thus provisional: while celebrating our roots we need to guard our future. This timing is underlined in verse 38 where detailed obedience is emphasized. We need to have a sense of God in control through the baffling and perplexing ebb and flow of history and not become fixated on the particular moment.

A solid structure (6:2-10)
The phrase 'built for the LORD' (v. 2) gives the motive for this undertaking; it was not for Solomon's aggrandizement. The description of the exterior is much briefer than that of the interior which suggests the greater importance of the inside, especially of the Holy of Holies (see diagram of the ground plan). Essentially, like the tabernacle, it had three divisions: the outer court; the main hall and the inner sanctuary. There were also side rooms all around

the outside wall to avoid making holes in the sanctuary wall (vv. 5-7); this showed scrupulous obedience to the Torah which forbade iron tools being used in the building of sanctuaries (Exod. 20:25; Deut. 27:5-6). The accompanying diagram should help the reader to picture the ground plan of the temple.

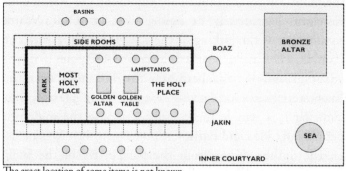

The exact location of some items is not known.

The emphasis on gold has been criticized, but this is unfair (the emphasis is different in 10:14ff). Here what is being emphasized is that Yahweh deserves the best and that these assets were better publicly displayed than hidden in some dark storeroom. This was a visible expression of devotion to Yahweh. As we apply this today, we do not say our buildings are to be lavish and aesthetic paradigms, but we do need to say that in our service for God there is a right kind of professionalism and what we offer to Him must not be shoddy. Our preparation and presentation need to be as good as lies within us. This applies across the board: singing, stewarding, cleaning, and serving of all kinds needs to be gold standard. Nothing shoddy or careless is good enough.

Conditions for God's presence (6:11-13)

Building and beautifying, however, is not the main concern. In the middle of the architectural plans there is a surprising intrusion, and when this kind of thing occurs in the Bible we do not assume a careless author or editor, but ask, Why this at this point? Remember the last few chapters have been particularly concerned with external manifestations of Solomon's wisdom, and now we are seeing the building of this glorious structure. At that very moment comes a Word from Yahweh as the temple building is going on. Yahweh is reminding Solomon what all this activity is about. In particular he is reminding him of David's words in 2:2-4 which, I suggested, give us our bearings in understanding the whole book. There is also the underlining of the promise to David in 2 Samuel 7:12-16 where faithfulness to the covenant is related to Yahweh's indwelling presence. Temple without Torah is a recipe for disaster.

The emphasis on the details of building which precede and follow these words of Yahweh show how important the project is, but this Word is a sharp reminder what all this building is for. We are not the anointed king, but we need to ponder the significance of this. We spend so much time on the things of God that God Himself can fade out of the picture. Our work can become an idol; something to boast about rather than to accept humbly and thankfully as a gift from God. Obedience is what the Lord commands and what ultimately reveals our love for Him. Thus we need to see beyond the porticos, the cedar and the gold, the services we lead and the work we undertake for the Lord Himself.

The heart of the building (6:14-36)

A summary statement in verse 14 moves us to the interior of the building. Many of the technical terms here are not well understood, but the loving detail shows the author's interest. The woodwork of the main hall is passed over briefly and his emphasis is on the heart of the building, the inner sanctuary also called the Holy of Holies or the Most Holy Place, the resting place of the Ark of the Covenant. This was the box in which were placed the tablets of the Law (Exod. 25:10-22). It was this ark before which the Philistine idol Dagon was smashed (1 Sam. 5:1-5) and which was brought to Jerusalem in 2 Samuel 6 (an event probably celebrated in Ps. 24) where it was touched by Uzzah with catastrophic results.

On this ark, Yahweh of hosts sat enthroned on the cherubim (see e.g., Ps. 80:1; 99:1). It is fascinating that the first mention of the cherubim is Genesis 3:24 where they guard the tree of life from sinful humanity. Here, as they overshadow the Ark of the Covenant, they point to Christ, the true Mercy Seat (a theme which we shall explore in more depth later). Further details of the furnishings of the temple are to be given in chapter 7, but the central importance of the Ark of the Covenant needs to be emphasized, for it was here that God's glory dwelt and where his voice was heard, symbolised by the tablets of the law (also see Num. 7:89). Chapter 6 ends with a brief historical note about the end of the seven-year building project and reminds us of the detailed care which Solomon took and his own personal involvement in it.

Another building project (7:1-12)
Plainly our author has inserted this little section in the account of temple-building for a particular reason, and what this reason is has caused disagreement. It has been argued that what the author intends in chapters 6 and 7 is to give a complete account of Solomon's building activities.

It is further argued that since the account of the palace is squeezed in the middle of the much longer account of the temple this indicates its lesser importance. On the other hand, it is pointed out that Solomon took twice as long on the palace as on the temple. Both are simply called 'house' and there is a contrast between Yahweh's house and Solomon's house. The Hebrew conjunction *waw* in verse 1 could be translated 'however' (not translated in the NIV) and thus draw attention to the contrast of the two 'houses'. Our interpretation will be related to how far we see Solomon as having weaknesses from the beginning (see further comments on chapter 11).

The 'Palace of the Forest of Lebanon' (v. 2) was in itself larger than the temple and probably served as royal treasury. The throne hall or Hall of Justice (v. 7) suggests the function of the king as personal dispenser of justice (see 3:16-28). Judging is a function of God Himself and the anointed king must therefore rule justly (see David's words in 2 Sam. 23:3). The palace for Solomon's queen is now mentioned and at this point without any comment by the narrator.

To return to the question about whether this passage is favourable or unfavourable to Solomon, I would make this observation. At this point (see especially chapter 8) it seems Solomon is still faithful to Yahweh and truly wants to worship Him and obey His words. However, there is the inherent danger of treating the temple as a royal chapel and thus pave the way for other chapels to other gods, as in chapter 11. This need not have happened; the danger here is potential rather than actual. Yet the symbolism can easily be seen to present Yahweh as tenant rather than landlord.

Temple furnishings (7:13-51)

As the account of the temple furnishings opens, we meet a new character, Huram, who comes from Tyre to supervise the work, and we are assured of his Israelite roots. The significance of this is that the language used of him recalls that of Bezalel, the chief craftsman of the tabernacle (Exod. 31:1-11; 35:30-35) which underlines the connection between these two events in salvation history. The words translated by the NIV as 'highly skilled and experienced' are more exactly 'full of wisdom and understanding and knowledge'. This picks up the wisdom theme which undergirds the story from chapter 3 onwards and without which no house will stand.

Prominence is now given to two giant pillars (vv. 15-22) which towered almost as high as the temple itself. Once again many obscure technical terms are used, but their significance embodied in their names is vital and clearly throws light on their purpose. 'Jakin' is a form of the verb *kwn* which means 'to be established' – a verb used of the covenant with David in 2 Samuel 7:12, 13, 16 and in 1 Kings 2:12, 24, 45, 46 of Solomon being established in the kingdom. The word means 'He [Yahweh] will establish', or, possibly as a prayer 'May He establish'. In either case it is a visible reminder of Yahweh's covenant promise to the royal line.

The name of the second pillar, 'Boaz', probably means 'in him [Yahweh] is strength', or perhaps 'in him [Yahweh] he [the king] is strong'. Some have linked it with Psalm 21 'O Yahweh, the king rejoices in your strength' (v. 1) and 'be exalted, O Yahweh, in your strength' (v. 13). The two hundred pomegranates represent the care and artistic skill lavished on these pillars.

This is a permanent reminder that this temple is built on Yahweh's promise and sustained by Yahweh's power. The first tells of His covenant love; the second of His power to fulfil His purpose. These remain the solid foundations on which our confidence is built. They, and the temple where they stood, have long gone, but in every age God's people need to trust God's promises and depend on His power.

The Bronze Sea (vv. 23-39) was plainly important for the author, both the Sea proper (vv. 23-26) and its mobile stands. This was a gigantic metal basin (the parallel passage in 2 Chron. 4:6 says it was for ritual washing by the priests). Probably there is also symbolic significance. The sea in Scripture is often a symbol of the forces of chaos and evil which God subdued in the creation of the world (see e.g. Ps. 74:12-17; 89:5-11; 93 and Job 38:8-11). Especially in this connection, Psalm 24 celebrates Yahweh founding the earth on the sea and establishing it on the rivers. This is the psalm traditionally associated with bringing the ark to Jerusalem. Huram excelled himself here in the construction of this superb artefact. The following verses (vv. 41-51) summarize the bronze and gold work which probably reflect temple archives with Huram supervising the bronze artefacts and Solomon the gold. Indeed the chapter ends with the spotlight falling once again on Solomon. Verse 51 establishes the continuity as we are reminded of the part David played in all this. In 2 Samuel 8:11-12 we read of how David dedicated the spoils of war. Significantly that chapter speaks of David's victories at the Euphrates and down in Philistine land on the borders of Egypt. These were the victories which made possible the peace of 1 Kings 4 which was the necessary condition for the building of the temple which is now ready to be dedicated for the worship of Yahweh.

Getting the message clear: the theme
The theme is Solomon's massive and elaborate building programmes which are another example of his wisdom and that of his craftsmen.

Getting the message clear: the aim
The aim of the passage is to show how building for God must conform to His guidance and reflect His glory.

A way in
Many churches engage in building work and fabric repair, trying to make old buildings more suitable for contemporary conditions. These are good insofar as they help the basic mission of the church and help it to be most effective in the community. What is not helpful is when a building is identified as a 'church' and the emphasis is on bricks and mortar rather than the living stones who make up the Temple of the Lord. The temple does not correspond to any of our modern church buildings, whether splendid cathedrals or Nissen huts. If there is to be a comparison, it is to a synagogue where worship centred around the reading and exposition of Scripture (see Luke 4:14-27). Yet, until Jesus turned His back on the temple, it remained the place where God met His people and this is why, after the Exile, Haggai essentially says that if they did not rebuild the temple, the people did not care whether God was among them or not. If we are going to expound the next chapters faithfully we need to keep all these considerations in mind.

Ideas for application
We have travelled a lot of territory which readers may have found more dull than entrancing and, as a preacher, I want

to try to convince the sceptical that here we have much to learn about the life of the kingdom.

+ Many of us will have problems with the amount of words devoted to the temple and especially want to avoid the idea of 'sacred space' exemplified in great buildings such as cathedrals where certain parts are deemed more 'holy' than others and God's presence identified with Gothic splendour, trained choirs, robes and processions. This is a legitimate reaction, but it can lead us to an unbalanced view of what the temple was for; remember, as we have already noted, it was the sacrament of God's presence among His people and a reminder of His grace and holiness. We need to remember Luther's famous characterization of humanity falling off a horse on one side, getting back on and immediately falling off on the other side. We rightly dread the deadness of formality, but can forget the deadness of informality. Our services can become totally horizontal with no sense of the transcendence of God (see further on chapter 8).

+ The beauty of the temple reflected the beauty of the divine wisdom which lay behind it. This means that it was a visual aid to point people to God. There is the poetry and drama of our faith which is often underplayed. The temple, like the tabernacle before it, reflected the splendour of the Creator even in its fallen state. Thus, although temporary and limited, it recalled Eden where the Lord walked with His people and pointed to the new creation where His presence will be permanent (Rev. 21:3). Fitting these chapters into that unfolding story will help to show their power.

+ But why all this detail? Most readers find these
chapters hard and not enough preachers tackle them.
The first thing to say is that the author clearly does
not find the detail boring; rather he lovingly and
carefully builds up a picture. Like creation itself, every
detail is part of God's providential attention. This is
the God without whom no sparrow falls to the ground
and who numbers the hairs of our heads. Everything
matters to Him, including the mass of things we do
not understand. There is the prose of our faith as
well as the poetry; the soaring magnificence which
reveals His glory and the tender, detailed care which is
concerned with what we eat and where we live. We can
trust a God like that! The theology of transcendence
and immanence is more fully developed in chapter 8.

+ All this work is not good works to earn the Lord's
favour, but a response to the grace He has shown us.
We firmly believe in justification by grace through faith,
but often we are so anxious that others know about
our work for the church that it appears we believe in
sanctification by works. That is why, although we are
not anointed kings, we need to keep on returning to
the covenant promises and luxuriate in the grace that
sought and found us.

+ Here, as everywhere in the Bible, our task is never
simply to 'explain the passage', but to proclaim Christ.
If that is not our aim we will end up either dishing out
moralizing platitudes or giving antiquarian lectures.
Christ is the true Temple, but we need to look at the
specific emphases of each passage to discern which of
the variegated glories of Christ are in view. Here the

emphasis given to the Holy of Holies where the Ark of the Covenant was to be placed (6:19) gives us our bearings. This was the place where the High Priest went on the Day of Atonement (Lev. 16) and, shielded by the blood of sacrifice, approached the mercy seat. Almost certainly the ark was destroyed when the Babylonians sacked the city and burned the temple. What happened then? Read Ezekiel 1 where the young prophet sees what is in effect the chariot throne of Yahweh, a portable ark. Yahweh is alive and well in Nebuchadnezzar's Babylon. All this is pointing to the time when the Word becomes flesh and pitches His tent among us (John 1:14) and the glory of Yahweh no longer hovers over a golden box, but is incarnate. In John 2:19ff Jesus speaks of his own body as the Temple. Thus we can appreciate that these chapters are full of Christ and that while the physical temple and the sacrificial system are long gone, the teaching about them remains a vital part of how we come to know Him.

Suggestions for preaching

Although there is a large amount of material here it is probably wise to take the two chapters together and expound their overall message. As we have noticed, there are a number of highlights which give us our bearings and a sermon could be constructed around these.

Sermon: Unless the Lord builds the house

This is not just a building, but the work of the kingdom initiated by God and sustained by His grace.

- **A date to celebrate** (especially 6:1, but also 6:37-38 and 7:51). The temple is a visual aid of the story of salvation and helps us remember our salvation, both exodus and new exodus (Luke 9:51). We also anticipate our new creation: this is a finished work (7:51) – just as at the first creation.

- **A word to obey** (6:11-13) where Solomon trusts the promises and obeys the commands in all their detail.

- **A place to meet God** (6:19). The place of the ark is important. In particular the mercy seat is significant, the place where God's anger is turned away.

- **A challenge to priorities**. This point may pick up on the contrast between the two 'houses'.

Suggestions for teaching
Questions to help understand the passage

1. What is the significance of the mention of the Exodus in 6:1?

2. Why are the dimensions of the temple described (6:2-6)?

3. Why does 6:11-13 interrupt the description of the building?

4. What does 6:19 suggest about the importance of the Ark of the Covenant?

5. What is the significance in comparing the length of time of building the temple (6:38) and building the palace (7:1)?

6. What is the importance of the pillars, Jakin and Boaz (7:21)?

7. Why do you think there is so much detail about the temple furniture (7:15-50)?

8. Why is David mentioned (7:51)?

Questions to help apply the passage

1. The Exodus (6:1) is at the heart of Israel's story and worship. How does the cross by which we were saved shape our whole approach to meeting with God?

2. While the temple is not a model for our church gatherings, what can we learn from the loving detail which reflects the glory of God?

3. The commands of 6:11-13 relate to obedience to the Word of God. How seriously do we take that Word as we approach God? How do we demonstrate our seriousness?

4. How do 6:38 and 7:1 (about the relative time of building temple and palace) give us guidance on priorities? (Remember that this is not ultimately about buildings.)

6

HEAVEN MEETING EARTH
(1 KINGS 8)

Introduction

When I was a child I did not want to go to heaven because I was told it would be like being in church. That was the most unappealing prospect I could imagine! What a delight it was to discover the verse: 'I saw no temple in the city' (Rev. 21:22). Much later I was puzzled how to reconcile this with Ezekiel 40–48 where the whole of the new creation is described using temple/city language. But then I realized that both referred to the same reality from a different angle and that reality was the unveiled presence of the living God; the true union of heaven and earth symbolized by the new Jerusalem coming down from heaven (Rev. 21:2-3). This is the fulfilment of the reality begun in Eden; then the tabernacle where Yahweh lives among His people (Exod. 25:8). Here now, in this chapter, in the temple is where heaven meets earth.

This is the high-water mark of Solomon's story, especially in his great dedication prayer. This prayer goes right to the heart of who God is and how, though enthroned above the cherubim, He condescends to live with His people. This anticipates the time when the Word would become flesh and take the form of a servant.

Listening to the text
Context and structure
It would be helpful to divide the text into five main sections:

+ Celebration as the ark finds a home (8:1-13)

+ Solomon blesses Israel (8:14-21)

+ Solomon's prayer of dedication (8:22-53)

+ Solomon blesses Israel (8:54-61)

+ Celebration as the temple is dedicated (8:62-66)

Praise and celebration are the bookends and remind us that everything is a gift of God's grace. In between, the prayer emphasizes the need of repentance and forgiveness.

Celebration as the ark finds a home (8:1-13)
This section is a blend of the everyday and the mystery of God's presence which runs through the chapter. It begins with a date 'in the month of Ethanim, the seventh month' (v. 2) which would be September/October, and, appropriately, the festival (v. 2) would be the Feast of Tabernacles (Lev. 23:33-43) which commemorated the desert wanderings. Now Yahweh had given them rest (v. 56) and put an end to their wanderings. This was further symbolized by the bringing of the tent of meeting with its sacred furnishings to remind them of their continuity with the past. The phrase 'they are still there today' (v. 8) clearly refers to a time before the destruction of the temple and

gives an air of factuality to the account. This is not a legend, but an account of something that happened.

But there is mystery as well. God cannot be put in a box. Verses 10 and 11 speak of the glory cloud filling the temple. This repeats what happened at the dedication of the tabernacle (Exod. 40:34-35). The cloud reveals God's presence, but also conceals it; the people do not see the full blaze of Yahweh's glory. This is picked up by Solomon in verse 12 in his reference to Yahweh dwelling in a dark cloud. Preachers and others would do well to have written on their hearts, if not on their desks, the words of Deuteronomy 29:29: 'The secret things belong to Yahweh our God, but the things revealed belong to us and to our children for ever, that we may follow all the words of this law'. What we know is what is revealed.

This is where mystery and clarity come together: in the Ark of the Covenant. The ark is mentioned eight times in nine verses, but it is verse 9 which gives us the key. Yahweh was not in the ark itself, but His Word *was* in the form of the decalogue, the heart of the covenant and expressing the people's response of gratitude for their salvation. The clarity is unmistakable: the people of God live by obedience to the Word of God. Thus though we do not know the full purposes of God to all eternity we know enough for ' life and godliness' (2 Pet. 1:3). The ark no longer contained the pot of manna or Aaron's rod which budded, probably because they were specifically associated with the desert wanderings. The Decalogue, however, remained their charter (2:2-4).

Mystery will always remain in the choices we have to make in the often perplexing circumstances of our lives, but we can always obey the commandments God has given us. Here again the fundamental teaching of the book of Kings about the necessity of obeying God's Word is underlined. At the heart of the temple is the Holy of Holies, at its heart is the Ark of the Covenant and in it is the Word of the living God.

Solomon blesses Israel (8:14-21)

As Solomon addresses the people, he focuses on the covenant with David, but again links this closely with the Exodus and thus with the Sinai covenant. As anointed king he blesses the people and the emphasis is on the faithfulness of Yahweh, which will be developed further in the dedication prayer. There is a particularly poignant detail in verse 18 when we are told of Nathan's words to David when the latter is told that he will not be allowed to build the temple – 'Because it was in your heart to build a temple for my Name, you did well to have this in your heart'. We shall return to this in *ideas for application*, but it is encouraging to notice that a godly ambition, even if unfulfilled, is remembered and acknowledged by the Lord.

The emphasis on the 'Name' of Yahweh is significant. The Name signifies Yahweh's owning of the building, but also emphasizes that He is not confined to it although His presence is real. This is to become explicit in the prayer which follows. This is 'a place for the Ark of the Covenant' (v. 21) which is the tangible symbol of Yahweh's promises.

Solomon's prayer of dedication (8:22-53)

Here is one of the great prayers of the Bible and of crucial importance both in the unfolding story of Solomon and of the book as a whole, with its emphasis on the nature of God, the place of the temple, and covenant blessings and curses. This is a prayer of an individual, but that individual is the anointed king and thus is offered on behalf of both his family and the whole nation. Also, its great truths teach us many important lessons about praying, both in its content and manner. Verse 22 shows us Solomon's approach to Yahweh. He stands before the bronze altar in the outer court where large numbers gathered to worship. Spreading out his hands shows the solemnity of the occasion. The prayer develops in two parts: first the nature of Yahweh (vv. 23-30) and then petitions on behalf of Yahweh's people (vv. 31-53).

The first part of the prayer is full of great and life-changing truths about God. He is the God of Israel bound to them by covenant promises, but more than that He is incomparable: 'there is no God like you in heaven above or on earth below' (v. 23). If you are looking for a sound bite (which, of course, you're not!) to sum up the Old Testament's picture of God, you could do worse than 'the incomparability of Yahweh'. This great truth is developed particularly in Isaiah 40ff, but is everywhere in the Old Testament. This is no abstract idea; it means that there is nowhere in heaven and earth where His writ does not run and this brings both tremendous reassurance and profound challenge.

Here, more specifically, His incomparability is linked to his total trustworthiness and complete fidelity to His covenant. His faithfulness in the past is the reason for confidence in the present and future. Faithfulness is not an accidental characteristic of God; it is at the heart of His being. It is encapsulated in Paul's statement in 1 Corinthians 1:9 – 'God is faithful'; not 'God is *sometimes* faithful', not even 'God is *mostly* faithful', but absolutely and to all eternity He keeps His promises. This is totally different from pagan gods who are fickle, capricious, bear grudges and are often malicious.

So, with Yahweh we can praise Him for all that is past, and trust Him for all that is to come. Probably, in another Exodus echo, Solomon is recalling the great hymn of praise after the crossing of the sea: 'Who among the gods is like you, O Yahweh, who is like you – majestic in holiness, awesome in glory, working wonders?' (Exod. 15:11).

In many ways verses 27 and 28 are the very heart of who Yahweh is as Solomon blends transcendence and immanence; God up there and God down here. This is the picture of God established right at the beginning of the Bible. Any student from Cornhill, Scotland – where I teach – will tell you about the God of Genesis 1 and the God of Genesis 2 and further tell you that what we read there is the key to understanding biblical theology. Not that there are two gods, but rather one God who is both transcendent (Gen. 1) and immanent (Gen. 2). He is big enough to control the universe and the sweep of history, but also comes right down into His creation. He is no absentee landlord.

In Genesis 1, God up there speaks and creation bursts into life: light shines; birds sing; earth, sea and sky are filled with His glory and all this because He speaks. In Genesis 2, that same God comes down into history and takes dust and shapes it into humanity. Take one or the other and you have a God of power, but do not know if He cares; or a God of compassion, but do not know if He has the power to carry out His purposes. Put the pictures together and we have the God who one day will become incarnate in the Lord Jesus Christ. That continues throughout the Bible: one or two references will have to suffice: Isaiah 40 – Yahweh measures the waters in the hollow of His hand (v. 12) and brings out the starry host (v. 26), but also gives strength to the weary (v. 29); in Psalm 147:3-4, He determines the number of the stars and heals the broken-hearted; in Revelation 1:17, John on Patmos falls as if dead before the Risen Lord, then that same Lord touches him and tells him not to be afraid.

So here Solomon looks at this magnificent temple on which so much work has been done and so much wealth lavished, and it all dwindles to insignificance in the presence of Yahweh. Indeed His majesty dwarfs the universe and our minds boggle and our hearts fail as we think of the myriad galaxies, the unthinkable distances and the insignificance of our most splendid projects. The words of Job 26:14 are a fitting expression of the immensity of this God: 'These are, but the outer fringe of his works, how faint the whisper we hear of him! Who then can understand the thunder of his power?'

So what hope is there for us? There is a way to approach a God like that, and Solomon in verse 28 speaks of 'your servant's prayer and plea for mercy'. He cannot be confined to the temple or any other box, but 'this place' (v. 29) is where He will listen and will keep a watchful eye and will do this continually, night and day. Just as He came down to Eden and to the lowly cattle shed so in wonderful grace He will come to His people. We cannot understand God fully, but by grace we can know Him, listen to Him and speak to Him. That is an immense God and I keep on saying to students that one of the most important words in theology is 'Wow!' This is a 'wow' passage.

The second part of the prayer (vv. 31-53) consists of seven petitions which envisage different scenarios in which grace and mercy would be particularly needed. These are

especially related to the covenant curses in Leviticus 26
and Deuteronomy 28. This is inevitable for 'there is no one
who does not sin' (v. 46). This prevents the tremendous
truths about Yahweh simply being pious phrases; there is
a cold dose of realism here. In each petition there is both
a reference to 'hear from heaven' and 'towards this place';
the twin truths of transcendence and immanence are at the
heart of true prayer. A brief look at each of these situations
show us circumstances in which people would pray.

The first petition (vv. 31-32) is about justice in society
and a case is envisaged where there is a lack of evidence
(such a case as Solomon had handled so brilliantly back
in 3:16-28). Possibly some kind of priestly ritual would be
involved as in the case of the unfaithful wife (Num. 5:11-31).
However the emphasis is on neither the king nor priest but
on God the Judge of all the earth.

The second petition refers to defeat in battle (vv. 33-34)
and echoes the defeat of Joshua's army because of the sin
of Achan (Josh. 7:11-12). But it also envisages the Exile –
'bring them back to the land'. The third (vv. 35-36) and the
fourth (vv. 37-40) refer to calamities often associated with
war. Drought is the spur for the Elijah stories in chapter 17
and is mentioned in Deuteronomy 28:23-24 as one of the
punishments for covenant disobedience. Famine and plague
are also signs of divine displeasure (Lev. 26:19-20 and 25;
Deut. 28:21-22 and 32:24); Yahweh is Lord of creation and
what we call 'natural forces' obey Him.

The fifth (vv. 41-43) moves us out from Israel to 'the
foreigner', reminding us of the promise to Abraham that
the blessing was to extend to all the nations on earth
(Gen. 12:3). The foreigner would have heard of the Exodus
for the phrase Yahweh's 'great name, mighty hand and

outstretched arm' echoes Deuteronomy 4:34 and 5:15. Since Yahweh is the incomparable God, all nations are summoned to worship Him.

The sixth (vv. 44-45) and the seventh (vv. 46-51) petitions deal with two mirror-image situations: the sixth, where God uses His people to defeat their enemies; and the seventh, where He uses their enemies to defeat them. The seventh is the longest and focuses on the danger of exile; although an earlier example of potential exile occurs in 2 Kings 5 where Yahweh uses Naaman, the Syrian general to punish His people. Here the Exile is seen (as in Dan. 1:2) as an act of Yahweh Himself.

However, it is this seventh petition which brings together the twin emphases on mercy and judgment which underlie all seven. Repentant prayer would lead to restoration and forgiveness. Daniel prays 'towards the city and temple' at a time when they were both still in ruins (Dan. 6:10) and Daniel 9:1-19 gives us such a prayer of repentance. The earlier cursing passages of Leviticus and Deuteronomy had also given assurance of restoration if there was repentance. This flows from the nature of the incomparable God who punishes Israel for her sins but provides a way back, unlike the petty and capricious godlets of paganism. Again the foundational words given to Moses are emphasized (v. 53).

Solomon blesses the people (8:54-61)
This blessing continues and focuses the theme of the prayer. It is worth noting in passing that the details of verses 54 and 55 read like the report of an eyewitness account and give an air of realism to the proceedings. There are two particular notes here. The first is a powerful sense of God at work in history. Again gratitude for the faithfulness of God

particularly shown to Moses (v. 56) is shown by Solomon
echoing words of Joshua 21:45: 'Not one word has failed of
all the good promises he gave through his servant Moses'. In
the same verse the reference to rest reflects the victories of
David which had brought it about.

But Solomon is also looking to the far future when 'all
peoples of the earth will know that Yahweh is God and
that there is no other'. But side by side with the big picture,
Solomon does not forget the demands of every day. This is
the emphasis of verse 59: 'the cause of his servant and the
cause of his people Israel according to each day's need'. This
again illustrates the magnificence of Yahweh who knows
the end from the beginning and works everything according
to the counsel of His will. But He also cares for the daily
grind, the personal joys and sorrows and numbers the hairs
of our head. Not only is He the Lord of history, He is the
Lord of every day. He will bring in His kingdom, but He
will also care about your hospital appointment, your daily
work and your fears about tomorrow.

That is why verse 59 is so important. It is not only the
cause of His anointed king, but the cause of His people
Israel which Yahweh is pledged to uphold. How deeply has
Solomon grasped both the awesome majesty of Yahweh
and His tender care! It is no accident that these convictions
were shaped in prayer because these are better apprehended
on our knees than anywhere else. The reminder of heart
commitment and obedience (v. 61) reminds us that covenant
obedience is the key to enjoying covenant blessings.

This is the other emphasis: the nature of obedience
to the Torah. This is no routine legalism; rather it is the
obedience of a heart and life shown in transformed living.
This is the emphasis of verse 58 – 'May he turn our hearts

to him'; keeping the law is a gift of grace not a means of earning salvation. This will be a powerful witness to 'all the peoples of the earth' that Yahweh is the true God. Verse 61 concludes this section with its summary of the true balance of the life of faith: warm loyalty and scrupulous obedience. Here is not shallow emotionalism on the one hand or pedantic legalism on the other but heart and mind united in the service of Yahweh.

Celebration as the Temple is dedicated (8:62-66)

The bookends of this chapter (vv. 1-13 and vv. 62-66) are about rejoicing and celebration. The first noteworthy point is the mass participation in the sacrifices; so many indeed that the bronze altar was insufficient for the task and part of the courtyard had to be consecrated as well. The people came from Lebo Hamath in the north on the Euphrates and the Wadi of Egypt in the far south. This is a reminder of chapter 4 and how the kingdom had reached the boundaries promised to Abraham (Gen. 15:18). But even more it points to the future when blessing will flow from the eternal temple (Ezek. 47). This is a trailer for the time when all the lands will worship.

The other emphasis is on God's covenant with David and his faithfulness to David's house (v. 66). It is still possible to detect in this ancient record the sense of jubilation and excitement at this moving and memorable occasion. At that moment king and people were united in their praise of Yahweh, their confidence in His past faithfulness and future blessing, and in their resolve to obey the revelation given to Moses. It is a tantalizing glimpse of what might have been and impels us beyond it to look for a true obedience and a lasting worship.

From text to message

Getting the message clear: the theme

God is both in heaven and on earth and thus the temple, magnificent as it was, cannot reveal Him fully.

Getting the message clear: the aim

The aim of a sermon on this passage might be to emphasize both the majesty of God and the way we can approach Him in prayer.

A way in

'The Lord of heaven and earth … does not live in temples built by hands' (Acts 17:24). These words of Paul to the Athenian philosophers are already anticipated in this chapter in 8:27-30. Solomon, at the peak of his glory and in touch with Yahweh, shows us the very heart of what this temple-building is about. No more than Paul does Solomon believe that God lives in man-made buildings (8:27). Indeed, God cannot be limited even by the vast universe He has made. The temple does not confine God; a point Jeremiah was to make forcefully in the temple sermon (Jer. 7:1-11). Thus, the temple only gains its significance when Yahweh is there. Heaven is God's dwelling place and it is to there that Solomon addresses his prayer.

Yet God is gracious and, as in Eden, He does provide a place where His servants on earth can meet Him (8:29). One day, in the new creation, heaven and earth will blend, and the reality to which the temple points will permanently live with redeemed humanity (Rev. 21:3, 22). Ultimately these chapters are about God in His majesty and mystery, but also in his condescension as He reveals Himself to humans.

Ideas for application

+ In a sense the other applications of this chapter are special examples of the most important emphasis, which is God up there and God down here. To hold these in tension is vital. If all our emphasis is on God up there, our view of Him will become more and more remote. Our worship of Him will become stilted and pompous and our relationship will be cold and formal. We will identify solemnity with elaborate ritual, and reverence with ornate liturgy and ancient buildings. However, if all our emphasis is on God down here we will become more and more familiar, and the type of 'Jesus is my boyfriend' kind of song will predominate. We will end up with the 'vulnerable God' beloved of much contemporary theology. But hold both together and our lives and worship will be transformed; we will both love and fear; rejoice and weep; know we are welcome at the Father's table and repent of our sin.

+ The theme of worship which has been the subject of debate among evangelicals in recent years needs to be governed by our view of God. Some have seen it as what happens 'in church' and more especially associated with liturgy. Others have seen it as the whole of life (Rom. 12:1) and meeting together as the occasion for teaching and encouragement. A true appreciation of God 'up there' and 'down here' would prevent either extreme. Of course worship must be 'seven whole days, not one in seven' (as the seventeenth-century hymn-writer George Herbert puts it), otherwise the 'one in seven' will be stilted and soon boring. But there needs to be special occasions where we focus our worship.

If I say 'I love my wife every day, so I don't need to remember her birthday', you would rightly assume the relationship had become a matter of routine.

+ The importance of the Word of God, here particularly the Torah, is emphasized and its emphasis on the great doctrines of creation and history underlined. These are practical: space and time belong to God and this has enormous implications on how we think and how we live our lives. They are also the bulwark of faith and give confidence that God will complete what He began.

+ The importance of communal assembling to worship God is emphasized here: 'all the men of Israel' (v. 2); 'the whole assembly' (v. 14, v. 22); 'all Israel' (v. 62, v. 65). This is not simply the people then present; it is all the people of God across space and throughout time and indeed in eternity.

+ 'You have come to Mount Zion, to the heavenly Jerusalem, the city of the living God. You have come to thousands upon thousands of angels in joyful assembly, to the church of the firstborn, whose names are written in heaven. You have come to God, the judge of all, to the spirits of the righteous made perfect, to Jesus the mediator of a new covenant, and to the sprinkled blood that speaks a better word than the blood of Abel' (Heb. 12:22-24). This event in tenth-century-B.C. Jerusalem is an expression and anticipation of that reality.

+ The importance of practising the presence of God is also emphasized. This involves finding God not only through the medium of regular worship, but in lives of faithfulness. The temple did not guarantee God's presence if people's hearts were disobedient and idolatrous (see Jer. 7). This is closely linked with prayer, and we have already seen how Solomon's prayer is in many ways a model of prayer beginning with who God is and yet focusing on the specific situation. Prayer as a way of life and as expressed in specific situations reflects the God of the everyday and of the special.

+ We have already noticed how the temple and ark point to Christ himself, the true Ark of the Covenant where heaven meets earth. This is gospel and leads to a deeper and fuller appreciation of Him. In one sense the whole of the Old Testament is a series of acted parables and visual aids which give us windows into the Word who was to be made flesh.

Suggestions for preaching

It would be possible to preach several sermons on this chapter on such topics as: The mystery and nearness of God; The True Temple; The prayer that reaches heaven. However, if you are preaching a series on the book, it probably would be better to preach on it as a whole.

Sermon: Heaven meeting earth or God coming down

An introduction needs to cover the place of the temple in the Bible story (Eden, Tabernacle, Temple, New Covenant, New Creation). It also can make the point that we are witnessing the high-water mark of Solomon's story, especially in his great dedication prayer.

+ **True obedience to the Word of God:** Here we see the ark as not only the place of revelation (containing the tablets of law), but as pointing towards the Living Word.

- ✦ **True understanding of God's covenant:** There is significance in highlighting both Moses and David. We see divine initiative and human response (especially vv. 31-53).

- ✦ **True understanding of who God is:** both a sense of awe and transcendence, and a sense of nearness.

Suggestions for teaching
Questions to help understand the passage

1. Why is the Ark of the Covenant so important? (8:1-9)?

2. How do verses 10-11 show that the priests, while important, are only secondary?

3. What do the king's words (8:15-21) show about the significance of David in the story?

4. How is the importance of God's covenant emphasized in 8:23-26?

5. How does Solomon show both the majesty and grace of Yahweh in 8:27-30?

6. In the prayer for forgiveness (8:31-53), Solomon asks several times that Yahweh would hear from heaven, his dwelling-place (8:39, 43, 49). How would this be an encouragement to people during the Exile?

7. How is the importance of obedience emphasized (8:56-61)?

8. Why is David rather than Solomon mentioned in 8:66?

Questions to help apply the passage

1. The Ark of the Covenant no longer exists, almost certainly destroyed by Nebuchadnezzar's armies when the temple was burned. The true Ark is Christ Himself who embodies the glory of God (John 1:14). Verse 9 speaks about the words given to Moses and their abiding significance. How do we make certain that our worship of Christ truly flows from the Word?

2. This chapter is ultimately about worshipping the true and living God who is both in heaven and on earth. What are the dangers of overemphasizing one of these truths to the detriment of the other?

3. What does this passage teach about prayer?

4. This is a chapter about celebration. Is this note sometimes missing in our worship? How can we reclaim it?

5. How can we, without ritual and ceremony, best convey our sense of the majesty of God? We rightly deplore the deadness of formality, but do we sufficiently see that informality can be just as dead?

7

BUILDING THAT WILL LAST?
(1 KINGS 9)

Introduction

Building and buying houses is one of the great contemporary interests here in the U.K. if the popularity of such television programmes as 'Location, Location, Location' and 'Escape to the Country' is anything to go by. Such shows often deal in loving detail with the niceties of materials, the shape and configuration of rooms, and the surrounding land. Solomon's story so far has been mainly about building and we are not yet finished. The word 'build' is one of the binding threads of this chapter (vv. 1, 3, 10, 15, 17, 19, 24 [twice], 25, 26). There is, as we shall see, a lot more than the physical act of building, hence the question mark in the title, but it clearly unifies the apparently disparate materials of the chapter. Also, both of the two main sections (vv. 1-9) and (vv. 10-28) include a reference to Yahweh's house and Solomon's house and this gives us our bearings.

Listening to the text
Context and structure

Taking these sections as the two main divisions of the chapter, we see that the first section, which is mainly the words of Yahweh, must control the second, which is mainly the activities of Solomon. This is a chapter which describes the situation in the middle of Solomon's reign (v. 10), and is a reflection on the past and looking at prospects for the future. It is a place where the author gives us our bearings (along with chapter 10) before we come to the closing years of the reign.

Working through the text
A second appearance of the Lord (9:1-9)

God now appears again to Solomon and this forms an inclusio with chapter 3:4-15 and reminds us of that occasion when he was given the heavenly wisdom whose fruits have been evident up to now. The content of what Yahweh says develops in three stages.

First, in verse 3 the dedication of the temple is put in context. Solomon may have dedicated it, but only God can make it holy: 'I have consecrated it'. Ultimately this goes back to the making holy of the Sabbath (Gen. 2:3). The Sabbath anticipates the new creation, as does the temple when God dwells with His people (Rev. 21:3). With that in mind the putting of God's name in the temple 'for ever' makes sense. The physical structure may go, but the heavenly Temple, the house not made with hands, is eternal. If Solomon and the people had remembered that it was the Lord's temple, later heartbreak and disaster would have been avoided (see comments on chapter 11).

Second, in verses 4 and 5, God emphasizes the need for Solomon to walk in the ways of David. Emphasis is placed on 'integrity of heart and uprightness'. Back in chapter 2:3-4, David had urged Solomon to walk in the ways of the Torah and linked that with both the prosperity of his kingdom and the future of his dynasty; so it is here.

Third, there is the note of warning in verses 6-9 where the high cost of disobedience is spelled out. The land will be lost and the promises to Abraham threatened. The temple, the visible sacrament of God's presence among them, will be destroyed. The throne itself will vanish and all the covenant promises will seem empty.

Solomon could not complain that he had not been warned and that the consequences had not been identified. The end of verse 9 is especially striking: 'The LORD brought all this disaster on them'. This ominous chain of events would not simply be the product of political, economic and military factors (although doubtless these operate as secondary factors) but the Lord's judgment (see also Dan. 1:1-2).

Politics and Planning (9:10-28)

This is not so much in chronological sequence as a parallel to verses 1-9, showing us the outward business of the kingdom as the earlier verses had given us a glimpse of Solomon's inner life. We are in the middle of the reign and four issues are mentioned by the author.

There is first a voice from the past (vv. 10-14). Solomon again enlists Hiram king of Tyre (see 5:10) and again the man from Tyre is very much the junior partner. Here Solomon gives Hiram a number of towns in Galilee of dubious worth. There is an ambivalence about this action;

was Solomon wise in ceding part of the promised land? No comment is made but it is hardly the action of someone who sees that the land is Yahweh's and that the king is merely the tenant. Hiram's disappointment with the villages ('Cabul' suggests useless and pointless) does not prevent him giving a huge amount of gold to Solomon (v. 28). The exact amount was colossal: about four tons of the stuff. This is a theme that will surface again in chapter 10. Again there is ambiguity; God had promised Solomon riches but there may be a hint here, and certainly in chapter 10, of a growing love for luxury and excess.

Second, in verses 15-24, matters of defence and further building are outlined. A number of issues are significant and the first is the use of forced labour. This has already been mentioned in 5:13-18 as being involved in the building of the temple and now it emerges that other building projects had been taking place; although foreigners were conscripted from the old Canaanite inhabitants of the land, no Israelites were slaves (v. 22). Solomon also shows himself the true son of David in his concern for defence, fortifying the strategic cities of Hazor and Megiddo, both at key points on the highway between Egypt and Mesopotamia. The twofold mention of Pharaoh and his daughter (vv. 16, 24) reminds us of this potentially disastrous liaison with Egypt which becomes a reality in chapter 11. Plainly, building activities were a major emphasis of Solomon's reign and here we see these in a wider context.

The third element of those years (v. 25) was Solomon's punctilious observations of the three annual festivals of Passover, Pentecost and Tabernacles (Exod. 23:14-17). So far, idolatry is avoided and orthodoxy practised.

Fourth (vv. 26-28), we read about Solomon's commercial and trading enterprises. Solomon now controlled the main trade routes, both maritime and overland, again with the assistance of Hiram. Ezion Geber was on the Gulf of Aqaba, as was Elath (near modern Eilat) and they controlled the caravan routes from Arabia. Ophir (famous for its gold – see Job 28:16; Isa. 13:12) was probably in south Arabia, although other locations such as India have been suggested (because of the two to three-year voyage mentioned in 10:22).

These summaries of the business of government are on the whole positive, although with a few warning bells ringing, as already noted. The placing of them in parallel to God's words to Solomon in the first part of the chapter helps us to study priorities and we shall explore these as we look at application.

From text to message

Getting the message clear: the theme
Solomon has another vision of the LORD and is reminded of true priorities; meanwhile his other activities continue.

Getting the message clear: the aim
The aim of a sermon on this passage should be to underline the importance of true priorities in our work for the kingdom.

A way in
With these chapters we reach the middle years of Solomon's reign. We might want to emphasize the opportunities and pitfalls of middle life. These are the years often associated with teenage children, mortgages, pressures of work and a time to take stock. Chapters 9 and 10 speak of Solomon's

achievements, his building works and his international prestige. As we have seen in the exposition, there are warning bells, although the picture is mainly positive.

Thus an emphasis on the importance of taking stock on where our lives are going is valuable for everyone. To young people there will be the importance of not frittering away time; to the middle-aged a serious look at priorities; to the old a determination to finish well. These could easily become moralizing platitudes but the emphasis of 9:3-7 on covenant faithfulness drives these chapters. Again, as in chapters 4 and 5 the whole of life is covered; politics as well as temple; diplomacy as well as worship.

Ideas for application

If we are going to get the most benefit from a chapter like this we need to see that verses 1-9 with God speaking to Solomon are parallel to, and give us our bearings in interpreting, verses 10-28. Otherwise we will end up with moralizing platitudes or unapplied historical observations.

+ The important point this chapter emphasizes is that the obedience of faith needs to dominate every part of life. The kingdom is flourishing both in its domestic and foreign policy, but the warning of verses 6-9 reminds us that it could all evaporate if characterized by faithless disobedience. This not only true of kings. We have this warning universalized by the Lord Himself: 'What good is it for a man to gain the whole world and forfeit his soul?' (Mark 8:36). At every stage of life we need this constant reminder of having eternal and not simply temporal priorities.

✦ A complementary point is that these 'secular' concerns *do* matter. It is very easy as ministers and preachers to become preoccupied narrowly with issues of 'ministry' and forget that these are not the preoccupations of most of our listeners. Electricians, teachers, doctors, cleaners, carers, lawyers and those involved in every task under the sun need help to live their lives for the glory of God, and passages such as this showing the juxtaposition of prayer and work are important reminders that God cares for the schoolroom as well as the sanctuary, the workshop as well as worship and the holiday as well as the holy day. As preachers too, we live in this world with families, mortgages, bills, problems and privileges. We must not draw unscriptural dichotomies; God is Lord of all life.

✦ The importance of building for God, as we have seen, dominates the chapter. This is not only the temple, but the other projects for defence and security. It is important that we see this in the light of the above point. The building of living stones in the eternal Temple is the supreme concern but building for God is wider and involves the daily, unglamorous building of character which will last for eternity. A chorus of a Victorian hymn by Fanny Crosby makes the point well.

> We are building day by day as the moments glide away,
> Our temple which the world may not see.
> Every victory won by grace will be sure to find its place
> In our building for eternity.

✦ The importance of listening to God's voice is clear. It is true that twenty years and more have passed since God appeared to Solomon at Gibeon and this was an initiative of the Lord rather than a seeking on Solomon's part. However, the words of God in verse 4, as already noted, echo the words of David in chapter 2 with their emphasis on following the Torah. The special appearance of the Lord, in other words, is to reinforce the fundamental principle of obedience to the Word of God. It is all too easy to become fixated on special guidance and forget that all we need for life and godliness is in the Scriptures, and that daily obedience will help us to avoid the pitfalls and dangers of everyday life. Indeed this is a major theme as we teach Kings (see *Introducing Kings*) and thus a continual reminder to us and those who hear us that reading the Bible prayerfully and diligently and hearing it expounded faithfully will be the major way we will hear God's voice.

✦ The continual danger of idolatry is emphasized (v. 9). The word 'embraced' is important; this is not simply an intellectual change but a breaking of covenant as Israel falls out of love with Yahweh and has affairs with other gods. This will happen most spectacularly with Solomon himself. We are in continual danger of this and no mere intellectual commitment to 'teaching the Bible' will save us from idolatry if we fall out of love with the Lord. Indeed, that very teaching can itself become idolatrous as we trust our techniques, ape our gurus, become obsessed with a particular methodology and pridefully talk about the admiring comments our teaching has attracted. Whether we are preachers or not we can become proud of our churches and our part in them without giving honour to the Lord.

+ In case the previous comment seems like pious moralizing, we need to see that this is a chapter about grace and God's initiative. By his Word and Spirit He can keep us from the above weaknesses. This is emphasized here by His consecrating of the temple, the reminder of His promises to David and the causing of Solomon's activities to prosper. It is also shown by His warnings of judgment. The teaching and preaching of judgment is a sign of grace because it warns people to avoid disaster and enjoy the blessings which follow obedience.

Suggestions for preaching
Sermon: Living all of life for God's glory

Possibly the obvious way is to take the two sections as the two main teaching points:

+ **God's agenda** (9:1-9). This is an important occasion with a second appearance of God:
    + Remember the true meaning of the temple –not man's building but God's presence.
    + Remember the covenant with David – this is the true foundation of Solomon's kingdom.
    + Remember what will be lost if Solomon disobeys.

+ **Solomon's agenda** (9:10-28) still largely governed by verses 1-9:
    + Concern for building.
    + Concern for worship.
    + Concern for prosperity of kingdom.

Suggestions for teaching

Suggestions for leading a Bible Study will come after comments on chapter 10 where there will also be suggestions on how we might preach the two chapters together.

8

The World Beating a Track to Solomon's Door
(1 Kings 10)

Introduction

The Queen of Sheba, along with Cleopatra, evokes images of the exotic and opulent East and perhaps Hollywood films of an earlier age. Certainly she has fascinated film producers and novelists, often with the subtext that this was the beginning of Solomon's decline which culminates in chapter 11. The sense is that he was seduced away from his earlier springtime faith and came to love luxury and even decadence. There may be some truth in this as we shall see (and indeed have already picked up some such hints in chapter 9) but this must not be exaggerated. For one thing, there is no hint in the text of a seductive, oriental queen coming to lead a simple, rustic chieftain astray. Rather this queen is drawn here to be overwhelmed and overawed at the splendour of Solomon and his court. Also we need to take seriously what Jesus says about this episode in Matthew 12:42 and, as we shall see, that suggests a different slant on the story.

Listening to the text
Context and structure

The chapter falls into two clear parts: the queen's visit (10:1-13) and Solomon's golden age (10:14-29). There are echoes of chapter 4 where the wisdom and wealth of Solomon's court and its growing international reputation were underlined.

There is no doubt the main focus of the author is on the breathtaking nature of Solomon's wisdom and riches, and, as in all narrative, we will need to be alert to the pointers to the true perspective for viewing this pageant, as well as seeing how it fits into the wider narrative.

Working through the text
The royal visit (10:1-13)

We are familiar today with the protocol that surrounds the visits of heads of state and presidents and prime ministers, with the feverish attempts of the leaders' entourages to build up the importance of their particular boss. Did the president give the Prime Minister a full state reception? What was the significance of having lunch rather than dinner? Often beleaguered national leaders look to foreign visits as a way of boosting their status at home.

Here the Queen of Sheba is given the full works. The detail does not read like legend or exaggeration of something essentially modest; rather the occasion is an important trade mission from Sheba (probably an area in modern-day Yemen about 1,000 miles south of Jerusalem). So here is a serious and important diplomatic visit.

However, the author's emphasis is not simply on Solomon's splendour but on his wisdom. The 'hard questions' (v. 1) would not simply be riddles but would have included political and ethical issues, and we have seen in chapters 3 and 4 how these were handled by Solomon and were the cause of his growing fame both at home and abroad. Verse 3 shows that the queen was not disappointed in her search, and indeed verse 7 shows that his fame had been underplayed rather than overdone. Yahweh had clearly fulfilled his promise to give Solomon abundant wisdom (see 3:12) and the tone here is of gladness and thankfulness, which recaptures something of the springtime of chapters 3 and 4 at this much later point in the reign. We are, in effect, being given a series of snapshots of Solomon in all his glory.

The emphasis on wealth is also continued and linked with wisdom (v. 4) and the queen herself is no pauper, as seen in the lavish gift of gold, jewels and spices (v. 10), although this would be partly, at least, a commercial transaction. This is probably confirmed by the parenthesis in verses 11-12 which mentions Hiram's continuing participation in joint trading ventures involving luxuries as well as everyday goods. This echoes the emphases of 4:22-24 and 27-28 where the wealth of the court overflows to bless the whole nation.

The queen's assessment of all this wisdom and wealth is an important part of this section. The first thing of note is her mention of Yahweh as the one who placed Solomon on his throne and from whom flowed all the spiritual and material gifts of the king (v. 9). This is more than diplomatic courtesy. It is not altogether clear what is meant by 'his relation to the name of the LORD' (v. 1), but if we remember the emphasis of 8:15-21 where the newly built temple is especially associated with the Name of Yahweh, it is likely that something of the unique significance of that temple and its God, who does not live in it but is intimately associated with it, is implied. This impression is further strengthened by the queen's words in verse 9 where not only does she praise Israel's God but uses expressions such as 'eternal love for Israel', 'justice' and 'righteousness' which are at the heart of Israel's faith. This suggests that Solomon had spoken to her of such things. We shall look at this further in ideas for application on the chapter as a whole.

Solomon's Golden Age (10:14-29)

The key word in this section is 'gold', mentioned ten times (vv. 14, 16-18, 21, 22, 25). This can be seen in a negative way in that it is used for the further beautifying of his residences and the construction of an elaborate throne, as well as shields. Indeed 'silver was considered of little value' (v. 21). The sense of luxury is intensified by the trade in exotic animals (v. 22). Solomon's political and economic significance grows greater: revenues from Arabian kings and governors (v. 15); trade with Egypt and Kue (probably Cilicia) and with the Hittites in Asia Minor and with Syria (10:28-29). What are we to make of all this?

Clearly warning bells ring in the multiplicity of chariots and horses (v. 26). Deuteronomy 17:16 warns that a king is not 'to acquire great numbers of horses for himself' because of the danger of trusting in superior military strength of which chariots, along with horses, are the symbol. However, at the moment, this is a warning rather than condemnation. This becomes clear when we look at verse 23 which talks of 'the wisdom God had put in his heart', which surely means that wisdom is still the dominating factor in all Solomon's activities and decisions. It is difficult to avoid the impression that the author is admiring Solomon along with the Queen of Sheba and also is impressed and even inspired by the wisdom and splendour of the court.

The author is not simply repeating data and statistics but creating a sense of the wise king, widely praised and sought after for his wisdom as well as being at the centre of an extensive trading empire. Many questions are left unanswered but the selectivity of the storyteller is admirable and the literary art superb.

From text to message
Getting the message right: the theme
The theme of this passage is the way the Lord has blessed Solomon in granting him wisdom and wealth which has brought him international praise. There are dangers in all this impressive splendour, not least in the temptation to trust in power and uncertain riches and it is important now as then to realize that when God blesses greatly we need to accept such blessings as gifts and not make them idols.

Getting the message right: the aim
The aim is to show that wealth is not wrong in itself (1 Tim. 6:10 is often misquoted omitting the word 'love') but emphasizing that wisdom in handling responsibility and money is a product of humble faith.

A way in
Spin was not an invention of the present day, but is characteristic of the human tendency to rewrite and repackage history (including contemporary history) and to read into texts our own perceptions rather than listen to what is there. As noted at the beginning of the chapter, films and novels have made this into a story of seduction and sex, in some

cases suggesting that Solomon had a child by the queen. To avoid this we need to emphasize the chapter's emphasis on wisdom (vv. 4, 7, 23, 24) as well as the New Testament's references to the queen. A big part of our task is not only to read the text faithfully ourselves but help others to do so.

Ideas for application

It would be easy to read this chapter simply as a good example of the author's skill and ignore the applications. We need now to examine the tone and detail of the narrative and find its abiding message.

Wisdom is emphasized here before wealth and power (vv. 3 & 4). This suggests we need to read the chapter in the light of God's gift of wisdom to Solomon in 3:12. This is the wisdom from above (James 3:17). Solomon's wisdom is not the wisdom which is earthly and unspiritual; not yet anyway. Another reference in James makes plain that God's gift of wisdom is not for some only. 'If any of you lacks wisdom, he should ask God, who gives generously to all' (James 1:5). Thus we need to emphasize the need to ask for wisdom in all parts of our lives.

+ Wealth is not to be seen as bad in itself and inevitably turning people's hearts away from the Lord. As is well known, it is the *love* of money which leads to disaster (1 Tim. 6:10). There is no evidence that Solomon has departed from the Lord (even in chapter 11 it is his *wives* not his *money* who lead to his downfall). We must therefore avoid moralizing platitudes about wealth, still less urging our hearers to give to the church rather than themselves. Of course that is a legitimate point to make but it is not here and we are not being faithful to the text if we smuggle it in. Rather we need to emphasize that many a good Christian work would disappear were it not for one or two individuals whom the Lord has blessed with wealth and who use that generously in His service.

* Further to the above, while we rightly reject the 'prosperity gospel' we must not feel envious of God blessing some with material wealth or indeed feel guilty if God blesses us in that way. We cannot ignore the words of Proverbs 10:22 – 'the blessing of the Lord brings wealth'. The problem arises when we think we won the prosperity unaided and do not thank the Lord and trust in His continued blessing.

* This is further a story of gospel grace and blessing. The queen coming with her gifts is a picture of the day when the Gentiles will come to Zion when, as Isaiah says, 'the wealth of the nations like a flooding stream' (Isa. 66:12) will pour into Jerusalem. Even more significantly, Psalm 72, associated with Solomon, says 'may gold from Sheba be given to him' (v. 15). What the Queen of Sheba saw was a foretaste of the King seated on the throne of His universal kingdom; she herself was a preview of the day when all nations will come and worship and 'the kings of the earth will bring their splendour' into the new Jerusalem (Rev. 21:24). I don't mean the Queen of Sheba went home singing *Crown him with many crowns*, but that what she saw was a true glimpse of the kingdom which is to come.

* There is a further point from the teaching of Christ. We must not ignore the New Testament challenge of the story. The Lord Jesus Christ warns us not to ignore or neglect the Queen of Sheba. 'The Queen of the South

will rise at the judgment with this generation and condemn it; for she came from the ends of the earth to listen to Solomon's wisdom, and now one greater than Solomon is here' (Matt. 12:42). In Matthew 11 and 12, Jesus has highlighted the faithlessness and unbelief of Israel's leaders and now, along with Jonah, He mentions the queen as one who will condemn them on the day of judgment. He says that she saw and knew less than they did but still believed. This is even more pointed to us because we live after the cross and the Resurrection and thus know more than the Jewish leaders of that day did. So that is the ultimate significance of this fragment of the queen's story in 1 Kings 10; there is a day of judgment and those who know more than she ever knew and fail to believe will be judged more severely. Don't consign her to an exotic Hollywood past; she is a pointer to the future.

Preaching Christ faithfully (chapters 5 to 8)

Jesus Himself is the true Temple (John 2:19-22) and His people living stones (e.g. 1 Cor. 3:16). Thus, as we study these chapters, we should expect to find pointers to these truths. The involvement of Hiram, king of Tyre, in chapter 5 points to the ingathering of the nations under the King. The temple itself reflects (as did the tabernacle) the beauty and splendour of the Lord. This can be overdone and lead to wild and unbalanced speculation, but there is a genuine typology. The linking with the Exodus story (6:1) reminds us that only redeemed people can truly worship God. The king/priest function of Solomon is only fully united in Christ and only in Him do we find the answer to the Exile foretold in 8:22-53.

Suggestions for preaching

It would probably be useful to take the two broad divisions of the chapter as indicating the two main divisions of the sermon.

Sermon 1: A foretaste of the true kingdom

The snapshot here is not just of Solomon's ancient kingdom but of the kingdom to come – and it is important to emphasize that this is a genuine foreshadowing of that kingdom in all its wonder.

- **A woman with an open mind and heart (10:1-13).** We can see the significance of the queen's visit. Not only is it an important commercial trip but it also anticipates Gentiles coming into the kingdom of God. There is also surprise in the visit. It is a far better than anticipated foreshadowing of the grace of the kingdom.

- **A man with a wide vision (10:14-29).** Solomon is great in both wisdom and wealth (note the importance of verse 23). However, the king is still not self-sufficient and there are one or two doubts about the trajectory of his reign, for example references to the horses and chariots. However, he is certainly generous in spirit – there are echoes here of chapter 4 where the wealth of the king overflows to the kingdom.

Sermon 2: Still following the Lord

It would also be possible to preach on chapters 9 and 10 together; this would be a more thematic sermon. The emphasis of this sermon would be the covenant undergirding the whole relationship with the Lord and Solomon, and the need for obedience.

+ **The importance of obedience and trust.** This is especially clear in 9:1-9 but also seen in 10:9 and 23. All Solomon's splendour and prosperity depends on covenant obedience and being a humble and grateful servant – wisdom is a gift not a right.

+ **The attractiveness of covenant living.** This is seen, for example, in the fortifying of Jerusalem and other strategic sites (9:15-19), the amazed reaction of the Queen of Sheba (10:4-9) and the desire of others to benefit from Solomon's wisdom (10:24).

+ **The need for vigilance.** We begin to see the warnings of the danger of covenant-breaking.

Suggestions for teaching

I suggested earlier that it would be a good idea to take these two chapters together as they deal with the middle years of Solomon's reign and raise similar issues. One thing the Bible study leader will need to do is to demonstrate their relevance as the key question, spoken or unspoken, is how we connect with the story of this fabulously wealthy ancient king. As always we need to emphasize that this is the story of God, not the story of Solomon, and that we have the same God and indeed the same covenant promises as Solomon. These promises, in our case, do not relate to sitting on the throne of Israel but they do relate to the coming kingdom and our living now needs to be in the light of that kingdom.

Questions to help understand the passage

1.   What is the significance of the author mentioning chapter 3 at this point in 9:1-2?

2.   How does 9:4-9 show how God's unconditional faithfulness relates to human obedience?

3. What do the building activities (9:15-18) tell us about Solomon's priorities?

4. Why do you think the author includes the visit of the Queen of Sheba (10:1-13)?

5. What do you think is the point of the description of Solomon's luxurious lifestyle (10:14-29)? Is this a passage warning of danger or is it celebrating the goodness of God?

Questions to help apply the passage

1. Yahweh warns Solomon of the dangers of disobedience even though grace is unconditional. How do we neglect holiness in the life of grace?

2. Solomon's other building activities are not seen separately from temple-building. How can we avoid compartmentalizing our lives into 'sacred' and 'secular'?

3. The Queen of Sheba sees that Solomon's greatness comes from Yahweh. Our churches, especially if we seem to be doing relatively well, can often become conceited and self-satisfied, and this can be reflected in the self-congratulatory tone of our websites. How do we avoid this and give glory to Christ?

4. How does this passage, and indeed the story up to now, help us to understand true wisdom and live by it?

9

THE TRAGEDY OF A DIVIDED HEART
(1 KINGS 11)

Introduction

Many years ago I remember going to the site of my old
primary school which was shortly to be demolished and
was then derelict, silent and empty. The memories of young
life, laughter and bustle made the building seem even
more desolate. A comparison of chapter 11 with chapter 3
evokes a similar feeling of melancholy. This chapter, with its
autumnal note, contrasts starkly with the early springtime
of Solomon's love for the Lord and the high midsummer
pomp of the dedication of the temple (chapter 8). It is very
important to listen carefully to what the text is saying and
to see the connections with the previous chapters.

Some commentators who have seen Solomon in a very
affirming way up to this point have difficulty in explaining
the almost total about-turn here. Others who have been
negative see this simply as an inevitable result of earlier
compromises. I think neither view is satisfactory. As for
the first, we do not go to bed one night loving the Lord

and wake up the next morning virtually apostate. As for the second, it takes insufficient account of verse 4, 'As Solomon grew old'.

Both views contain truth, but what the flow of the whole story from the beginning of the book suggests is that, from the start, Solomon was tempted to compromise in matters such as marrying Pharaoh's daughter and failing to remove the high places, and perhaps in the increasing material splendour of the court. However, these were occasions of temptation rather than actual faults, but a compromising spirit and a consequent weakening of commitment over the years eventually resulted in full-blown idolatry. Just as an old chair worn out with repeated use one day collapses, so here Solomon's collapse was the result of years of drifting.

Listening to the text
Context and structure
The chapter develops in five movements:

1. Solomon's idolatry (11:1-8)

2. God's anger (11:9-13)

3. External opposition (11:14-25)

4. The emergence of Jeroboam (11:26-40)

5. Solomon's death (11:41-43)

It is also worth noting how the author shows this is the end of a longer section which began in 3:3, 'Solomon loved the LORD, walking in the statutes of his father David', and ends here with 'his heart was not fully devoted to the LORD his God, as the heart of David his father had been' (v. 4).

Working through the text

This is a long but very carefully organized chapter where Solomon's spiritual failures parallel closely the beginning of the political disintegration of the kingdom.

Solomon's idolatry (11:1-8)

Plainly the word 'heart' dominates this section. This is spelled out further by such words as 'held fast' and 'devoted'. In the depths of Solomon's being there was a fatal weakness; he was capable of great affection and real devotion but his heart was not fully committed to Yahweh. David had sinned in technicolour, but his repentance was as spectacular as his sin (see Ps. 51) and he never wandered from his love for Yahweh, however much his affections for people might have strayed. How little Solomon had taken heed of his own words, 'Above all else, guard your heart, for it is the wellspring of life' (Prov. 4:23). The heart in the Bible is not simply the emotions and feelings, it is the very self and involves the will and the reason; it is who we are.

We must not distance this story from ourselves by seeing here only lust and an uncontrolled sex drive, although that is undoubtedly there and serves as a warning. Rather, we need to see the wider issue and how this fits in within the overall story. Moses had warned that 'the king must not take many wives or his heart will be led astray' (Deut. 17:17). That would even have applied to orthodox Israelite wives, but here this is compounded by the multiplicity of pagan wives, as we learn that the only difference between Pharaoh's daughter and the other pagan women was the eminence of her parentage. Also in Deuteronomy (7:3-4), Moses warns against such intermarriage. It was to these women that Solomon 'held fast' (v. 3) in love. The word translated 'held fast' is the word also used in Genesis 2:24 about the unique love which makes a man and a woman 'one flesh'. The extravagance of the royal harem is a tragic visual evidence of the sad divided heart.

However, what the author is most concerned about is not illicit sex, but pagan worship, in which Solomon himself was involved (v. 5). 'Ashtoreth the goddess of the Sidonians' was the goddess of love and fertility, and Molech was the grim demon god whose worship was marked by child sacrifice. Here begins that slippery slope that is to lead to full-blown idolatry with Ahab (1 Kings 16–18) and Manasseh (2 Kings 21). So far it is syncretism which is shown by Yahweh still being part of this pagan exercise in ecumenism. It is easy to see how this could have been excused as an exercise in wise diplomacy: temples for pagan gods would also double up as embassies and Solomon's spin doctors would laud this wise and shrewd international statesman who showed such broadmindedness and tolerance.

The phrase, 'As Solomon grew old', should not be ignored. It is so easy as we grow older to depart almost imperceptibly from our first love and in pressurized middle age and complacent old age drift far away from the devotion of our youth. This is not inevitable: Psalm 103:5 speaks of youth being renewed like the eagle's; but it *is* a danger. We rightly see the importance of youth ministry and the shaping of lives which, in God's grace, will have many fruitful years ahead of them. However, one rather neglected ministry is supporting those who have so far run the race well and helping them to finish still going strong.

God's anger (11:9-13)
The godlets who now jostled for space on the temple mount were dumb and ineffective but Yahweh could and

did speak, and His Word is one of judgment. This comes as no surprise. The covenant Lord who pledges blessing to all who obey also pronounces curses on those who do not (Deut. 6:14-15). His claims are universal and will not be shared, just as a loving husband or wife will not share their spouse with anyone else. This is important if we are going to understand covenant and how the Lord's unbreakable promises relate to the necessity of obedience. The kingdom *will* come; David's son *will* reign, but those of his sons who disobey will come under the covenant curses. This is spelled out most clearly in Psalm 89:28-37 where God's faithfulness to the Davidic line is unconditional but those who disobey will be punished.

Here David's son is more like the rejected Saul (1 Sam. 15:28) than he is like David. Here too emerges the concept of the remnant through whom God's purposes will be fulfilled. One tribe (Benjamin here being regarded as part of Judah) will remain to David's sons and from and to that remnant great David's Greater Son will come (see Luke 1–3).

Solomon's failure is exacerbated by the fact that God had appeared to him twice (v. 9) and given His Word (v. 10). This means that even the most privileged are liable to fall away unless they remain humble and alert. Solomon did not lack for good teaching or good example, but his heart was hopelessly divided.

External opposition (11:14-25)
We are left in no doubt that, as the vultures gather, the opposition is no accident. Yahweh himself has raised up these enemies of Solomon (vv. 14 and 23). It will not be long before a divided heart leads to a divided kingdom.

The problem with Hadad the Edomite began in David's time with the defeat of Edom; however, there we read that 'The LORD gave David victory' (2 Sam. 8:14); it is to be very different here. As an interesting aside, Joab is seen here as engaged in a massacre. Little good came to either David or Solomon from the activities of this hard, though gifted, general.

We now have a glimpse of political intrigues at the Egyptian court. Solomon may have married Pharaoh's daughter, but Pharaoh is quite willing to give aid and comfort to his enemies. Solomon's attempts to build lasting peace on dodgy alliances are now exposed as a failure. In Egypt, feted and honoured, Hadad's resentment against Israel simmers and he sees with the death of David and Joab a chance to return home, doubtless to create mischief.

The second adversary, Rezon son of Eliada (v. 23) also resurfaces from David's wars. In 2 Samuel 8:3-8, David conquered Zobah near the Euphrates, and Rezon (with a band of guerrilla fighters) fled and temporarily took over Damascus, which was subsequently taken by David (2 Sam. 8:6). Probably this had remained the situation early in Solomon's reign but now the vultures are beginning to gather as the golden age of peace and prosperity moves towards its end. The real significance of these adversaries is to lie in the future and we have no account of actual wars waged by Solomon. Edom is to be not only an old enemy but becomes an object of particular detestation for giving help to the Babylonians when Jerusalem was destroyed (see Ps. 137:7 and Obadiah). Aram/Syria is to become a major thorn in Israel's flesh (see, for example, 1 Kings 20–22 and 2 Kings 6–13).

The emergence of Jeroboam (11:26-40)

For the moment, these external enemies are more irritations than real threats, but a far more formidable internal enemy now emerges. Hadad and Rezon are shadowy figures but Jeroboam is a more substantial figure who is to cast a long shadow over the rest of the book. He is to become the archetypal apostate king who led Israel into sin; many future kings are described as 'walking in the ways of Jeroboam' (15:34; 16:2, 19, 26). He is the more dangerous enemy because of his great abilities. The description 'a man of standing' probably refers to his great energies and abilities as he oversaw some of Solomon's building projects. His particular oversight of 'the whole labour force of the house of Joseph' (i.e. the northern tribes) hints at his particular standing there and would facilitate his takeover of the north.

But the main interest here is the emergence of the prophet Ahijah and the importance of prophetic ministry, which is to be so important in the rest of the book. Like Elijah, he appears suddenly and abruptly, and both his words and actions are dramatic. It is important to see the relationship of word and action. The apparently bizarre action of tearing a new cloak certainly would grab Jeroboam's attention, but without the explanation it would be incomprehensible. The alert reader will recall 1 Samuel 15:27-28 with the torn cloak a symbol of the kingdom being torn from Saul. However, there is one major difference; David is willing to wait for Yahweh to give him the kingdom; Jeroboam will seize it for himself.

This instantly raises questions. How will the promise to David of an everlasting throne (2 Sam. 7:12-16) now be fulfilled? The answer is in the fine detail of the prophecy. It will not happen in Solomon's time and the judgment will not be total. Yet judgment is real. Yahweh will deny neither His holiness nor His love and the subsequent history is to demonstrate this. The idolatry of Solomon is again emphasized (v. 33) with a significant added detail: *they have forsaken me and worshipped false gods*. The king may have given the lead but the apostasy was far wider although, as ever, there was a faithful remnant represented here by Ahijah.

God's faithfulness to His covenant is symbolized by the lamp (v. 36) which is a powerful reminder that this is part of a bigger story. It recalls that great moment (1 Sam. 3:3) when the still burning lamp, a reminder of the fire of God which burned at the call of Moses (Exod. 3:2-3), is now heralding the call of young Samuel. The same image occurs in 2 Samuel 14:7 symbolizing a continuous line of descendants. 'Not for ever' (v. 39) is the abiding principle: there will be punishment, but David's line will not be abandoned.

Moreover, there could have been two faithful lines of kings and two faithful kingdoms if Jeroboam had obeyed and been humble (v. 38) and thus the theme of human responsibility is again underlined. If Jeroboam is to enjoy the blessings of David, he must walk in the ways of David. His line could then have been stable rather than the four dynasties which rose and fell in the northern kingdom before it fell to Assyria. We do not know the sequence of events which followed Jeroboam receiving Ahijah's message, simply that Jeroboam fled to Egypt where he bided his time.

Solomon's death (11:41-43)

Little more remains to be said, for Solomon's sun has set and with it the last hope for a prosperous and united kingdom.

Never again would it be said of a king in his obituary that he 'reigned over all Israel'. The brief notes here are to become a formula marking the end of subsequent reigns: other sources for the king's reign are mentioned; the length of the reign and the phrase 'rested/slept with his fathers'; a notice of burial; the name of the successor.

There is grace here also. In the final notice of Solomon, the evil he did is unmentioned. This does not mean it was insignificant. Rather, the conclusion is part of a wider picture. We will return to that in the following notes.

From text to message

Getting the message right: the theme

The theme is Solomon's divided heart which led to personal departure from the Lord and to a threatened kingdom. The inexorable decline towards the judgment of exile is emphasized but also the faithfulness of God who will not abandon His promises to David.

Getting the message right: the aim

The aim is to show the danger of a divided heart which leads to faithlessness and foolishness. But this contrasts with the covenant faithfulness of God.

A way in

A good starting point would be Hebrews 2:1, 'We must pay more careful attention, therefore, to what we have heard, so that we do not drift away'. The metaphor here is of a ship drifting away to destruction because it has been carelessly moored. Solomon did not arrive at this sad state overnight, but has lapsed into idolatry.

Ideas for application

As we try to apply the teaching of this chapter we need to avoid moralizing. But we also need to acknowledge some of the issues that arise despite the difference in Solomon's situation and ours. Particularly we need to realize that the life of faith is a marathon with the challenge of persevering and helping others to do so.

+ Keeping our heart is the most important thing we can do (Prov. 4:23). Without that no godly teaching, good role models or great gifts will keep us faithful. Solomon had all these in abundance but in the end repeated compromises and a desensitizing of his spiritual insight undid him. We might want to emphasize that our inner life will sooner or later show itself for what it is. Without resorting to legalism we need to emphasize the importance of spiritual discipline. What distinguishes true discipline from legalism is that it is inward and between us and the Lord, not an ostentatious parade which panders to our sense of self-importance and makes others feel guilty. A continual biblical emphasis is on the importance of what is inward and what motivates us: 'out of the heart come evil thoughts, sexual immorality ... and folly. All these evils come from inside and make a man unclean' (Mark 7:21-23). These words of Jesus apply Solomon's inner heart trouble to us all.

+ Closely related is the danger of idolatry. The heart which is divided and provides only certain rooms for Yahweh will soon find tenants for the others. The temples to Chemosh and Molech on a hill outside Jerusalem were simply outward signs that the royal heart had become divided. That this is no ancient problem is shown by the last words of 1 John: 'Dear children keep yourselves from idols' (1 John 5:21).

+ Another related point is that the Word which we neglect or defy has a way of catching up with us; this is shown here by the appearance of Ahijah the prophet. The Lord has ways of bringing His Word dramatically alive and showing that He has been no idle bystander while Solomon has slid into idolatry. This is a reminder not only to obey that Word, but to have confidence in its power to accomplish its purpose (Isa. 55:11).

+ Great privileges and gifts bring great responsibilities. Those of us who have the enormous privilege of preaching and teaching the Word need to remember continually the judgment associated with that (James 3:1). Yet this is scarcely less so for evangelicals in the West who have complete access not only to the Scriptures but to a plethora of aids to understanding it: preaching; commentaries; study guides and the resources of electronic media. In these circumstances the responsibility to hear and obey is very great.

+ God overrules the failures of His people. This needs to be taken in parallel with the previous points which have emphasized human responsibility. That emphasis taken on its own can lead to the gospel of good works being smuggled in the back door or, on the other hand, to despair and the lassitude which follows. We need to remember that we will not bring in the kingdom and that the very best of God's servants only make it by grace. The combination of these twin truths: that God demands faithfulness, and that He gives more grace, will keep us going in tough times.

Preaching Christ faithfully (chapters 9 to 11)
As Solomon's building and diplomatic activities continue, we see further evidence of a kingdom ruled by wisdom. Yet in chapter 11 tragedy strikes and the kingdom begins to fall apart. Here we must preach that no earthly anticipation of the kingdom, no church, however flourishing, is immune from apostasy. This calls for greater heart devotion to the true Son of David because it is the heart of the problem (11:4). Yet this is also the chapter which reaffirms the future reign of David's son (11:36). No human leader will bring in the kingdom; we must trust the true leader.

Suggestions for preaching
Sermon 1: *The tragedy of half-heartedness*
If the sermon reflects the text, it must concentrate on the overwhelming importance of the heart and the danger of inner compromises which eventually result in full-blown idolatry.

- **Solomon's divided heart** (11:1-13). Note the book-ends in Solomon's story, 'Solomon loved the LORD' (3:3) and 'Solomon held fast to them in love' (11:2).

    - The idolatry Solomon practised, both adultery and apostasy intertwined.

    - The Word Solomon rejected, especially verse 9. Remember that God had appeared to him twice.

- **Solomon's divided kingdom** (11:14-28). Contrast this chapter with the peace and prosperity of chapter 4. There are two complementary truths:

+ Yahweh controls history – twice (vv. 14 and 23) – He raises up an adversary.

+ People have choices to make – especially in the Jeroboam part of the story.

+ **God's undivided grace** (11:11-13; 29-43).

+ Gracious preaching of judgment by Ahijah and judgment mixed with mercy.

+ Throughout there is the faithfulness of Yahweh to His promises. He has chosen David and Jerusalem, and will not go back on His promise (vv. 34-36).

Suggestions for teaching

This will be an opportunity to sum up briefly the overall message of the Solomon story and its place in the developing narrative.

Understanding the passage

1. How is Solomon's failure linked with failure to obey the words of Moses? (See Exod. 34:16 and Deut. 17:17 and compare with 1 Kings 2:3 & 4.)

2. What does verse 2 tell us about both Solomon and David, and how does this fit with 2 Samuel 11 & 12?

3. What does verse 9 show about the seriousness of Solomon's sin?

4. How does verse 14 link verses 1-13 with the military and political situation?

5. How do verses 29-39 show both God's judgment and mercy?

6. What is the final assessment of Solomon?

Applying the passage

1.   What were the earlier signs of Solomon's divided heart and how can we recognize similar symptoms in ourselves?

2.   What are our idols?

3.   How do we divide up into compartments our lives with the Lord in one room, perhaps a rather attractive guest room, but not truly Lord of our lives?

4.   How can we encourage those who are reaching the autumn years of life?

5.   Most importantly as we come to the end of our study of Solomon, what have we learned about God, about His covenant, His grace and judgment, and His purposes both in history and personal lives?

Getting our bearings

At the end of Solomon's story we are almost halfway through 1 Kings and one fifth of the way through 1 and 2 Kings. No other king is to be given such extensive coverage, and while mere length is not in itself an index of importance, plainly we have here markers for interpreting the rest of the book.

•   In a sense, Solomon sums up in himself the range of all subsequent kings. This is not only because he is most directly 'son of David' and the last to sit on the throne of the united kingdom, but that good and bad qualities are expressed most starkly in him. Many of the kings 'do evil in the eyes of the Lord'; a few, notably Hezekiah and Josiah, 'walk in the ways of David'. Solomon does both and this needs to be taken into account in considering the often-raised question as to whether Solomon was condemned to eternal judgment as an apostate. We have to acknowledge that the Bible is silent on this question. The preservation in Scripture of Proverbs and other wisdom books may suggest that in the end he repented. This may be confirmed by the absence of negative comment in the New Testament. However, often behind this lurks another question: how far can I dabble with forbidden things and get away with it? That is the wrong approach: the story of Solomon is not telling us that we can sin as much as we want and come back when we choose; rather it tells us to recognize our own weaknesses and frailties and trust in the grace of our Advocate who is able to keep us from falling.

+ The vital importance of the prophetic Word is underlined at the beginning with the words of Moses (v. 2), which are the words of God, as the charter both for king and people, and at the end with the words of Ahijah. The ministry of prophets, named and unnamed, is to be a feature of the book. No one is to remain in ignorance of God's Word as these brave messengers speak with power and conviction.

+ The importance of the Davidic covenant (see 2 Sam. 7) is central to the book. The tension between God's unconditional promises to David and his line on the one hand, and the repeated unfaithfulness and idolatry of many of the kings on the other, is to be a major theme culminating in the Exile. This is intertwined with Yahweh's control of history and the responsibility of the individuals and communities who are part of that history. Written over the narrative are the words of Psalm 89, echoing 2 Sam. 7: 'If his sons forsake my

law ... I will punish their sin with the rod ... I will
not lie to David – that his line will continue for ever'
(Ps. 89:30-35).

+ The Christ-centred nature of the story is vital.
Solomon in his glory, and the peace of the earlier part
of his reign, points to the King who is to come (Ps. 72)
and who will rule the whole world and renew creation.
It is important to realize that such times are genuine
glimpses of the coming kingdom. Putting this in its
widest context we can flash forward to Acts 1:6, 'Lord
are you at this time going to restore the kingdom to
Israel?'. The Lord's answer does not rebuke the disciples
for silliness but rather shows that their vision was too
small. The kingdom would indeed come but was not
going to be confined to Jerusalem, Judea and Samaria,
but was to extend to 'the ends of the earth'. As we read
1 and 2 Kings we need to see what is happening there
as part of that process as Yahweh steadily moves to the
time when great David's Greater Son will reign for ever.

Part 3

THE DIVIDED KINGDOM
(1 KINGS 12–22)

This next major section of the book covers some seventy years from the death of Solomon to the beginning of Ahab's reign in the northern kingdom. It is not a happy story but, as we shall see, the purposes of God continue in spite of rebellion and failure. Three issues are prominent in this section.

The first is the divided kingdom itself. Hardly has Solomon gone when his son Rehoboam's foolishness causes the northern tribes to rebel. From now on the story is going to switch back and forwards between the two tribes of Judah and Benjamin in the south, with Jerusalem as capital, and the ten northern tribes, with the capital successively Shechem, Tirzah and then, for most of the time, Samaria. The southern kingdom is usually known as Judah and the northern as Israel. This story continues until Israel falls to Assyria (2 Kings 17:6) and thereafter the story of Judah alone is told until her own exile to Babylon (2 Kings 25:21b).

However, though that story is dispiriting, we have already been encouraged to see it in a wider perspective. Chapter 11:29-39 tells how the prophet Ahijah had told Jeroboam that the northern kingdom would be his and that the LORD would bless him if he kept the Torah. He had further told him that the south would also be blessed for David's sake. So ultimately it is a story of grace.

The second notable feature is the continued slide into apostasy and idolatry. Jeroboam is to earn the unenviable epithet of the man who caused Israel to sin (1 Kings 14:16). This behaviour is to continue in the short-lived and uninspiring reigns of the kings in chapters 14 and 15 and to culminate in the full-blown idolatry of Ahab 'who did more to provoke the LORD, the God of Israel, to anger than did all the kings of Israel before him' (16:33). Yet even this must be seen against the background of continuous warnings by prophets, known and unknown, who hold out the opportunity of repentance.

The third feature of these chapters (which is to be characteristic of the story as a whole) is the occasional glimpse of anticipations of the kingdom to come. In this section this is particularly seen in the unnamed man of God who confronts Jeroboam in chapter 13 and in King Asa of Judah (15:9-24). Neither is perfect but both show that it is still possible to be faithful among the surrounding apostasy.

From a literary point of view there is long, leisurely narrative from 13:1–14:19 which sets out the issues of unbelief and rebellion of Jeroboam's reign. Much of the rest is brief notes as the consequences unfold.

I

SEPARATING WHAT GOD HAS JOINED
(1 KINGS 12)

Introduction

The golden age of Solomon has ended and the events which cause the disintegration of the united kingdom are now described rapidly. Chapter 11 has already shown the fatal slide of Solomon into idolatry and the fraying at the edges of the once-powerful kingdom as enemies begin to circle. However, the sovereignty of God overshadows everything (12:15) and this prevents what follows simply being a depressing account of human stupidity and malevolence.

Listening to the text

Context and Structure

The events leading to the divided kingdom are outlined clearly and concisely. The narrative develops in four main movements:

1. Stupidity and Sovereignty (12:1-15)

2. The north breaks away (12:16-20)

3. Rehoboam prevented from further stupidity
    (12:21-24)

4. Jeroboam invents a new religion (12:25-33)

Probably there is material for two sermons here, with the
Jeroboam material taken separately. The Jeroboam material
is fundamental for understanding the lapse into idolatry of
both kingdoms and is thus a useful place to get our bearings
for the rest of the book.

Working through the text
1. Stupidity and Sovereignty (12:1-15)
The stupidity is Rehoboam's and the sovereignty is
Yahweh's. The tension between these two drives the
narrative. Rehoboam is responsible for his attitudes and
actions which threaten to derail Yahweh's purposes, but
while he can and does do immense damage to the kingdom,
its final destiny is in higher hands. Rehoboam needs
endorsement by the northern tribes (probably already
restive in the later years of Solomon's reign) so that the
kingdom can remain united. 'All the Israelites' (v. 1) picks
up the 'all Israel' (11:42) over which Solomon had reigned.

Shechem was probably chosen because of its association
with the patriarchs. The Lord had appeared to Abraham
there (Gen. 12:6) and Jacob settled there and built an altar
after his encounter with Esau (Gen. 33:18-20). Joshua had
a great covenant renewal ceremony there with all the tribes
just before his death (Josh. 24).

An ominous note is struck in verse 2 with the re-
emergence of Jeroboam who now returns from Egypt (see
11:40). The implication of verse 3 is that he had consider-
able support among the people. It seems likely that he is the

main author of the protest against Solomon's severity (v. 4) but there is at least as much spin here as objective truth and Rehoboam asks for time to confer with his advisers.

There follows (vv. 6-11) an account of that consultation in which his late father's advisers advocate a conciliatory approach (v. 7). They realize that the essence of leadership is to be a servant, a view which is later to be underwritten by Jesus Himself: 'whoever wants to become great among you must be your servant' (Mark 10:43). This side of David perhaps particularly comes out in 2 Samuel 23:8-39 where the king honours and celebrates the loyalty and achievements of the men who had stood with him, rather than taking all the credit himself. This advice, however, is unpalatable to Rehoboam and he turns to 'the young men who had grown up with him', a group with whom he more readily identifies.

Their approach is that intimidation is the way, and they give Rehoboam a slogan to use which will prove his virility. What they say shows little understanding of human nature and little concern for the unity of the kingdom. Rehoboam, with crass insensitivity, not only follows their advice but also uses their bullying language. We know that the chance to save the situation by diplomacy has been blown.

Thus far the stupidity of Rehoboam has been evident. We must not moralize the story and say that this episode shows the folly of listening to youth instead of following the advice of older men. In any case, 'elders' were not necessarily old men; rather they were mature and experienced, and were a feature of the leadership in communities. Instead, Rehoboam is a man who will not listen to anyone's advice, but is stupidly determined to follow his own course.

However, there is something deeper here; stupidity is under the control of sovereignty.'For this turn of events was from the LORD' (v. 15) shows that, far from this upsetting Yahweh's purpose, it was in fact the end He had in view. The prophecy of Ahijah (11:29-39) had predicted this outcome. There was, however, nothing mechanical here; Rehoboam made his decision freely yet carried out God's Word. This is the consistent teaching of the Bible. God is not taken by surprise but people are responsible for their actions.

2. The north breaks away (12:16-20)

What is interesting about this little section is not that the northern kingdoms have decisively rejected Rehoboam but that they have rejected David. The negative reference to 'the house of David' at the beginning and end of the section (vv. 16 and 20) shows a determination to look for a different identity and a different destiny. Yet nothing can set aside the covenant promises which Yahweh, through Nathan, spoke to David: 'Your house and your kingdom shall endure for ever before me; your throne shall be established for ever.' (2 Sam. 7:16).

Faced with this situation Rehoboam again acts foolishly. The choice of Adinoram (see 4:6; 5:14) was tactless because of his association with forced labour. Again there is theological comment in verse 19 about the rebellion of Israel against the God-appointed Davidic line. Jeroboam is installed as king and the stage is set for the drama of the two kingdoms.

3. Rehoboam prevented from further stupidity (12:21-24)

Again we see clearly the two levels of human activity and God's purposes revealed by His Word. In verse 21 Rehoboam continues on his blundering way; diplomacy (such as it is) has failed and now he wants to try war. However, a 'man of God' intervenes and says that Yahweh forbids violence. 'Man of God' essentially draws attention to the fact that this individual stands in the succession of 'Moses the man of God' (Deut. 33:1; Josh. 14:6; Ezra 3:2; Ps. 90 (title); 1 Chron. 23:14; 2 Chron. 30:16). Paul's use of the term in relation to Timothy (1 Tim. 6:11; 2 Tim. 3:17) probably reflects this usage. Perhaps surprisingly, Rehoboam obeys, but it is clear that the Word of Yahweh is controlling this whole situation.

4. Jeroboam invents a new religion (12:25-33)

Jeroboam starts vigorously fortifying Shechem as a rival capital to Jerusalem. Peniel was a little east of where the brook Jabbok joined Jordan (the place where Jacob wrestled with God, Gen. 32:30) and would guard the eastern frontier. That is a sensible start, but then it becomes clear he is going set up a whole rival religion.

This involved first setting up two golden calves and repeating the sin of Aaron, and indeed echoing his words (Exod. 32:4). This blatant breaking of the second commandment is also leading the people into Canaanite religion where the bull or calf was used as a fertility symbol. The change is further disguised as sympathetic concern for people who had to make the long journey to Jerusalem. This would be a possible reason for the location of the bull/calves at Bethel in the south and Dan in the north. But probably Jeroboam was also exploiting the patriarchal connections of Bethel (with Abraham in Gen. 12:8; 13:3-4 and with Jacob in Gen. 28:10-22; 31:13; 35:1-15). As for Dan, a priest who was a grandson of Moses had operated there (Judg. 18:30-31). Doubtless Jeroboam's spin doctors would not be slow in pointing out these connections. What Jeroboam does is to institutionalize the break-up of God's people spiritually as well as physically.

He goes on to establish all the paraphernalia of a rival cult with the multiplication of shrines and expansion of the notorious 'high places' (see notes on 3:2). He starts a rival calendar (as Antiochus Epiphanes does – see Dan. 7:25). He makes the priesthood a job for anybody. In short he completely rejects Yahweh's revelation about the place, time and personnel for worship. This is underlined by the word 'made' (v. 28); the Hebrew word is repeated several times but translated variously as 'built', 'set up' and 'appointed'. This religion is a human invention and has no authority other than Jeroboam's whims. Politics has triumphed over principle and within a short time the commands of Yahweh are totally ignored.

From text to message
Getting the message clear: the theme
This chapter vividly dramatizes how quickly the unity of God's people can be broken and how radically disobedience takes the place of faithfulness. It is not unexpected; the tragic decline of Solomon's later years (11:1-13) has made this scenario probable. However, probable does not mean inevitable and, as we have seen, a major part of the emphasis has been God's overruling providence which does not remove human responsibility. It is a pivotal chapter and sets the pattern for much that is to follow in the rest of the story. The continual danger of departing from God's Word is at the heart of the narrative.

Getting the message clear: the aim

As Christians we need to realize that the health, indeed the survival, of our communities is in continual obedience to the Word of God. Once that begins to slip there are no limits to which we cannot go. This is especially true of our church communities. There is little doubt that the capitulation of the churches to unbiblical thinking on sexuality has made it easier for governments to do so.

A way in

It would be easy to moralize about the importance of listening to advice and not taking hasty decisions, to overload our sermons with antiquarian detail about Shechem. A chapter like this needs to be seen in terms of how we listen to the Word of God in every aspect of our lives throughout the week. In particular how do we make godly decisions. The key is verse 15 – 'this turn of events was from the LORD to fulfil the word the LORD had spoken'. This tells us that in the end the Lord will have His way, however foolish human decisions and actions may be. The practical effect of that is not to give a sense of fatalism but a great concern that our attitudes and activities are positively working towards that end and that our fellowships are faithful to the Word.

Ideas for application

Loyalty to Scripture must be comprehensive and extend beyond preaching and prayer meetings to all aspects of corporate and individual living. Rehoboam does not (as his father had done in chapter 3) consult the Lord for wisdom in dealing with this situation but rushes to take advice from others and then does what he had intended to do in the first place. Our business meetings are a good index to how far our churches are gospel-driven.

+ The providence of God is not an abstract idea but a powerful impetus to make all our decisions prayerfully and see the enormous importance of following biblical principles in the assurance that God will ultimately overrule for good (see Gen. 50:20).

+ There is an ever-present danger of substituting our own ideas of what is sensible and appealing instead of following Scripture. The New Testament, of course, has no detailed blueprint of what to do when we meet together, but so often we are driven by our own preferences – whether trendy or traditional – which then harden into a new orthodoxy and Jeroboam-like turn the gospel into an alien religion.

+ The danger of abandoning the Word of God has disastrous effects on future generations as God's people drift further and further from their biblical moorings.

Suggestions for preaching

Many of the issues to be developed in the rest of the book surface here. The divided kingdom is to be a fact of life and Jeroboam is to be remembered as the one who was the archetypal apostate king who led Israel into sin (1 Kings 15:30; 16:2, 19, 26, 31; 22:52; 2 Kings 3:3; 9:9; 13:11; 15:28; 17:22). Plainly these issues of disunity, disobedience and bad models for future generations are vital for God's people in every generation.

Depending on the length of the series or the emphasis the preacher wants to make, we might preach one or two sermons.

Sermon 1: Dangerous disunity

This sermon takes the chapter as a whole and emphasizes disunity and its consequences.

+ **The sins of the father** (12:1-15). The reference to Solomon is a reminder of chapter 11 and how Solomon's inner departure from the Lord is matched by external whittling away of the once-great kingdom. The failure of Rehoboam to ask the Lord and the foolish decision he makes shows that he is not the man to stop the rot. Yet although the situation quickly spirals out of his control it is not out of the Lord's control.

+ **The foolishness of the son** (12:16-22). Rehoboam again sees bluster and violence as the solution and is only saved from this by the man of God, Shemaiah. The interplay of the king's foolishness and the authority of the prophetic Word raises issues of true leadership and authority.

+ **The emergence of a new authority** (12:25-33). The rashness and bad decision-making of Rehoboam were exploited skilfully by Jeroboam and a whole new religion was set up. Both the kings are driven by their own desires and passions, and this new kingdom almost immediately becomes a model of apostasy. Neither rule 'in the fear of God' (2 Sam. 23:3) and both show that authority devoid of godliness and humility is deadly.

Sermon 2: Man proposes, God disposes
We could take verses 1-24 as a sermon on its own and
develop more fully the ideas of divine sovereignty and
human responsibility. The introduction (vv. 1 and 2) would
underline the bad example Rehoboam's father set in his
later years.

+ **Rehoboam is stupid, but God is sovereign** (12:1-15).
  Focus on the key verse (15) and show how this
  determined the outcome but that Rehoboam remained
  responsible.

+ **The kingdom is divided, but the house of David
  remains** (12:16-20). Focus on the 'house of David'
  – verses 16, 19 and 20. The people have gone their
  own way but the covenant kingdom will survive.
  The preacher needs to point to how the kingdom of
  David's Greater Son will come although regularly
  under attack.

+ **The king remains rash, but God's Word prevails**
  (12:21-24). Prophetic warning prevents further folly
  – this in itself is a sign of God's grace.

Sermon 3: The man who invented his own religion
We could devote a sermon to Jeroboam (12:25-33), given
his notoriety in the story. Also this section provides a
helpful anatomy of idolatry. Jeroboam is a big player and his
military plans are shrewd, as are his diplomatic skills. Good
leadership is a great blessing but when it lacks godliness it
becomes deadly.

+ **His displacement of Yahweh.** Jeroboam repeats the
  sin of Aaron and makes visibility the sign of Yahweh's
  presence, thus diminishing Him and trapping Him in

His own creation, leading to worshipping the creation rather than the Creator (Rom. 1:25).

+ **His setting up a rival calendar.** Jeroboam rewrites Yahweh's ordering of time and festivals to suit himself.

+ **His making the priesthood a job**, ignoring the divine qualifications that God Himself has established.

Suggestions for teaching

Understanding the passage

1. Why was it important for 'all the Israelites' to crown Rehoboam?

2. What have we already learned about Jeroboam which makes us sense trouble? (see 11:26-40)

3. Why does Rehoboam reject wise advice? (12:7-14)

4. Why is 'the house of David' mentioned three times in verses 16-20?

5. Why does Rehoboam listen to Shemaiah? (12:22-24)

6. What are Jeroboam's motives in setting up a rival capital and an alternative temple? (12:25-30)

7. What are the essential elements of this new religion he sets up? (12:31-33)

Applying the passage

1. What are the signs that an individual or a church are beginning to drift away from God? You might like to read and reflect on 2:2-4 alongside this passage.

2. In what ways is verse 15 encouraging when this drifting away from God happens?

3. In what way does the repeated reference to 'the house of David' (vv. 16-20) point to the bigger picture? You may want to read such Psalms as 2 and 72 and look at Revelation 22:16.

4. What was at stake in Jeroboam setting up a rival temple? (12:26-27)

5. What does Jeroboam's wholesale rewriting of the Law of God say to us today? You might want to consider how often in our churches we follow secular models of leadership or psychological methods more related to non-Christian counselling. You might also want to consider such matters as rewriting the definition of marriage and the rush to political correctness.

2

STIFF-NECKED AFTER MANY REBUKES
(1 KINGS 13)

Introduction

If Jeroboam is to descend completely into apostasy it is not to be without repeated warnings. Already Ahijah has spoken to him (11:29-33) and will again in 14:6-16. This is a chapter of prophetic activity which heightens awareness of God's Word and the fatal consequences of rejecting it. The continuing story of Jeroboam here and into chapter 14 is a striking illustration of Proverbs 29:1: 'A man who remains stiff necked after many rebukes will suddenly be destroyed – without remedy.'

The chapter is rich and powerful and raises many questions which are difficult to answer, such as what was the old prophet's motive?; why was the man of God killed for what seems like a minor fault?, and the like. From a literary standpoint the story is superb: the plot is crisp and fast-moving; there is deft characterization and plenty of suspense.

Listening to the text
Context and structure
This chapter flows directly from the end of chapter 12 where Jeroboam had set up a rival sanctuary and altar in Bethel. Here he is officiating at a ceremony beside the altar when the proceedings are rudely interrupted by a man of God from Judah. Plainly this chapter is dominated by the Word of Yahweh (vv. 1, 2, 5, 9, 17, 18, 20, 26, 32) and this is the theme of the story. We shall look at how it unfolds in three scenes.

1. Word and sign   13:1-6

2. True and false words   13:7-30

3. The Word and the future   13:31-34

Working through the text
Word and sign 13:1-6
Powerfully and dramatically, the Word that Jeroboam despises bursts into his liturgical ceremony. Here the king is given two forceful lessons about the power of that Word. The first is that the power of the Word is not confined to the moment that it is spoken. Josiah is to come centuries later (2 Kings 23:15-20) and plainly after the northern kingdom has gone and only the house of David remains. This is a powerful reminder that God's Word often works unseen for long periods but always accomplishes its purpose (Isa. 55:10-11).

The second lesson to Jeroboam is that the Word also works immediately and here with staggering effect. At that time no one knew how long in the future it would be before the Josiah prophecy would be fulfilled, but here is a sudden and startling present fulfilment of the prophecy about the altar showing that the God who can vindicate His Word immediately can also do so in the future. The torn altar may have recalled the tearing of the kingdom (in 11:11-13 the same verb, the Hebrew word *qara*, is used of the tearing of Ahijah's cloak which symbolizes the divided kingdom).

Here, as often in the Elijah/Elisha stories and in the ministry of Jesus and the apostles, the Word is accompanied by a sign or rather two signs, one of judgment and one of healing. This will be discussed more fully when we come to Elijah and Elisha. Two points can be made here. First, God sometimes authenticates His Word by signs. Indeed this is the fundamental truth of Genesis 1 that the creating Word brings about what it says. This is the emphasis of Hebrews 2:3-4 that God 'according to his will' accompanies the preached Word with 'signs, wonders and various miracles'. Second, even when such signs are not present God's Word works effectively. The gospel Word is not something accompanied by the power of God, it is itself the power of God (Rom. 1:16-17).

It is noteworthy that the prophetic Word focuses first on the altar rather than the house of Jeroboam. Having created his own religion, Jeroboam now acts as king/priest, probably deliberately imitating Solomon (1 Kings 8:2). The splitting of the altar and the shrivelling of his hand show Jeroboam that he cannot manipulate God nor silence His Word. He is weak and vulnerable.

It is only the man of God whom Jeroboam tries to destroy – someone who can bring healing as well as judgment. Here the man of God is shown as a true prophetic intercessor. Surely this shows the patience of Yahweh, who gives Jeroboam unmistakable evidences of both His judgment and mercy. Yet Jeroboam is heedless of both. The words and signs do not lead him to repentance and faith any more than they had done to Pharaoh in Exodus 7–11.

The links of this chapter with the wider story are clear. Josiah, of the house of David, is to undertake the most thorough reformation of national life (2 Kings 22 & 23) and to be one of the worthiest of David's sons to sit on his throne. The vital importance of obeying the Torah is emphasized, as in David's charge to Solomon (1 Kings 2:2-4) which we identified as the melodic line of Kings.

True and false words (13:7-30)

The long central section of the story is told with power and restraint, and many questions are left unanswered. Force has failed and now Jeroboam, who is no mindless thug, tries flattery. It may well be that the 'gift' (v. 7) was in fact a bribe and an attempt to avoid judgment. No reason is given for Yahweh's prohibition of the man of God receiving hospitality. It may be that this would mean that he was not to be under any obligation to the powerful. What is plain is that God requires complete obedience from His servants even when they do not understand His command. The man of God successfully overcomes the temptation to break God's Word and we could wish that the story might have ended here.

This section from verses 11-22 makes sad and disturbing reading. Why is the man of God summarily cut down and the old prophet, who had grown grey in deceit and unfaithfulness, allowed to live even after being responsible for the man of God's downfall? We shall return to that question but will consider some other questions first. The suspense of the narrative draws the reader imaginatively into the situation.

No reason is given for the old prophet's behaviour. Presumably he long turned a blind eye to Jeroboam's activities and perhaps even feared for his own position should Jeroboam repent. The text, however, is silent on these matters. The fact that he had a table (v. 20) is the sign of a wealthy home, perhaps an indication that he had grown rich by assiduous cultivation of the establishment. The next question is why he speaks as he does (v. 18). What he says there shows both deviousness and malevolence. He is too clever to claim direct revelation; here it is the Word of Yahweh mediated by an angel. Probably this would allow him to claim that he was not misrepresenting the direct Word of God. Perhaps now we can see more clearly the nature of the man of God's tragic mistake. He stood tall in a crisis, succumbing neither to intimidation nor flattery. Yet faced with a charlatan, he let down his guard. A clear Word of God cannot be set aside because someone claims to have further revelation.

Now the story takes yet another twist. What neither the old prophet nor the reader expected was that Yahweh would actually speak (vv. 21-22) and most certainly not that He would speak through the old prophet. The phrase 'he cried' shows the suddenness and seriousness of what is about to be said. Here is a striking demonstration of the independence of the Word of God from its human agents. This is a point we shall return to in discussing application.

In another of the chapter's silences, we are told nothing of the man of God's reaction to this devastating news. The death swiftly follows (v. 24) and in yet another twist, both the donkey and the lion stand still beside the body. God was in control; the lion had carried out his judgment but the lion's attack was halted there. The old prophet arranges the funeral and weeps over the man who had been brought to death by his lies. He now accepts that the man of God was telling the truth and now he fears, as he well might, for his own posthumous fate.

This chapter as we have seen, has long horizons and looks to the great reforms of Josiah. In the end the man of God spoke the true Word and the preserving of his body both now and in the future (2 Kings 23:16-18) is a sign of how truthfully he spoke. The final authority of God's Word is what this chapter is about and neither the foolishness of the man of God nor the deceit of the old prophet can alter that. God's Word stands above everything; no one faithful or faithless is exempt from obeying it. It is never safe to step outside that Word, however plausible may be the voices urging us to do so.

The Word and the future (13:31-34)

The prophet now fears greatly for himself and his posthumous fate. However, the main point of this short concluding section is to tie this story of the prophet back into the main Jeroboam narrative. The thrust of the chapter has been that the prophetic Word will bring about what it announces. The man of God's words will not only bring about the destruction of Bethel but all false altars and idolatrous shrines.

Yet Jeroboam, like Pharaoh (Exod. 9:35), once the immediate danger is over, reverts to his evil ways and indeed goes deeper into them. The 'high places' (see comment on 3:2) become more and more the focus of religious life. Jeroboam's dynasty did not survive the death of his son (15:29) but the memory of his sin was to live on.

From text to message

Getting the message clear: the theme

The key theme is the power of the Word of God and its independence of those who bring it. It is a particularly strong example of this major theme which runs right through 1 and 2 Kings. That Word is more powerful than kings and prophets.

Getting the message clear: the aim

The aim is well expressed in Isaiah 66:2 – 'This is the one I esteem: he who is humble and contrite in spirit, and trembles at my word'. The message is not simply that we need to listen to the Word of God but that we need to remember its power and tremble at what it can do.

A way in

A perennial problem in our churches is an apparent commitment to Scripture without truly believing or trembling before it. A good test of any fellowship's alleg-iance to the Bible is not what happens at Sunday services or prayer meetings but what happens in house groups and business meetings. Are our agendas driven there by Scripture as well? So often secular models and worldly attitudes undermine the direction of the pulpit ministry.

How do we become truly biblical churches where all we do is under the authority of Scripture? Sometimes we treat our preachers as gurus whose every opinion on everything is regarded as Holy Writ. When that happens, personality cult has replaced trembling before the Word. The messenger has become more important than the message. Sometimes the preached Word is regarded as what we care for in services but 'real life' is about buildings, budgets and gossip.

Ideas for application

+ Courage in bringing the Word of God is always important. At the beginning of the chapter, whatever may have happened later, the man of God showed great bravery in coming into a hostile and threatening environment.

+ The prayer for Jeroboam's healing is another evidence of grace in the story and ultimately points to the One who will pray 'Father, forgive them, for they do not know what they are doing' (Luke 23:34). These two points balance each other: speaking the Word without fear or favour and a prayerful concern for those to whom we speak.

+ There is a danger of being seduced by apparent new revelation which marginalizes the Word God has already spoken. We need to 'test the spirits' (1 John 4:1). This is not simply the danger of self-appointed prophets claiming to have a special line to the Lord denied to others. It happens in house groups when someone, who has clearly done little or no preparation, says 'I believe what the Lord is telling us from this passage is …' Apart from anything else, this brings the study to a grinding halt. After all, if that is what the Lord is saying then why listen further to the Word?

+ Those in the preaching ministry need to listen particularly carefully to this passage. We can be firm and uncompromising when we face the king's intimidation and indeed his flattery. But we can be so easily deceived by charlatans. Our only safety lies in staying within the bounds of the Word of God.

- The power of the Word is independent of those who preach it. The old prophet becomes a channel of the Word of God but that truth does not change him nor does he tremble before it. We all know sad cases of those who have preached with power and conviction but who were living double lives. None of us can be complacent for that could happen to any of us and in our hearts we know that sometimes we have come very near to that and only the grace of God has prevented disaster.

- We need to recover confidence in the life-changing power of the preached Word. We all are grateful for the recovery of expository preaching in the last decades. However, too often this has been collapsed into 'explaining the passage'. But preaching is about proclaiming Christ and showing how the written Word fully and faithfully points to the living Word. Bible in the head has often replaced Christ in the heart and the necessity of the Holy Spirit applying that Word has been neglected.

- We need to realize that even the Word in the power of the Spirit will not change everyone. Jeroboam continued on his merry way to judgment and the old prophet was concerned about his own future without showing any sign of repentance.

Suggestions for preaching
Sermon 1
One way would be to follow the suggested outline above and have some such title as 'The independent Word', drawing attention to the message rather than the messenger.

- ✦ **The powerful Word** (13:1-6). The point here is that the Word works both immediately and in the long term – see Isaiah 55:10-13. This is the Word which judges and is the only one which heals. The preacher needs to emphasize having confidence in that Word to do its work – perhaps using the parable in Mark 4:26-29 of the seed growing independently of the sower.

- ✦ **The true Word among lies** (13:7-30). We see faithfulness and then foolishness on the part of the man of God – the need to be discerning and 'test the spirits'. There is also the danger of prophecy or preaching as a job – Jeroboam appointed priests as if it were an ordinary job – probably he also appointed prophets as Ahab was to do (1 Kings 22:6). No wonder a Word of judgment breaks in.

- ✦ **The Word which controls the future** (13:31-34). The Word disobeyed becomes the Word which judges.

It would be helpful to show that what is happening here is a trailer of the final judgment and refers to the Olivet Discourse and the certainty of the Word being fulfilled. 'Heaven and earth will pass away, but my words will never pass away' (Matt. 24:35).

Sermon 2
Since the story revolves round three characters, another way of preaching it would be to examine how the Word is received by each of them. Some such title as 'Same Word; different responses' would underline that the message is the same but response to that message makes the difference of life and death.

+ **Jeroboam despised the Word** – neither judgment nor mercy moved him and he continued and intensified his apostasy.

+ **The man of God didn't take the Word seriously enough** – began well, but lacked discernment.

+ **The old prophet manipulated the Word** – to him it was just a job.

Suggestions for teaching
Questions to help understand the passage

1. What does the opening phrase of verse 1, 'By the word of the LORD' tell us about how to understand the events of this chapter?

2. What are the two things the man of God says about the effect of the Word of God?

3. What do we learn about Jeroboam's reaction to the Word (vv. 6 & 7)?

4. How do we learn that the old prophet is insincere?

5. How does God show both judgment and mercy in the death of the man of God? (see vv. 23 & 24)

6. What does verse 33 show us about Jeroboam's attitude to the Word of God?

Questions to help apply the passage

1. What do we learn in verses 2-3 about the power of the Word of God both in the short and long term?

2. How does the man of God show us by his behaviour that consistent obedience is vital?

3. In what ways are we deceived by those who claim to have a special 'line' to the Lord and what can we do about it?

4. How does this story show us the dangers of a wrong kind of 'professionalism' in our communities?

5. This chapter is a gospel chapter because it shows a God of mercy and judgment. How do we maintain both these elements in our presentations of the gospel?

6. After reading this chapter do we feel that we take the Word of God seriously and in what ways do our attitudes need to change?

3

ENDING BADLY

(1 KINGS 14)

Introduction

We are not yet finished with Jeroboam or with the prophetic Word which has so strikingly punctuated his reign.
We have also to read the later part of Rehoboam's story.
This chapter recounts the sorry tale of the swift decline
of godliness in both kingdoms, but the persistence of the
prophetic Word and the reminder of David (v. 8) shows us
that Yahweh is controlling matters, however unpromising
they may seem on the surface.

Listening to the text

Context and structure

This chapter follows on from the kingdom division in
chapter 12 and the prophetic drama of chapter 13. The
accounts of both kingdoms are to continue until the end
of chapter 16 when there is to be an increasing emphasis
on the northern kingdom and the prophetic ministry to it.

There are two main divisions:

+   The end of Jeroboam (14:1-20)

+   The end of Rehoboam (14:21-31)

Working through the text (14:1-20)
The end of Jeroboam (14:1-20).

The words of Isaiah 40:8 are a striking commentary on this story: 'The grass withers and the flowers fall, but the word of our God stands for ever'. The grass and flowers are not simply plants but metaphors of the kingdoms of the world. Here judgment is to be pronounced on Jeroboam and his house, but the Word that brings that condemnation is to stand. In many ways this is a parallel to chapter 13 and shows the Word of God working powerfully in both kingdoms. The story develops in four movements.

Scene 1 (14:1-5)

The first scene shows that God cannot be deceived. Jeroboam's reign had begun with a word from Ahijah the prophet (11:29-39) and the doom not only of the king but of his house is announced by the same prophet. The story is full of irony: Jeroboam, apparently so pragmatic and politically astute, behaves with incredible naivety. He imagines that the prophet, or rather the prophet's God, can be bribed and deceived. But this is no more than the inevitable result of his limiting God to an idol. He no longer believes – if he ever did – in the God who fills heaven and earth and sees and knows everything. Thus, again, the author reminds us that the kind of God we believe in determines how we think and behave.

Also, when true faith goes, superstition is always ready to fill the vacuum. The story has abundantly demonstrated that Jeroboam has no intention of obeying the Word of

God. Yet he hopes that same Word he despises will work in a magical way to help his dying son. The irony of telling his wife to disguise herself to visit a blind prophet seems to have escaped him. The disguise will no more deceive the prophet than the bread, cakes and honey will flatter him. His ear is open to the Word of Yahweh (v. 5). For him that Word was living reality.

Scene 2 (14:6-11)

The second scene shows that the future cannot be manipulated. Jeroboam's wife's disguise is no more successful than Adam and Eve's attempt to hide from God (Gen. 3:8-9) or Saul's disguise (1 Sam. 28:12). The blind prophet instantly turns the tables. Jeroboam had sent his wife; yet in fact it is the prophet himself who had been sent by Yahweh. Yahweh's words echo the first prophecy to Jeroboam (11:28ff) but are now dark with impending judgment. Far from Jeroboam being politically astute, here is a reminder that Yahweh had controlled the unfolding events even when they seemed to be spiralling into chaos. The verbs 'raised', 'made' and 'tore' (vv. 7-8) show the divine hand behind history.

Moreover, the reference to David (one of the many throughout Kings) helps us to get our bearings. The Davidic covenant is emphatic on two things. One is that God would never take His covenant love away from David (2 Sam. 7:15) and second is that disobedience would be punished (2 Sam. 7:14). Since Jeroboam had been promised a similar blessing (1 Kings 11:38), his apostasy is all the more culpable. He had despised Yahweh's goodness.

The indictment is spelled out in verse 9. Unlike the Thessalonians who 'had turned to God from idols to serve the living and true God' (1 Thess. 1:9), Jeroboam had pushed Yahweh out of the way and embraced idols. He had flouted the command to have no other gods besides Yahweh (Exod. 20:3) and the making of idols was simply the outward sign of his apostasy. He had plumbed new depths not to be seen again until Ahab (1 Kings 16:30-31).

The judgment is chilling and comprehensive (vv. 10-11). 'Every last male' is literally 'one who urinates against the wall' and this makes a clear parallel with burning dung. The house of Jeroboam stinks and needs to be cleansed. Thus the dynasty will be annihilated. To lie unburied was a curse (Deut. 28:26) and this was later to happen to Baasha (1 Kings 16:4) and Jezebel (2 Kings 9:35). The words 'the LORD has spoken' show the certainty of judgment.

Scene 3 (14:12-18)
The third scene shows again what was established in chapter 13, namely the effectiveness of the Word does not depend on time. 'As for you' (v. 12) brings us starkly back into the present and to the immediate death of Abijah. There is a real tenderness in verse 13 as the boy is mourned by 'all Israel' and the sense that, had he lived, he would have been a good king. But, like the young man of God of chapter 13, he is taken away from the evil and is the only one of Jeroboam's descendants to be buried. The unspecified 'good' in the boy's life is a reminder that the life of faith can be lived in the most uncongenial circumstances.

But the long-term implications of the Word are now spelled out in verses 14-16. One of these, the destruction of Jeroboam's dynasty has already been mentioned, but now the view is long-term, right to the Exile itself. However, the moves to destroy the dynasty are already afoot (v. 14). Baasha (15:27–16:7) will carry this out. However, this pro-

nouncement also concerns the fate of the northern kingdom
as a whole. The vine brought from Egypt (Psalm 80:8-11)
will be uprooted (fulfilling Deut. 29:28) and taken back to
the land Abraham left. The Asherah poles were symbols
of the Canaanite fertility goddess and are especially and
grimly ironic in a passage focusing on the death of a child.
The author will never let us forget the sin of Jeroboam (see
also 1 Kings 15:26, 30, 34; 16:19, 26; 22:52; 2 Kings 10:31;
13:6, 11; 14:24, 28; 15:18, 24, 28; 17:21-23). The reign of
Jeroboam was the beginning of the end. The boy dies and
the prophetic Word continues. Ahijah's prophecy dominates this chapter and gives us a summary of a sad story
which is to continue until 2 Kings 17.

Scene 4 (14:19-20)
The fourth scene is the brief note of the death of Jeroboam
and the accession of Nadab. 'The other events' of Jeroboam's
reign are destined to disappear like the annals which
recorded them. No details of his burial are given and, having
listened to the prophet, we know that Nadab his son reigns
on borrowed time.

The end of Rehoboam (14:21-31)
Rehoboam's story which began in chapter 12 has been
postponed until Jeroboam's is over. From now on, Judah
is to be used as the title for the southern kingdom and
Israel for the northern. A summary verse (21) reminds us
of the two major emphases of this whole section. Yahweh's
choice of and commitment to Jerusalem is the undergirding
providence which, in the end, is to triumph over human
sin and failure. The other is the reference to Rehoboam's
mother being an Ammonite, a fact which is mentioned

again at the end of the section (v. 31). Here we see again the tragic consequence of Solomon's idolatry and fear for the future of a throne surrounded by pagan influences.

The rest of this section develops in three movements. The first (vv. 22-24) moves away from Rehoboam personally to emphasize that this apostasy is national. Indeed these verses give us a window into the whole of the history of Judah as it slides into apostasy. Both northern and southern kingdoms are headed for disaster. Rehoboam and Jeroboam set the pattern for their kingdoms. Full-blown Canaanite religion is alive and well in Judah and Israel. The 'high places' (see 1 Kings 3:2) flourish unchecked as do fertility rites and debased practices.

In the second movement (vv. 25-28), idolatrous practices are accompanied by political reversal. We have already seen this at the end of Solomon's reign (11:26-40). What the author implies here is made explicit in the parallel account in 2 Chronicles 12:1-12 where Shishak's invasion is seen as a punishment for abandoning Yahweh's law. Shishak was Pharaoh from 945-924 B.C. and was probably mainly concerned with securing the coastal trade routes. Solomon's attempt to neutralize Egypt by marrying an earlier Pharaoh's daughter had not ultimately worked. Probably this was a warning shot rather than a full-scale invasion, and indeed Shishak may have been bought off by the temple treasures.

Yet there is a sad commentary on the decline of Judah, especially in the reference to Solomon's gold shields being replaced by Rehoboam's bronze ones. This is both an actual incident but also an eloquent comment on the shabby and downbeat nature of the kingdom. They may have looked the same from a distance but the reality was that the splendour was fading. Yet temple ritual was maintained (vv. 27-28).

Yahweh's house and its ordinances must be maintained in a pick-and-mix supermarket of religions. So it is that formal religion, albeit in a more grubby form, continues, with no commitment of heart or engagement of mind.

The third movement (vv. 29-31) is a brief note of Rehoboam's death and the accession of his son. But clearly this is a deliberate parallel with 'the annals of the kings of Israel' (v. 19). Like Jeroboam, Rehoboam may have done many other things, but the implication is that they were of little significance. The incessant warfare contrasts vividly with the peace of much of Solomon's reign. David's reign had indeed been marked with wars but those were for the sake of the kingdom. Here it is internecine battle between two proud and stubborn rivals. The repetition of Rehoboam's mother's name suggests that she was a major influence in his idolatry. He is succeeded by Abijah (the same name as Jeroboam's short-lived son). But while the earlier Abijah is taken away to avoid being caught up in the judgment of the dynasty, this one lives to carry on his father's dismal legacy.

From text to message

Getting the message clear: the theme

The apparently irresistible tendency to self-destruct on the part of leaders and people establishes an unhappy pattern which is to run from here until Exile. The root cause is, then and now, disobedience to the Word of God. The pattern established here at the beginning of the divided kingdom is a stark warning.

Getting the message clear: the aim

While 'narrative is not normative' (see discussion on preaching narrative in the Introduction) we have to balance that by seeing how we need to learn general principles of how God deals with His people in every age. Here we are learning specifically what to avoid.

A way in
We need to be careful to preach God's judgment and not our judgmentalism. It would be good to focus on God's unchanging and unbreakable purposes but to show how enjoyment of these will be forfeited by people who choose their own way. The conviction that God will triumph will prevent defeatism but also complacency as we realize our boundless capacity to get it wrong.

Ideas for application

+ The fact that the Word of God is freely available does not mean it will be obeyed. The prophet Ahijah spoke persistently and consistently but his words fell on deaf ears. Today, with the ready availability of Bible translations and a multiplicity of helps to understand the text, as well as the proliferation of preachers determined to teach and apply Scripture, we have no real excuse. What we need to ask and keep on asking is how this is changing communities and individuals.

+ An important balance to the above point is that God's Word will triumph in spite of the opposition of its detractors and the weakness of its defenders. If we preach and God graciously blesses with visible fruit, then we must thank Him and not become conceited. If we preach and no visible fruit attends, then we need to trust God and believe that the Word is still doing its unstoppable work.

+ Bad leaders create bad communities. This is most clearly seen in verses 22-24 where the people collectively depart from God. But it is more subtle than that. Then, as now, people tend to get the leaders they deserve and all too easily follow those who offer an apparently easier lifestyle and more accommodating beliefs. God's people are collectively responsible for godly living.

+ It is foolish to try to disguise our real selves, shown here by Jeroboam's wife disguising herself to deceive a blind man. 'What you see is what you get' ought to be the norm. How often we deceive ourselves and others by pious talk and a flurry of activity. The opposite of deceiving is 'walking in the light'.

+ The kingdom is advancing even while the nations rage and the rulers imagine a vain thing (Ps. 2:1, KJV). The references to David point to his Greater Son and thus encourage kingdom-living in the present.

Suggestions for preaching
Sermon 1
One possible sermon would focus on the verses which emphasize God's commitment to the Davidic covenant and emphasize the divine providence which overcomes human failure. A title could be *His kingdom cannot fail.*

+ **Introduction:** grace is stronger and more persistent than sin – although it seems as if the kingdom will never come, here we have strong indications that it will do so, like lights shining in the darkness.

+ **God will not forget His promise to David.** The reminder of the covenant, the prophetic Word and the description of Jerusalem as 'the city of David' drive the story and point to its eventual outcome.

+ **God will not share His throne with other gods.** This points to the day when every knee will bow and every tongue confess Jesus Christ as Lord.

+ **God controls events**, even including the Pharaoh's invasion.

Sermon 2

Another approach is to tackle the passage from the other direction and focus on the inability of the human leaders to bring in the kingdom. A title could be *Little men in big positions*.

+ **Introduction:** there is a catastrophic failure to obey God's Word and therefore disaster reigns.

+ **Disobedience punished:** the death of a child; the fate of Jeroboam's dynasty; the exile of Judah.

+ **Covenant disregarded:** the abandoning of exclusive loyalty to Yahweh.

+ **Protection removed:** peace is now an empty word.

Both these sermons emphasize providence and responsibility from different angles.

There is more than one way to divide the material, and after we have considered chapters 15 and 16, I shall suggest another sermon which takes 14:21–15:8 as a unit about Rehoboam and his son.

Suggestions for teaching
Questions to help understand the passage

1. What is particularly stupid about Jeroboam's wife disguising herself?

2. How do we know that Jeroboam brought this judgment on himself and his dynasty? Compare verses 7-8 with 11:29-39.

3. Why does the boy die?

4. How does Judah show that it is as bad as Israel?

5. What does the Shishak episode (vv. 25-28) show about the deterioration of Rehoboam's kingdom?

6. Why is Rehoboam's mother mentioned twice (vv. 21 & 31)?

Questions to help apply the passage

1. Why do we have a continual tendency to try to deceive and be lacking in openness both with the Lord and each other?

2. How is the Word of God independent of time and human failures both in the short and long term?

3. How does this passage show that it is still possible to honour God in a godless society (look at v. 13)?

4. Leaders and people both go wrong here. In what ways can both parties help each other to be faithful?

5. How can we avoid ending up like this disreputable pair?

4

THE SLIDE CONTINUES
(1 KINGS 15–16)

Introduction

In 1938, a film was made of Victoria's reign entitled *Sixty Glorious Years*. Similar comments were made in 2012 about the reign of our present Queen. Here, by contrast, in these chapters, we have sixty miserable years, with one significant exception. Those who are not excited by Old Testament history are not likely to have their enthusiasm fired by a first reading of chapters 15 and 16. Hasty notes on parentage, length of reigns and the occasional mention of significant events seem unpromising and barren territory. However, the author knows what he is about and establishes principles, especially about the hidden hand of Yahweh, which are at the heart of the book's message.

These chapters bring to a close the second major section of 1 and 2 Kings and show continued decline, with the significant exception of Asa, as well as recording the working out of the judgment on Jeroboam's dynasty. Part of the unattractiveness of these chapters lies in their relentless portrait of sin and rebellion as tedious. We need our noses rubbed in this, for the devil loves to invest sin with a spurious glamour.

Listening to the text
Context and structure
The story covers some sixty years from the death of Rehoboam of Judah to the rise of Ahab of Israel and develops in eight sections:

+ Abijah: like father, like son (15:1-8)

+ Asa: better days (15:9-24)

+ Nadab: the end of Jeroboam's house (15:25-32)

+ Baasha: the slide continues (15:33–16:7)

+ Elah: another dead end (16:8-14)

+ Zimri: a short week (16:15-20)

+ Omri: firm but godless rule (16:21-28)

+ Ahab: worse still (16:29-34)

Working through the text
Abijah: like father, like son (15:1-8)
Abijah's reign was neither long nor distinguished. Virtually nothing is said about him other than that he was faithless and idolatrous. Right from the beginning he was marked by that fatally divided heart which had led Solomon astray in his later years (11:4). The key to his character is verse 3 where he slavishly followed the sins of his immediate progenitor, Rehoboam, but failed to walk in the ways of his 'forefather' (more precisely great-grandfather), David. Abijah chose the wrong father to follow.

However, grace is greater than sin and providence overrules human weakness. The divine choice of David's house is not set aside by the unworthiness of his sons, or indeed by his own sin. The 'case of Uriah the Hittite' (v. 5) reminds us simultaneously of the weakness of God's best servants and the faithfulness of Yahweh to His promises. The 'lamp' first refers to David himself (2 Sam. 22:29) and has formed part of Ahijah's prophecy (11:36): it is a symbol of continuing life and of continuous succession. It also refers to the guidance given by God's Word (e.g., Psalm 119:105) and is a reminder of the inextricable link between following that Word and ruling well. Humanly speaking, it is because of David that there is a kingdom in Jerusalem, and that points to the greater kingdom which will come.

2 Chronicles 13:1-22 gives a more positive account of Abijah, especially in his defiance of Jeroboam. This does not contradict the Kings account because both books are making different points. Chronicles is comparing Abijah to Jeroboam, and in that light he seems reasonably orthodox; Kings is comparing him to David and, on that basis, he falls woefully short. The brief note of Abijah's death rounds off the summary account of this lacklustre reign and makes way for a far more impressive figure.

Asa: better days (15:9-24)

The appearance of Asa shows the power of grace to flourish in unexpected places. Nothing in the life of his hapless father or formidable grandfather explains his openness to God or his substantial reforms. Godliness is not carried in the genes. The story unfolds in three scenes:

Scene 1 (15:9-15)

The first scene concerns Asa's reforms. Here we breathe a different atmosphere and something of the freshness of Solomon's springtime from chapter 3. For the first time we have a king who 'did what was right in the eyes of Yahweh, as David his father had done' (v. 11). This thoroughgoing reformation began, as all reformations must, with a wholesale clearing out of the practitioners and objects of idolatry. Cultic functionaries at fertility rites were sent packing. The 'repulsive Asherah pole' (v. 13) – the symbol of the fertility goddess whose worship Jezebel was to sponsor (18:19) – was destroyed. Even his grandmother was shown the door because of her involvement in Asherah worship. Admittedly, like Solomon before him, he did not remove the high places. Yet the key to his reforming zeal is that, unlike his father and grandfather, his heart was undivided in his loyalty to Yahweh. Positively, he valued and refurbished the temple.

Scene 2 (15:16-22)

The second scene concerns Asa's politics. During his long reign he was to see five kings of Israel come and go (15:25–16:28). Baasha was the second of these and he picked a fight. Ramah was a strategic place about six miles north of Jerusalem and controlled the western access to the coastal plain. Asa's response was to send for help to the king of Syria who agreed to attack northern Israel and took various towns north and west of the Sea of Galilee. Then Asa had the materials from Baasha's abortive fortifications at Ramah carried away to build up Judah's southern outposts.

In the parallel account in 2 Chronicles 16:7-10, a seer called Hanani rebukes Asa for trusting in armies rather than Yahweh. Here there is no overt comment, but the use of the word 'bribe' in verse 19 is significant. The translations tend to use the word 'gift' but the Hebrew word *sohad* means 'bribe' in its other appearances (for example, Deut. 16:19). Moreover, Asa is urging Ben-Hadad to break a previous treaty. This is opportunistic politics and the fact that it worked did not make it right. This is the wily politician rather than the zealous reformer.

Scene 3 (15:23-24)

The third scene narrates Asa's illness and death. The disease in his feet is attributed by the Chronicler to seeking help from physicians rather than Yahweh (2 Chron. 16:12). The Bible is not hostile to doctors but the account probably suggests that the king relied on human help as he had earlier done in the political realm. Asa was not the best of the kings but he was a good one and slowed down the slide into apostasy. His story is a salutary reminder that it is possible to live for God in dark times.

Nadab: the end of Jeroboam's house (15:25-32)

The narrative now returns to Israel and to the first of the five kings of Israel who are to rise and fall during Asa's long reign. Nadab has already been mentioned in 14:20, and the only notable thing about him is that he was his father's son in disobedience and sin. Baasha, whom we have met already, is now introduced here as the author of the coup which not only deposed Nadab but exterminated the house of Jeroboam. Nadab may have been strong enough to attack a Philistine city but he could not withstand the judgment pronounced on him.

From this archive-like account two important principles emerge. The first is the fulfilment of the prophetic Word spoken by Ahijah (14:10-11). Baasha was simply the instrument of that Word. Jeroboam's reign had been punctuated by prophetic warnings but he had ignored them all. Now the word of Yahweh is doing its work.

The second principle is that God governs history. Yahweh uses evil people to punish other evil people, and then in turn punishes the evil instruments he has used. That is also clear in Isaiah 10:5-19 in relation to the Assyrians (conquering Israel) and Jeremiah 25 in relation to the Babylonians (conquering Judah). As promised, the house of Jeroboam is no more.

Baasha: the slide continues (15:33–16:7)

With Baasha in charge, things do not improve. There may be a change of house, but there is no change of heart as Baasha walks in the ways of Jeroboam. This was the main characteristic of his twenty-four-year reign and his 'achievements' (16:5) are, appropriately, lost to us for ever.

However, another prophet emerges and gives the divine perspective on these twenty four years. Jehu, otherwise unknown, tells Baasha that he reigns only by divine permission, and that he has despised and flouted the God who raised him up. The one who destroyed Jeroboam and all his house will meet the same fate.

The story is a grim one and shows how self-destructive sin and violence are. Nothing lasting is being built and no worthwhile legacy left behind. The sheer pointlessness of godless living is underlined here, as is the futility of power without faithfulness. Again the 'bookends' of this account with their reference to the Word of Yahweh by Jehu (16:1 and 7) show that the righteous judge is assessing this reign and commenting on it through His servant.

One problem in verse 7 is the last phrase – 'and also because he destroyed it.' Didn't Yahweh use Baasha to destroy Jeroboam's house? Yes. However, the point is that God punishes human evil even if he overrules that evil to bring about ultimate good.

Elah: another dead end (16:8-14)

Baasha's house is doomed but limps on during his son Elah's two-year reign. The one thing the narrator has to say about Elah is that he was getting drunk, partying like Adonijah back in 1:41, while his cause was collapsing about his ears. This is not to be taken as an opportunity for a moralizing rant on teetotalism but rather the irresponsibility of the king is shown in his self-indulgence.

In that state, he is an easy prey to Zimri, an army officer, who killed the drunk man and took over the kingdom. He swiftly and ruthlessly eliminates Baasha's family and indeed proves himself an even more drastic butcher, killing friends as well. The brief note in verse 12 reminds us of the prophetic Word which continues to stand and the 'worthless idols' on which no lasting kingdom can be built.

Emphasis is again put on Zimri's fulfilment of the prophecy of Jehu, although he was almost certainly unaware of it. Yet again, it is impressive that the Word is being fulfilled in spite of human sin and wickedness. We need to trust the Bible to be the Bible more than we do.

Zimri: a short week (16:15-20)

A former British Prime Minister, Harold Wilson, famously said 'a week is a long time in politics'. Here we have a miniscule reign of seven days which most certainly altered the situation profoundly, but not for any achievement on Zimri's part. Zimri's lack of success raises failure to an art form: he reigns for a mere week; fails to have an heir and takes his own life in the blazing ruins of his palace. Zimri was a military man but made the cardinal error of organizing a coup without ensuring the loyalty of the army in the field who were pro-Omri, their commander.

It has been objected that a week was hardly long enough to follow the sins of Jeroboam. But seven days in that exalted position would show clearly the kind of man Zimri was. Also, in his previous position as a royal official, he would have shown his hand on numerous occasions, not least in his murder of the entire royal family. At the very least, he could have used these seven days to announce changes in policy rather than getting drunk. How futile power is unless exercised responsibly!

Omri: firm but godless rule (16:21-28)

Some four years of confusion with no king at all now follow. This can be seen by comparing verse 15, where Zimri comes to the throne in the twenty-seventh year of Asa, and verse 23, where Omri becomes king in Asa's thirty-first year. Tibni must have had sufficient popular support to offset Omri's support base in the army. However, Tibni died (helped on his way, perhaps?) and Omri became king. He was to prove both an effective builder and formidable warlord. He moved the capital from Tirzah to the hill of Samaria, where he built a new city. Samaria stood on a hill three hundred feet high with a commanding view of the plain beneath. Indeed, it was strong enough to withstand a three-year siege by the Assyrians (2 Kings 18:9-10). Probably he intended it to be an effective rival to Jerusalem.

Omri was a big player on the international stage. King Mesha of Moab tells on the Moabite stone (an ancient stele in the Louvre museum in Paris) that Omri 'humbled Moab many years'. It was probably as a result of his diplomatic initiatives with the Phoenicians that his son Ahab married Jezebel. More significantly, he impressed the rising power of Assyria which, even after the demise of his dynasty, referred to Israel as 'the house of Omri'. After the chaos of recent years, Israel now had a strong and effective ruler. He saved Israel from anarchy and his dynasty lasted forty years.

Yet the Bible assesses him very differently. He did evil on a massive scale and plumbed new depths of idolatry. In the end, seen in the light of eternity, these great achievements counted for nothing. Over his reign can be written 'what good is it for a man to gain the whole world, yet forfeit his soul?' (Mark 8:36).

Ahab: worse still (16:29-34)

But just when we imagine that things could not get worse, they do. Now there comes to the throne the most apostate of Israel's kings, who is to reign for twenty-one years. He is the fifth of the kings of Israel to overlap with Asa of Judah, now nearing the end of his long reign. On the surface, as in the reign of Omri, things looked rather good. No coups disturbed his twenty-one-year reign. His marriage to the Phoenician princess Jezebel, possibly engineered by dad Omri, would look a shrewd diplomatic move because this would strengthen Israel's economy by giving access to the

Phoenician ports. Those who had lived through the days of Elah and Zimri would appreciate the stability Omri established and Ahab continued.

But from the standpoint of the prophetic historian this king is the worst idolater ever, for Ahab surpasses his father Omri in apostasy, as the latter had surpassed Jeroboam (v. 30). The god Baal now enters centre-stage as the ground is prepared for the great contest with Yahweh in chapter 18. At that point we shall examine more closely what Baal worship actually involved, but here the emphasis is on the assembling of the panoply of idolatry. A temple and altar to Baal is set up in Samaria, plainly a rival to Yahweh's temple in Jerusalem. The Asherah pole, condemned in 14:15, makes its reappearance.

After the general introduction to the evil days of Ahab, the reference to the rebuilding of Jericho (v. 34) is rather puzzling. This is not directly attributed to Ahab but could hardly have been done without his permission as the phrase 'in Ahab's time' implies. The word spoken by Joshua did not prohibit people living there but it did forbid rebuilding it as a fortified city (Josh. 6:26). The author, therefore, is showing Ahab's cavalier disregard for the Word of Yahweh. This is a further reminder that the prophetic Word (in this case from Joshua) will be fulfilled even if several centuries pass. For Ahab, the Word of God does not count. So this little episode reveals the character of the regime, and Ahab's disregard for Yahweh's Word sets up the conflict of the following chapters.

We would expect, following the pattern of the last two chapters, that there would now be a general statement about Ahab's 'achievements' and a brief notice of his death. Instead the remaining chapters of 1 Kings are to be devoted to his reign, and events are about to take a dramatic turn.

From text to message

Getting the message clear: the theme

The diverse material in these chapters is unified by one main concern: events seem out of control but God is controlling events to bring about the ultimate triumph of His kingdom. The theme is that, while the nations rage and the people imagine a vain thing, God has set his king on the holy hill of Zion.

Getting the message clear: the aim

The text is both warning and encouragement. We need to warn Christians, including ourselves, not to sin away our mercies. However, there is great encouragement here to keep going in evil times and to look for the coming of the kingdom.

A way in

Many preachers might well shrink from these passages which lack a strong narrative drive and appear often to be just brief notes. But that is perhaps the point. They are rather like directors' notes for actors to show them how to read and perform the script. These chapters are indeed Director's notes giving us clues about how to read the unfolding drama. They show us not to be depressed at the state of God's people; God is in control and may raise up an Asa. We are not to take the route of idolatry which runs into a dead end. We are not to be intimidated by worldly power, even if it as impressive as Omri and Ahab.

Ideas for application

+ Life often seems a series of unrelated events without discernible pattern. The conviction that the Lord rules history helps people to keep on going.

+ Idolatry is futile and silly; hence the references here to 'worthless idols'. This is why the 'achievements' of various kings count for nothing because their houses have been built on sand. That is a problem for all of us when things, often right in themselves, begin to dominate our attitudes and lifestyle.

+ The power of the living Word is independent of the individuals who speak and operates long after they have gone, illustrated most strikingly here by the Word Yahweh spoke through Joshua (16:34).

+ We need to be realistic about our own weaknesses; Asa was a good king but he had flaws and, although he was a man of faith, he sometimes walked by sight. This emphasizes that the kingdom does not ultimately depend on our faith but on God's faithfulness.

+ However, in Asa we have a glimpse of the king and the kingdom to come. However imperfectly, this son of David points to David's Greater Son.

Preaching Christ faithfully (chapters 12 to 16)

The situation deteriorates rapidly with the tearing apart of the northern and southern kingdoms, faithless kings and false prophets. There is to be a serious concern in the prophets for the unity of God's people, for example in Ezekiel 37:15-28 where Judah and Israel are to be reunited and 'my servant David will be king over them and they will all have one shepherd'. This anticipates John 10:16 – 'one flock and one shepherd' – and John 17:20, where Jesus prays for the unity of His people.

These chapters show a depressing cluster of false shepherds, both in bad kings and false prophets (especially chapter 13), which points to the need for the true Shepherd. Yet in the midst of all this depressing scenario we have glimpses of true shepherds, imperfect as they are. There is the man of God from Judah (ch. 13); the prophet Ahijah (ch. 14) and King Asa (ch. 15). Neither the malevolence of bad shepherds nor the limitations of true shepherds can prevent the coming of the good Shepherd.

Suggestions for preaching
There is a lot of material here, and if preachers tackle both chapters they cannot pick up every detail. First, here is a suggestion for tackling the two chapters together.

Sermon 1
This sermon takes up the broad themes already mentioned of God's control of history and human chaos.

+ **The futile choices of humans:** This would underline that, although God controls everything, humans are not puppets and are responsible for the choices they make and the ways they follow:

    + Foolish idolatry. We see the slavish copying of Jeroboam's ways, although no doubt it is described as new and liberated.

    + Unstable government. The fall of two dynasties and short-lived and ineffective kings are inextricably linked with idolatry and weak personalities, e.g. Elah's drunkenness (16:9) or Zimri's failure to secure his power base (16:16).

    + Firm but godless government. Omri and Ahab did not share the futile ineffectiveness of Elah and Zimri, but their otherwise impressive achievements are neutralized by massive idolatry.

+ Sin is multi-coloured but underneath it ends in death and leaves a bitter legacy.

+ **The overriding providence of God:** Joseph's words 'God meant it for good' (Gen. 50:20) could be written over these stories. Without being compromised by evil, God works everything into His perfect plan to bring in the kingdom:

+ Emphasis on the promise to David (15:3-5). This promise effectively dominates the rest of the Kings story; his sons may be a bad lot and will suffer but David's kingdom will come.

+ The unexpected appearance of a Davidic king (15:9-24). Even in the dark days of the five kings of Israel who were his contemporaries, Asa is a lamp in Jerusalem. Like David himself, he was flawed but faithful.

+ The persistence of the Word of God. The text contains prophetic words from Jehu (16:1-7) and Joshua (16:34); God's Word will accomplish His purpose (Isa. 55:11).

Sermon 2

As already suggested, it would be possible to divide the material differently and take 14:21–15:8 and look at the end of Rehoboam's reign and Abijah's reign together. Probably we could take the title from 15:4 –*A lamp in Jerusalem* – the emphasis here is on Judah and Jerusalem.

+ Judgment is certain:

    + Judgment is anticipated in lesser judgments such as Shishak's invasion (14:25-28).

    + Exile is threatened (14:24). There is a suggestion that Judah will suffer the same fate as the Canaanites.

    + War is perpetual, not for the sake of the kingdom but due to internecine rivalry (15:6).

+ **The kingdom will come**, especially 15:3-5:

    + Grace is greater than sin – 'Uriah the Hittite'.

    + Keeping the commands – compare John 15:14, 'You are my friends if you do what I command'.

    + God keeps His promises, so trust and obey.

The rest of the chapters could be covered in much the way suggested in Sermon 1.

Sermon 3

The story of Asa (15:9-24) could be treated as a sermon on its own with some such title as *God's unexpected grace*:

+ **A zealous reformer** (15:11-15). Asa feared neither the establishment nor was he influenced by family ties as he pursued a vigorous clearing out of idolatry and positive support of the temple.

+ **A shrewd diplomat** (15:16-22). This may be good politics but it represents a stepping back from the high ground of faith.

+ **An ambiguous end** (15:23-24). Asa was flawed but gave stability for forty years and was a true Davidic king.

Suggestions for teaching
Questions to help understand the passage

1. Why is David mentioned in 15:3-7?

2. What is the significance of the reference to the continual war between Rehoboam and Jeroboam (15:6)?

3. What is the effect of introducing the story of Asa at this point (15:4)?

4. What is the final assessment of Asa?

5. Why was the whole of Jeroboam's dynasty destroyed (15:29-30)?

6. What is the author saying about the state of Israel in 16:1-20 and the lack of firm leadership?

7. How does the author build up a double portrait of Omri (16:21-27)?

8. How does the author in a few verses (16:29-34) show us the kind of man Ahab was?

Questions to help apply the passage

1. What do these chapters teach about idolatry? You may want to consider the implications of 1 John 5:21, 'dear children keep yourselves from idols'.

2. How does the Word of God triumph even in circumstances where it has been driven underground?

3. What indications are there that, while God is in control, people are still responsible for their actions?

4. What evidence is there in these chapters that sin, far from being glamorous, is boringly repetitive?

5. How does this passage show us that God's kingdom in Christ will surely come?

5

GOD'S COUNTER-ATTACK
(1 KINGS 17)

Introduction

Often in this age of sound bites, even if our business is preaching and teaching, we forget the power of the spoken word. At a critical period in our history, Winston Churchill effectively fought the Second World War with words at a time when there was nothing else to fight with. And what words they were! Even listening to recordings of them is a stirring experience. But if words are not simply human eloquence (as in the case of Churchill), but the words of God Himself, then they have the power to save and judge. Already in Kings we have seen a number of prophets and men of God whose words have spoken into their own time as well as into the future. Now the titanic figure of Elijah treads on to the stage, and the most evil of the kings is confronted by the most formidable of the prophets.

This is the unexpected turn in events referred to in the exposition of 16:29-34. Just as in Luke 3:1-2, the Word of God bypasses the imperial, local and religious leaders and comes to John the Baptist in the desert, so here the Word ignored by Omri and Ahab is to come in devastating power. This is the beginning of the long central section of 1 and 2 Kings which is to run to 2 Kings 13, Elijah dominating the story until 2 Kings 2, and Elisha until 2 Kings 13. There is more here than Elijah and Elisha alone, not least the courageous Micaiah in 1 Kings 22, but these men represent God's counter-attack as they bring His Word in dangerous times.

Listening to the text
Context and structure
The appearance of Elijah as God's spokesman thrusts the theme of the Word of Yahweh centre-stage. Elijah is to announce doom on Ahab's house but that does not come until 21:21-24. The emphasis here and in chapter 18 is Yahweh's response to the Baal worship Ahab introduced (16:31-32). This will be in two stages: the background in chapter 17 and the public contest in chapter 18. Elijah's name means 'Yahweh is my God' and this sets the tone for what follows.

The story develops in four movements:

+ Enter Elijah (17:1)

+ Strange providers (17:2-6)

+ Help from the helpless (17:7-16)

+ Life out of death (17:17-24)

Working through the text
Enter Elijah (17:1)
The abruptness of Elijah's appearance will be paralleled by the abruptness of his departure (2 Kings 2); in a very

real sense he came from God and went to God. The 'now' (Hebrew *waw*) could be translated 'however', showing that even as Baal seemed to be in charge Yahweh already had His man set to go. He is not reacting in panic; He is on the throne. The only piece of background we are given is that Elijah is from Tishbe in Gilead (north Transjordan). We are not told where he met Ahab.

What is vital is that he comes from Yahweh and brings His Word. The phrase 'whom I serve' is literally 'before whom I stand'. The prophet stands in the court of heaven where he hears God's voice and comes to humans with it. Elijah does not fear Ahab since he has stood in the presence of the King of kings. That word is one of judgment and echoes the words of Moses in Deuteronomy 11:16-17 and 28:23-24 where drought is a judgment for covenant disobedience. Thus already the battle lines are drawn between Yahweh and Baal. Baal, in Canaanite mythology, was the god of wind and weather, and now Israelites are going to see exactly what kind of fertility god he is. As dry day followed dry day and the grass shrivelled and the livestock died, Baal's reputation must have shrivelled with it. So right at the beginning of the story, before the great contest in chapter 18 we are confronted with the question 'which God is the true one?'

Strange providers (17:2-6)
Elijah is the first to be tested by the word he gives. Indeed it is the Word of God which is the connecting thread in this chapter and the bookends (vv. 1 and 24) underline this. This means first that the main channel of that Word is being removed from the public scene throughout the drought. So there is a double judgment here: the drought itself and what

Amos is to call 'a famine of hearing the words of Yahweh' (Amos 8:11).

For Elijah this is an abrupt instruction because Yahweh tells him where to go before saying how he will provide for him. Nor does a 'brook' or 'wadi' which dries up at the best of times seem a promising refuge at a time of drought. Moreover, the use of ravens as providers, which apart from being unclean (Lev. 11:15; Deut. 14:14) are more accustomed to steal than to provide, seems bizarre. But the key is surely verse 5, 'so he did what the LORD had told him'. He is going to obey that Word, however strange it seems.

Help from the helpless (17:7-16)

We might have expected that when the brook dried up, Yahweh would send rain; but no, He provides a widow. Widows were not providers; rather they needed to be provided for. Moreover, the command 'go to Zarephath' must have been about as welcome to Elijah as 'go to Nineveh' was to Jonah. This is going into the lion's den, for the king of Sidon was Ethbaal, Ahab's father-in-law. But not only is Elijah to be kept safe in enemy territory, God's grace is to overflow into that place.

The story is movingly told. Verses 10-12 linger over the details of abject poverty and vulnerability. Indeed, at first sight, Elijah seems to have added to her problems by bringing another mouth to feed when there was barely enough to feed the two already there. The widow's hopelessness is total; there is one scanty meal between her and her son and death. The pathetic hopelessness of her situation is told with agonizing detail in verse 12, and Elijah seems to be heartless in such destitute circumstances.

We see, however, in verse 13 that it is indeed Yahweh who is at work. How often in the Bible, the Lord or His servants speak the reassuring words 'Don't be afraid', words which bring hope that the situation is not as dire as it seems. This nameless widow acts on these words and thus joins the great cloud of witnesses who stake everything on God's Word and act believing that He is faithful. The widow does as Elijah says and daily finds new provision from a generous God. It was not that a massive supply of flour and oil appeared at once, but that every day, like the manna in the desert, the food was there, both needing faith for every day and showing new mercies every morning.

Again the Word of Yahweh dominates the story. That Word sends Elijah to Zarephath (v. 8); promises food (v. 14) and proves to be totally reliable. Yahweh has taken the battle into enemy territory and shown His power in Baal's heartland.

Life out of death (17:17-24)

We might feel that the widow's problems were over as day by day she finds the food has come. However, here we have a situation reproduced so often in the life of faith: a miraculous answer to one need is followed by the emergence of another and greater need. Indeed Yahweh's promise (v. 14) surely carries the implication that her own death and her son's death would not happen. Now the question is stark. Can the God who defeated famine, death's harbinger, defeat death itself?

The author underlines the bleak hopelessness of the situation. Verse 17 spells out the inexorable approach of death. The text makes it very plain that the boy actually died; this was not a coma. The widow is discovering early that the life of faith has dark valleys as well as sunlit uplands. It is hardly surprising that she sees this as a judgment of God; many far more advanced on the journey have reacted to such events in the same way. This is yet another example of the Bible's realism which refuses to sentimentalize the hardships of the life of faith. Our temptation here is to imagine that we would have been gentler than God and allowed her to grow in her faith before bringing her into such a bleak and tragic experience.

The story as it unfolds shows our author's character-istic blend of literary art and theological depth. Elijah enters the situation physically as well as spiritually, and not only prays but acts out his prayer by stretching his living body three times over the boy's dead body. This is not magic; this is Elijah the intercessor identifying himself with the boy and in his weakness crying on Yahweh to act. He is as perplexed as the widow (v. 20) and finds the ways of God baffling.

The symmetry of the story is impressive. Elijah carries up a lifeless body (19) and returns with a living boy (23). 'Give me your son' (19) is paralleled by 'look your son is alive' (23). There are in fact two climaxes: the raising of the boy to life and the recognition by the widow that Yahweh's Word is life-giving and totally reliable. Yahweh, unlike Baal, is not fickle and capricious; He keeps His Word and honours the Word He speaks through His prophets. Yahweh is Lord of life and death in the land of Baal as well as in the land of Israel. In Canaanite myth, the ferocious Mot, god of death, whose jaws reach from heaven to earth, defeats Baal (the good guy in that mythology) but he cannot defeat Yahweh.

This story points beyond itself to a greater Resurrection which will disable death and open the kingdom of heaven to all who will believe in Jesus. It is a sign, like the raising of Jairus' daughter (Mark 5:21-43), the only son of the widow of Nain (Luke 7:11-17) and Lazarus (John 11). These show the power of Jesus over death and anticipate the destroying of death which will bring in the new creation.

From text to message

Getting the message clear: the theme

The key idea is the power of the Lord's Word in circumstances of famine, despair and death itself. There have been many earlier examples of the power of that Word but now in the reign of the most apostate of kings, and with Baal worship in the ascendant, the battle lines are drawn starkly.

Getting the message clear: the aim

We need to have confidence in dark days that God's work will triumph. We can trust in the power of His Word to defeat unbelief and bring life and hope.

A way in

Consider the power of words for good and ill. If you say to someone, 'Will you marry me?', nothing will be the same again, whatever the answer. Or think of waiting for the consultant to tell the result of the scan and hoping to hear 'I'm glad to tell you it's not malignant'. Now these are human words; but if the words are God's words they are living and powerful and bring about what they state. In particular, the way the Lord uses the Word to convert and cause growth must be emphasized.

Ideas for application

+ Since the miraculous is to abound in the stories of Elijah and Elisha, this would be a good point to discuss the issue. There are two dead ends to avoid. The first is *rationalism*: the ravens who fed Elijah could by a slight change in the Hebrew word become the Bedouin; the neighbours rallied round and helped the widow with flour and oil; the boy was in a swoon, and Elijah gave him the kiss of life. Well, that's not going to fill anyone with wonder, love and praise!

+ The second is *sensationalism*: we need to expect such miraculous signs today and then people would believe, and the work of God would surge ahead. We need to remember that miracles cluster at the great moments such as the Exodus; here in the attempt to replace Yahweh by Baal; our Lord's earthly ministry and the early church in the first part of Acts. Here they are part of authenticating Elijah's ministry; but that accompaniment does not invariably happen. Jeremiah did not have such outward evidence. God in His wisdom gives or withholds miraculous signs as He pleases.

+ This is linked with another point about the Word of God. The gospel Word is not something accompanied by the power of God; it is *itself* that power (Rom. 1:16-17). We need to trust the Bible to be the Bible.

+ The place of prayer in Elijah's life is emphasized in James 5:17-18 where it is specifically linked with the beginning and ending of the drought. Here his prayer over the dead boy is mentioned. Plainly it is in the atmosphere of prayer that Elijah hears and obeys Yahweh. The sense of the unseen world is very strong, and Elijah is drawing his strength from a source other than the politicking and military adventuring of the last chapters.

+ We need to look beyond this story to the defeat of death and the empty tomb. The fear of death is a real one and only the glorious Prince of Life can give true hope. What happens here locally and occasionally points to death, the last enemy, being destroyed.

Suggestions for preaching

This is a powerful series of stories with the binding theme of the power of the Word of God and this must be reflected in our treatment of the chapter.

Sermon 1

This will focus on the change brought about by God's Word in the challenging circumstances of the chapter. A title like 'The life-changing power of the Word' could be used.

+ **Challenging the establishment** (v. 1) – the represent-ative of the King of kings stands before the king of Israel and speaks an authoritative Word.

+ **Bringing drought and coping with famine** (vv. 2-16) – first the judgment in the withdrawing of the Word as Elijah disappears from public view. Then miraculous provision and the widow's response of faith to Yahweh's Word.

+ **Conquering death** (vv. 17-24) – The Word of Yahweh defeats death and points to the day of resurrection.

Sermon 2

This sermon, while emphasizing the power of the Word focuses more on the prophet, using the idea from James, 'a man just like us' (James 5:17).

- **What kind of man brought God's Word?** (v. 1) – Elijah's authority is from the court of heaven expressed on earth. He is not afraid of the king.

- **What gave him his strength?** This may be a good place to talk about the intimate connection of the Word of God and prayer.

- **What did God do through him?** We see miracles of provision and new life and the response of faith.

Sermon 3

This takes 16:29–17:6 as a unit and shows the connection between the dreadful circumstances of Ahab's reign and the emergence of Elijah as God's voice for the times. A title could be 'God's Word challenges the establishment'.

Two broad points could be made:

- **The mess humans create** (16:29-34): the uniquely evil reign of Ahab; the worship of Baal polluting national life; the defiance of God's Word (see exposition of 16:29-34).

- **The remedy God provides** (17:1-6): the authority of God's Word; the authenticity of Elijah; the reality of judgment and mercy.

If this last outline were followed, then the rest of chapter 17 could be preached on along the lines suggested in sermons 1 and 2.

Suggestions for teaching
Questions to help understand the passage

1. How do Elijah's words (v. 1) show us that Baal worship leads to disaster?

2. What is surprising about the first way God provides for Elijah's needs? (vv. 2-6)

3. What is the significance of Elijah being sent to Zarephath? Look again at 16:31.

4. How does the author emphasize the plight of the widow and thus the apparent craziness of her being a provider?

5. How does the author show us beyond doubt that the boy is dead and not simply in a faint?

6. Why does Elijah stretch himself out on the boy?

7. How does the widow respond to her son being restored to her? Look especially at verse 24.

8. Trace through the story the clear emphasis on God's Word. What does this tell you about what the author is trying to convey?

Questions to help apply the passage

1. What does the appearance of Elijah tell us about how God responds to apostasy and mass unbelief? What might this have to say to us about how to respond to unbelief in our day?

2. What does this chapter teach us about the life of faith? We might think about God's unusual provision; the various challenges to faith as the Lord appears to give with one hand and take with another, and the need for daily faith.

3. What are we shown about the worldwide nature of the gospel? Study Luke 4:25-26 in this connection.

4.   What does this chapter teach us about prayer?

5.   In what way is Elijah 'just like us'?

6
WHO IS THE TRUE GOD?
(1 KINGS 18)

Introduction

In the previous chapter we had scarcely met Elijah before he was removed from the public arena and, first by a lonely wadi and then in a widow's home, had seen the power of Yahweh to relieve hunger and defeat death itself. Meanwhile the worship of Baal continued in spite of his manifest inability to send rain. Yet it was not enough for Baal to be privately discredited, he needed to be publicly humiliated because if the rain had simply come, many would have seen this as a sign that Baal had got his act together. Thus Baal has to be routed in a public contest with Yahweh.

As Yahweh's representative, Elijah now has to appear on the public stage and arrange for a confrontation which will not only prove to the widow of Zarephath that Yahweh's Word is true (17:24), but that all Israel will be forced to ask who is the true God. This is underlined in verses 21, 24, 36, 37, 39. This is a chapter about where our true loyalties lie and about the ever-present danger of idolatry.

Listening to the text
Context and structure

This is the second of three chapters which introduce Elijah as the prophet who is to challenge Baalism and its espousal by Ahab's apostate court. However, while chapters 17 and 19 are off-stage, this one brings into the open the stark choice faced by people of every age as the true God declares Himself. The bookends of the chapter are about the Creator sending rain: this is announced in verses 1-2 and reported in verses 41-46. The bulk of the chapter is concerned with the confrontation, first between Elijah and Ahab, which is the prelude to the greater contest between Yahweh and Baal.

We can divide the chapter into five parts including the brief introduction and conclusion and the main narrative from verses 3-40:

+ Promise of rain (18:1-2)

+ Elijah and Obadiah (18:3-15)

+ Elijah, Ahab and the prophets of Baal (18:16-29)

+ The true God answers (18:30-40)

+ Rain is sent (18:41-46)

Working through the text
Promise of rain (18:1-2)

Something of the frustration and hardship of the three-year drought is captured in the opening words 'After a long time, in the third year'. But the waiting time is over, and just as Elijah's first appearance to Ahab had heralded the drought, so this second appearance is to bring about its end. In both cases Ahab, like Baal, is impotent; it is Yahweh through His servant who takes the initiative.

Elijah and Obadiah (18:3-15)

Here we are introduced to the fascinating figure of Obadiah, Ahab's steward. His name means 'Yahweh's servant'; the parenthesis in verses 3b and 4 shows that his fear of Yahweh was no private piety but that he used his official position to save prophets of Yahweh from Jezebel's policy of extermination. He is a provider like the ravens (17:4) and the widow (17:9) – the same verb is used of all these activities. There is an implied contrast with Ahab: while Obadiah keeps people alive, Ahab is more concerned about horses and mules. Obadiah is not into confrontation, but works quietly behind the scenes to obstruct Jezebel.

The meeting with Elijah shows that Obadiah is not only different from Ahab but different from the prophet. Here there is a meeting of two very different kinds of individuals. Plainly Obadiah is afraid that his association with Elijah would cause Ahab to kill him and some see this as compromise. That is rather unreasonable; someone does not have to be a coward to be afraid of being killed. Obadiah had already shown his courage and no doubt felt that, by remaining alive and in his responsible position, he could continue to do a lot of good behind the scenes.

Obadiah is one of those faithful people who, in positions of responsibility, work quietly for God. Paul speaks of the saints in Caesar's household (Phil. 4:22) who in that hostile environment were keeping the faith. The times needed a rugged confrontationalist like Elijah but there was also a place for an Obadiah working faithfully behind the scenes.

Significantly the section closes with Elijah's oath in the name of 'the LORD of hosts', the first mention of this title of Yahweh in Kings. This is the Commander of the heavenly armies enthroned above the cherubim who is about to judge the false god.

Elijah, Ahab and the prophets of Baal (18:16-29)

There are two confrontations here: the meeting of Elijah and Ahab, and the stand-off between Elijah and the prophets of Baal. The key word in verses 16-19 is –'troubler', a word used in Joshua 7:25 of Achan who, by his sin, had brought defeat and disgrace upon Israel. Both Ahab and Elijah agree that Israel is troubled; what they disagree on is the cause: Elijah sees it as a failure to obey the Torah and filling the vacuum with Baalism. 'All Israel' (probably senior representatives from each community) is to be summoned to witness a contest between Yahweh and Baal. Baal is to be represented by 450 prophets supported by 400 prophets of Asherah. These were the prophets of Astarte, sometimes seen as Baal's consort, and the 'Asherah pole' was a symbol of her worship. The place of the confrontation is interesting: Mount Carmel, like Zarephath, was in Baal's territory. It was a centre of worship of Baal and indeed sometimes is referred to as 'Baal's mountain'. Baal is being publicly challenged in his heartland. The prophets of Asherah, like Jezebel herself, fail to appear and Ahab drops into the background as the great contest begins.

This is the place to say something about Baal worship so that we can understand clearly what this contest was about. 'Baal', as already pointed out, is in the first place a general title meaning 'lord' or 'master' and as such applied to a variety of gods (see v. 18). But here this god is the Phoenician storm and fertility god who was supposed to send rain and bring growth to the earth. But why was Baal worship so popular? Plainly there would be pragmatic considerations. Not only the 450 prophets, but all who wanted to be in positions of influence in Ahab's regime would find it convenient to be Baal worshippers. There would be traditionalists who would point out (as many liberal scholars have since) that Baalism was the traditional worship of the land (see Judges 2:11-13) and that Yahwism was an alien import. Baal worship, with its emphasis on the mysterious forces of nature: the power of the wind; the unseen processes of growth and the terrifying force of thunder and lightning would appeal to the sense of the 'other' – the unknown and awesome force behind the natural order.

But Baalism also appealed strongly to sensual pleasure and offered unbridled indulgence unhindered by any inconvenient moral demands. There was no Decalogue in the Canaanite texts. This kind of religion, then and now, is always going to prove a popular package. Probably, many of the people occupied a vague, sentimental muddle where Yahweh and Baal were simply alternative names for a pick-and-mix religion which appealed to self-indulgence and was comfortably lacking in a message of judgment.

Into this muddle strides Elijah who says, in effect, 'decision day has come'. The real question is not if Baalism is popular and apparently relevant; what matters is whether he or Yahweh is the true God. Elijah further shows this is not a matter of opinion – 'you've got your god and I've got mine' – but a matter of life-changing choice (v. 21). The true God calls to discipleship – 'follow Him'. It can't be Yahweh *and* Baal; it has to be Yahweh *or* Baal. There is a massive simplicity here: not different gods for work and leisure, for Sundays and weekdays, for life and death. The pagan heart is hopelessly divided (as Solomon found in 1 Kings 11:3-6).

As the contest begins, Elijah bends over backwards. He emphasizes the solitary nature of his stand as Yahweh's prophet; our opinion pollsters would have written off Yahweh as in line for total humiliation. Baal's prophets in their massed array are allowed a choice of altars and bullocks, and given the first go at summoning their god to demonstrate his power. The narrative is superb: its slow pace allows suspense to build up and we hold our breath as the tension mounts.

An interesting question arises in verse 24. Why is it to be 'the god who answers by fire' who proves to be the true God? After all, the problem had been the lack of rain. Fire in Scripture is a sign of the presence of the true God in both salvation and judgment. Its appearance at the gates of Eden (Gen. 3:24) guarding the way to the tree of life; in the bush that burned but was not consumed (Exod. 3:2) and in the theophany at Sinai (Exod. 19:18) show that fire is a sign that Yahweh Himself is present.

The preparations of Baal's prophets happen in two stages. The first is the routine business of preparing the animal and the altar. The second is the increasingly frantic attempt to persuade Baal to answer. They start an all-day prayer meeting marked by increasing volume and fanaticism. They hammer at Baal's door, but Baal is not in. Elijah begins to mock them (v. 27): he tells them they need to turn up the volume. His words are deeply ironical, but they make a serious point. What kind of a god is it who is so self-obsessed that he will not listen to his frantic worshippers; who has to go to the little boys' room; who has left the district; or who nods off when you need him? Baal's prophets, probably grimly serious men with no sense of humour, take this advice with deadly earnestness. Not content with shouting and raving, they begin a mad orgy of self-mutilation and frenzy which goes on until mid-afternoon.

The stark comment in verse 29 is designed as a deliberate contrast to the noise and fury of the preceding verses. This wild and prolonged cacophony had zero result. And why was there no result? Baal did not answer because Baal did not exist. Outside of Yahweh there is only emptiness and judgment. The suspense is unbearable and we turn now to Yahweh and His true prophet.

The true God answers (18:30-40)
Now it is Elijah's turn and he is determined to show there is no trickery. He summons the crowd (v. 30) so that they can watch exactly what he is doing. His first action is to repair the altar, symbolizing the way to God through sacrifice. The twelve stones symbolize the unity of the kingdom (see Exod. 24:4: Josh. 4:1-10) and show the prophetic disapproval of the divided kingdom (see also Ezek. 37:15-28). The message of Elijah is to the whole people of God. This is done in the name and under the authority of Yahweh who rules in Baal's home territory.

Suspense is evident again as Elijah painstakingly builds a trench, cuts up the bull and orders water to be poured over everything. Some have quibbled at the apparent abundance of water but there are springs on Mount Carmel, so this need not be queried. Plainly Elijah's action raises the stakes: sodden wood does not burn so if fire comes it can only be an act of the true God.

Elijah now prays and it is a world away from the frantic ravings of Baal's prophets. He calls on Yahweh, the covenant, keeping God, Lord of the past, who had revealed Himself to the patriarchs. But he knows that Yahweh is also God of the present and asks for vindication, not for his own sake but that people will know that Yahweh is truly God. He prays that there will be a radical conversion as the people turn in allegiance to the true God.

Then, dramatically and spectacularly, fire falls from heaven. This is the authentic sign that the God of Israel is present. The same thing had happened after the ordination of Aaron and his sons when fire from Yahweh consumed the sacrifice and thus showed His gracious acceptance of the sacrificial system. Again it happened when David sacrificed at the threshing floor of Araunah (1 Chron. 21:26) and declared it to be the site of the temple. This is underlined when Solomon's temple is completed and dedicated, and fire falls on the altar once again. Here the fire shows that Yahweh has accepted Elijah's sacrifice and there is a way back to God from the dark paths of sin.

The sign of the presence of the true God is followed by swift judgment on the prophets of Baal. Many have seen this as vindictiveness and fanaticism where Elijah goes beyond the divine command. But Elijah is not being personally vindictive; he is seeking to establish the Word of Yahweh as the rule in the land. Deut. 13:1-5 says that prophets who lead the people to worship other gods are to be put to death (as Moses himself had done in Exod. 32:27). We regard apostasy with less seriousness because we take sin lightly.

Rain is sent (18:41-46)

The narrative now returns to what has been the main theme of chapter 17, underlined in 18:1, which is that God *will* send rain. In a sense the dramatic contest on Carmel has been a digression (although a necessary one). The power of the true God has been unmistakably demonstrated but we have still to see His gracious provision.

Elijah here is an authoritative figure in relation to Ahab, but in relation to Yahweh he is a humble petitioner. He knows that God is about to send rain (v. 41) but he still prays. His posture – 'bent down to the ground and put his face between his knees' – is an outward expression of his total helplessness and dependence on God. There are suspense-laden moments for Elijah to live through as the promised rain is delayed and six times his servant returns from the scrutiny of sea and sky to say there is nothing. True, Elijah could have overall confidence in the words of Solomon's prayer at the dedication of the temple in 1 Kings 8:35-36 which link the ending of drought with prayer and repentance. Also in 18:1 he had Yahweh's specific promise that He would send rain. Yet there is still need for faith and believing prayer because the answer, unlike the sending of fire, is slow in coming.

There is mystery at the heart of prayer. God's promises are unbreakable yet He encourages us to pray for their fulfilment and thus gives us the amazing privilege of having a little part in the outworking of His purposes. We are reminded too that Elijah had no power in himself to summon either fire or rain from heaven. It is not his formidable personality and courage, important as these are, which are at the heart of the story, but that Elijah takes everything to the Lord in prayer (see James 5:17-18).

The other theme in this section is the impotence of Ahab, who has seen spectacular examples of Yahweh's power: sending the drought; fire from heaven. He is plainly a man in some awe of Elijah; how is he to respond? Elijah shows kindness in telling him to eat and drink. Then as heavy rain begins to fall, Elijah's earnest prayer is replaced by vigorous action. Again some have questioned Elijah running ahead of Ahab's chariot, as Carmel to Jezreel is some seventeen miles. The text makes it clear that this was no human feat – 'the power of Yahweh came upon Elijah' (v. 46). As Elijah runs ahead of the chariot, he symbolizes that the king must be subject to the Word of the prophet. Here the king is given a chance to respond to the Word of Yahweh and to reject Baal. The next chapter will show how he refused the offered grace.

From text to message

Getting the message clear: the theme

The theme is clear and essentially twofold. The first is what do we really mean when we talk of 'God' and how do we recognize the true God among the myriad competing voices? The second is that this is no mere intellectual ascent, but is discipleship: 'if the Lord is God, follow Him'.

Getting the message clear: the aim

The aim of the passage is to challenge allegiance of heart which is expressed in a changed lifestyle. We need to avoid muddle and imagining we can give allegiance to two 'gods'. The kind of God we believe in will determine how we pray and how we live.

A way in

We might use a football analogy and see this as the kind of contest where a team at the top of the Premier League takes on one heading for relegation. The top team is playing at home with crowds of cheering supporters and the away team have few who will bother to make the journey to see their team humiliated. Here team Baal is playing on home territory with all the odds stacked in their favour,but they lose and lose spectacularly. They have fatally underestimated the Captain who has come to reclaim His territory.

We might talk of the difficulty of hearing the voice of the true God amid the babble of seductive voices, not least on the Internet. We need to pray often, listen to God's voice and think clearly.

Ideas for application

+ At the heart of this passage is the need to listen to and obey the true God who speaks through His prophets. Daily, we are bombarded visually as well as verbally by a myriad of calls to attitudes and lifestyles which are alien to the gospel. Clear thinking and faithful hearts are needed.

+ This is related to the danger of Baalism. As Christians we find it so easy to feel detached from the danger of idolatry in ourselves as well as very adept in detecting it in others. We don't bow down to wood and stone; our churches are bare and plain; we don't have icons and symbols, and we are Bible people. We go to church twice on a Sunday and are regulars at the prayer meeting. Our personal evangelism is flourishing; our week is filled with activities and we are at the heart of flourishing gospel churches. All these are good in themselves, but it is so easy to become so involved in the things of God that we forget God Himself. Doing good slips so easily into 'God must really be pleased with me', and then we are thanking the Lord that we are not like other men.

+ This chapter teaches us a lot about prayer and here there is also the danger of making prayer itself into a meritorious work. There is a tendency to think that if we have all-day prayer meetings that God will bless us, and prayer is seen as emotional hype trying to persuade a reluctant God to work. Here, Baal's prophets held an all-day prayer meeting marked by increasing emotional frenzy without result. The phrase 'prayer changes things' sounds pious but is misleading. In fact, prayer changes nothing; the vital importance of prayer is that it places us in touch with God who changes things. The emphasis needs to be on 'the God who answers', not on the prayer. He does not always answer by fire (see chapter 19), but He answers and He speaks.

+ A further emphasis in this chapter is that all God's servants are different. There is the dynamic and forceful Elijah and the more diffident Obadiah. Both were needed and both are needed today; and many others as well.

+ The seriousness of sin and judgment are emphasized. We are probably horrified at the destruction of Baal's prophets because we do not take sin as seriously as God takes it.

+ This story points beyond itself. The fire fell 'at the time of the evening sacrifice' (v. 36). It was at that time that Jesus offered Himself to God as a sacrifice for sin and the fire of God's anger fell on Him as He took our place.

Suggestions for preaching

This is a long and rich chapter, and many sermons concentrate on the middle section. It would also be possible to preach three sermons; this will vary according to the length of your series.

Sermon 1

A title such as 'God's Word forces us to face up to our true loyalties' would put the emphasis on hearing and responding to God's Word.

- **Introduction:** to set the scene could make the point that the Word of Yahweh which withheld rain now sends it (18:1 & 45). It may also be useful to hint at the place of faithful Obadiah behind the scenes.

- **Who is the true God?** (18:17-21). The nature of Baal worship is both seductive yet muddled. Thus there is a need for public declaration of loyalty – the preacher might refer to Romans 10:9: 'confess with your mouth'.

- **How do we know who the true God is?** (18:22-29). The fire is significant. Other Bible examples include (as above) Eden, the burning bush, Sinai and the dedication of tabernacle and temple. Contrast this with the impotence of Baal in spite of the frenzy of his priests.

- **What does the true God want from us?** (18:30-46). Notice how the text emphasizes the repairing of the altar and believing prayer. We need to realize that sin is judged.

Sermon 2

A title such as 'The God who answers' would cover much the same ground as sermon 1 but the emphasis would be on the true God being the one who answers. For example:

+ **Introduction** – much the same as for sermon 1, although more emphasis on the God who answers prayer. The preacher would need to emphasize what is at stake (v. 21) and who is the true God. We will know because He will be the one who answers.

+ **Futile prayer:**

    + is marked by frenzy and fanaticism, and believing that multiplying words will bring results

    + is praying to a god who does not exist

+ **Faithful prayer:**

    + praises God for all that is past and trusts Him for all that's to come

    + expresses humble dependence upon God

    + believes in a God who listens and answers

Suggestions for teaching
Questions to help understand the passage

1. What are the implications of such a long drought (v. 1)?

2. How does the passage about Obadiah give us a clearer picture of what is happening in Israel at a time when Baal worship is rampant?

3. What does verse 10 tell us about Ahab's attitude to Elijah?

4. Both Ahab and Elijah realize Israel is 'troubled' (vv. 17-18). How do they differ in their analysis of the cause of that trouble?

5. Why is it necessary to have a public contest between Baal and Yahweh?

6.   Why is the true God the one 'who answers by fire'?

7.   What is the point of Elijah's mockery of Baal's prophets (v. 27)?

8.   Why does Elijah rebuild the altar and emphasize the unity of God's people?

9.   Why does he pour water on the altar?

10. Why does Elijah run in front of Ahab's chariot?

Questions to help apply the passage

1.   What does verse 1 tell us about how Elijah needed to live the life of faith in spite of the miraculous events of chapter 17?

2.   The mention of Obadiah shows a different kind of ministry to that of Elijah. Why do we need both kinds of leadership (and indeed other kinds)? How do they complement each other?

3.   What are the ways in which we easily slide into false worship and what can we do to resist it?

4.   Both Baal's prophets and Elijah pray, but their prayers are vastly different. What do their prayers reveal about the kind of god they believe in?

5.   How does our reaction to the killing of the prophets of Baal reveal our true attitude to sin and judgment?

6.   We have two very different responses to prayer here: the sudden and dramatic sending of the fire and the painfully slow sending of the rain. What do these teach us about how God answers prayer?

7.   How does this story lead us to Christ who won the great victory on the cross?

7

LOSING THE WILL TO LIVE
(1 KINGS 19)

Introduction

It is a regrettable human tendency to cut people down to size, especially if we are a little jealous of their status. In our churches we are not, on the whole, routing Baalism and riding in triumph over the land. Thus when we come to chapter 19, we feel this is an Elijah we can handle; he is indeed 'just like us' (James 5:17) and his much-vaunted faith is shown to be weak and inadequate, and he is a spent force. There is a tendency for preachers and teachers to go down two wrong roads and we need to look at these as a ground-clearing exercise before we come to the exposition proper.

The first cul-de-sac is moralizing, the view already hinted at. This view sees Elijah as a failure, who, having confronted Ahab and the priests of Baal, now runs in panic at a threat from Jezebel. This view ignores the flow as well as the detail of the narrative, and places the emphasis on the human response rather than the divine initiative. Elijah does indeed run, he does indeed despair, and we shall look at these issues as they arise in the text. Not wanting to die is scarcely an ignoble reason for taking evasive action.

The second cul-de-sac is sentimentalism. Elijah, we are told, needs to turn away from the fire of the spectacular and listen in silence to the 'still small voice'. Doubtless we do need rest and refreshment, and this does occur in the story but, as it takes a primary line, it takes us on a wrong track as we expound the narrative. Also the 'still, small voice' (an evocative but misleading translation) is brought into the wrong part of the story and seen as an order to rest, rather than a call to renewed action. We shall understand the narrative better if we study it as it unfolds, rather than approaching it with our minds already made up about verses 11-14.

Listening to the text
Context and structure
This chapter is a fine example of the storyteller's art and we shall look at it as it unfolds in four stages:

+ Running away (19:1-5a)

+ Food for the road (19:5b-9a)

+ Where is Elijah? (19:9b-14)

+ Roads to the future (19:15 -21)

Working through the text
Running away (19:1-5a)
A much more formidable antagonist now emerges; Jezebel has had no change of heart over the demonstration of Yahweh's power at Carmel and she sets in motion a train of events which she imagines she can control. She sends a 'messenger'; the same word is used in verses 5 and 7 where

it is translated 'angel'. Bigger things are afoot than Jezebel realizes, but for now everything seems to be going her way. In any case she is hedging her bets; if she was as certain as she seemed to be she could have sent an assassin instead of a messenger.

Elijah, according to most of the versions, 'was afraid'; an imperfect form of the verb *yare* – 'to fear, be afraid'. However, some manuscripts read a form of the verb *ra'ah* – 'to see'. In the imperfect, these verbs are easily confused and the text could mean he 'saw' in the sense that he assessed the situation and saw that nothing had changed in the attitude of the court, and thus took evading action. It is not a sign of spirituality but of stupidity to hang around to be killed when there is an escape route available.

However, it soon becomes clear that Elijah is not merely running away; consciously or subconsciously he is on a pilgrimage. Beersheba is not even in Israel, it is in the extreme south of Judah, well away from any possibility of Jezebel's revenge. He is on a journey back to Moses' country; the place where the great lawgiver met Yahweh. He is being prepared for a significant encounter with God. He is plainly exhausted physically, and drained spiritually from the encounter with Baalism and all this brings on a profound dejection (v. 4). He pleads with God to be the executioner Jezebel had failed to be. He is not so much abandoning his ministry as throwing himself on the mercy of God. In exhaustion he collapses under a broom tree and falls asleep.

Elijah here is a figure of genuine humanity and great vulnerability, as well as searing honesty. He is most certainly not *running* from God; rather in the desert he is determined to encounter Him even if that leads to his own death.

Food for the road (19:5b-9a)

If this were a film, the music would begin to sound more loudly and we would sense that something significant was about to happen. 'All at once' another 'messenger' appears, but this time not from Jezebel. Just as Yahweh had previously sent His messengers (ravens and a widow in chapter 17), now He sends another messenger. Indeed the very words deliberately echo the story of the widow's provision with a cake (cf 17:13) and a jug (cf 17:12, 14, 16).

It is important to notice that the Lord cares for the physical and emotional needs of His servants. He does not expect them to be superhuman and superior to the normal demands of the body. Elijah needs, at this moment, not a rebuke but food and sleep. This is a fine illustration of Psalm 103:14 – 'For he knows how we are formed, he remembers we are dust'.

But there is more. The second time a meal is provided (v. 7), the words 'for the journey is too much for you' are added, suggesting that the angel is anticipating and approving of the journey to Horeb. Indeed, we could go further and see the journey as arranged by the Lord. Just as the Israelites had been miraculously sustained by bread from heaven, so now Elijah is fed and sustained until he reaches 'Horeb, the mountain of God' (v. 8), the place where the Lord had appeared to Moses (Exod. 3:1). Horeb/Sinai are often used in parallel, with Sinai being the most prominent peak in the Horeb range. Far from Elijah running from God, he has now come to the very place where Yahweh is going to meet him.

Where is Elijah? (19:9b-14)

The key to understanding this section is Yahweh's repeated question: 'What are you doing here, Elijah?' (vv. 9b and 13).

Those who condemn Elijah here for his lack of faith take these as implied rebukes and argue that Yahweh is in effect telling Elijah he should be somewhere else, and that he was in dereliction of duty. That ignores the underlying thrust of the narrative, as already suggested, that it was God Himself who orchestrated this journey precisely to bring Elijah to Horeb and, like Moses, to meet Him and be further strengthened for what lay ahead. Thus Yahweh knew what Elijah was doing there, but Elijah himself did not fully know. How we interpret Yahweh's question is going to determine how we interpret Elijah's replies (vv. 10, 14).

If I have interpreted this correctly, then Yahweh's repeated question, far from being a rebuke, is an invitation to Elijah to be totally honest and pour out his frustration and hurt. This will prevent us from insisting that Elijah is nursing a bruised ego and indulging in self-pity. Thus verse 10 can only be taken that way if we have decided in advance that God's question is a rebuke. However, if we read the verse carefully we see that Elijah's passion is for the glory of Yahweh and only at the end does he come to his own danger. What appals him is that the people's hearts are wrong – 'rejected your covenant', leading to outward apostasy – 'broken your altars' and rejection of both message and messengers – 'put your prophets to death'. It is in that context that he sees his own peril. Even when he says 'I am the only one left', he is especially thinking of the public contest with Baal in chapter 18, where he indeed stood alone. This is the same man who confronted Ahab and Baalism, and he is raw and hurting. But we need to get this into perspective; most of us, if we are being honest, fear more for our personal safety and comfort than we do for the honour of the Lord. It suits us to criticize Elijah here; not least sitting writing sermons (or commentaries) in the peace and comfort of our studies.

Yahweh is about to pass by Elijah as he had passed by Moses (Exod. 34:6-7) and wind, earthquake and fire, as at Sinai, are to occur. In that lonely place these phenomena would have been terrifying. Yet God is not in any of these powerful elements. We would want to reject the view that God cannot appear in these phenomena, as He did at Sinai, and thus make this episode an implied criticism of the previous chapter. However, we should not go to the opposite extreme and expect signs and wonders round every corner. After all, we did notice in the exposition of chapter 18 that the fire from heaven was a sign that the true God of the burning bush and Sinai was present, but that the main point was that He is the God who answers: then by fire but not always, indeed not often, in that particular way.

The point here is that He speaks. Verse 12c – 'a gentle whisper' has been immortalized by the evocative KJV rendering 'and after the fire a still small voice'. We instinctively feel the power of these words but we must examine more closely what they mean. Literally the text reads 'a voice/ sound, a scarcely audible whisper'. This is something like Job 37:1–38:1 where Yahweh's coming is heralded by thunder and lightning, but then He speaks and that speech is revelation. The whisper and silence provides a space where Elijah can listen. Elijah is in no doubt that God is present, so, covering his face, he goes to the opening of the cave to hear what Yahweh will say, and this is followed by a repetition of the first question and answer.

There is plainly a contrast between the earthquake, wind and fire and the gentle voice that speaks into the silence. Yet the contrast does not lie in the marginalizing of the event on Carmel but rather in the fact that whether spectacular events occur or not, Yahweh's Word remains powerful. The contrast is between the times it is accompanied by outward signs and when it is not. We need to remember this when we give the impression that the Lord is more glorified when we make a lot of noise. That Word is now to lead Elijah into the future.

Roads into the future (19:15-21)

This section develops in two movements: God's new commission to Elijah (vv. 15-18) and the call of Elisha (vv. 19-21). If the interpretation offered above is correct, then 'Go back the way you came' is not an implication that Elijah was wrong to have been there in the first place. Rather, refreshed and invigorated, Elijah is being sent back to carry out his future ministry. God has further work for Elijah to do; he is not yesterday's man.

Before we consider how Elijah carried out his new commission, we must pause at what is probably the most striking feature of verses 15-18. These verses show us that the Word of God is more powerful than kings or nations, even when it comes in a quiet and unspectacular way. Also the Word is not just for Israel, but the whole world: 'anoint Hazael king over Aram'. This is to be a marked feature of the later-writing prophets who speak not only to Israel and Judah but contain 'oracles against the nations' (see especially Amos 1 and 2; Isa. 13–23; Jer. 46–51; Ezek. 25–32; Zeph. 2:4-15).

The reference to the seven thousand who have not bowed to Baal is reassurance rather than rebuke. The verb should be translated 'I will reserve' because, like everything else in this section, it is looking to the future. God will have His remnant and no Jezebel can prevent this. Further, Elijah would be reassured that his ministry was not a failure. This remains true; God will always have, and will always preserve, His people.

A common criticism is that Elijah carried out only one of the tasks: the anointing of Elisha. Two things can be said. The anointing of the prophet is more important than the anointing of the kings. It is by the Word that kings rise and fall. Also, whether it is Elijah or Elisha, it is the authority of that Word which matters. Indeed, in 2 Kings 9:1-3 it is not Elisha personally but one of 'the company of the prophets' who anoints Jehu. It was Elisha who prophesied the rise of Hazael (2 Kings 8:7-15). Thus it is not the identity of the prophet but the authority of his Word that matters.

So we come to the call of Elisha (vv. 19-21) and it comes in the context of his daily work just as it does to the disciples by the Sea of Galilee (Matt. 4:18-22) and to many another. We must not misinterpret this story by reading it through the lens of Luke 9:61-62 where Jesus says, 'No-one who puts his hand to the plough and looks back is fit for service in the kingdom of God'. There the situation is of someone who is uncertain in his discipleship and thus continually looking back. Here Elisha is about to leave his past decisively and symbolizes this by kissing his father and mother goodbye. This costly commitment is underlined in the slaughter of the oxen and the burning of the yoke, which is followed by a farewell meal. The past is behind him.

As so often, the answering of God's call does not begin with glamorous exploits but with serving: 'he set out to follow Elijah and became his attendant'. This is not the way we prefer; we love celebrity and the lure of the limelight, and following the servant's way has little appeal.

From text to message
Getting the message clear: the theme
Throughout 1 Kings, a major theme has been the relation between God's providence and human responsibility. Here that theme occurs with a particular slant. The kindly sovereignty of God is active even when His servants falter, and His gentleness and reassurance is given when these servants reach breaking point.

Getting the message clear: the aim
The aim is to show that God will carry out His will and call and preserve His people. Intertwined with that is the assurance that the Lord comes to His exhausted servants with help, reassurance and plans for the future.

A way in
We need to remind people that it is all too easy to condemn people for flaws and weaknesses as if we had none of our own. It might be useful to begin with James' illustration of the Bible as a mirror (1:23-25) in which our sins are plainly and painfully revealed. Often, not always publicly, we prefer to use it as a stick to punish others for their sins. Our love of moralizing would make a self-respecting Pharisee blush.

More particularly, as preachers and teachers we need to be far more honest about our weaknesses. We would, of course, rather call down fire from heaven than painfully and honestly express our fears and frustrations, and it would have to be said that contemporary evangelical celebrity culture does not encourage us to share failures and doubts.

Also, this story properly understood is a great blessing to those suffering from spiritual depression. To see that the great saints are people like us, and suffered from the same fears, frustrations and sense of uselessness as we do, can be enormously liberating.

Perhaps here as well we might humbly and reverently go to Gethsemane. There our Lord, facing the cross, chose to enter deeply into the experience of His most vulnerable servants, asking that the cup might be taken away and yet, like Elijah here, was strengthened by an angel (Luke 22:43) and went on to complete the task. The servant is not greater than the Master and here Elijah learns something of Gethsemane and Calvary.

Ideas for application

- ◆ The Lord cares for His people when circumstances are dire. We are not Elijah, but the care of the covenant Lord extends to all His people in every circumstance.

- ◆ This story is realistic about physical needs such as food and sleep and how these relate to our spiritual well-being. God cares for us as whole people.

- ◆ The Lord is gentle and yet wants us after a crisis, perhaps a serious illness, bereavement or emotional trauma, to keep going after rest and recuperation.

- ◆ God is always looking to the future and calling His people to follow Him there.

Preaching Christ faithfully

First John 2:18 tells us that 'many antichrists have come'. John specifically links this with 'the last hour', but even before Christ came such figures were around trying to destroy the kingdom of God; John himself argues this in speaking of 'that woman Jezebel' (Rev. 2:20 – see also 2:14 and

Jude 5-16). Here in Ahab and Jezebel's Israel, Antichrist reigns. However, Elijah, who foreshadows the Baptist, is raised up to confront him, with the miraculous events of these chapters pointing us to the signs of the Gospels.

Suggestions for preaching

It is probably best to take the natural flow of the story as indicating the main teaching points. Thus we could preach a sermon with a title like 'Down but not out'.

+ **God preserves the prophet from death** (19:1-9a). See how Jezebel thinks she is in control when she is not. Elijah is also protected from hunger and exhaustion, and God graciously brings him to Horeb.

+ **God probes the true situation** (19:9b-14). The Lord's questions help Elijah see the situation to its depths. We also see a demonstration of how God is not confined to phenomena, however powerful they may be.

+ **God points to the future** (19:15-21). There is a power in the Word over kings and nations, and power in the Word to call a new prophet, even when there is still work for the old one to do.

Suggestions for teaching

Questions to help understand the passage

1. What do verses 1 and 2 tell us about both Jezebel's power and her underlying insecurity?

2. How do we know that the popular view which sees Elijah as being cowardly is not right?

3. What evidence is there that God still cared for Elijah?

4. What is the point of God's repeated question? (vv. 9 & 13)

5. What is the reason for the wind, earthquake and fire?

6. How does the Lord reassure Elijah that his work is not over?

7. What does Elisha's response to the call show about the kind of man he was?

8. Why does Elisha kill the oxen and burn the yoke?

Questions to help apply the passage

1. What does the story show about the humanity of God's servants?

2. What does it show about how to handle people with spiritual and emotional problems?

3. Why are we so ready to denigrate Elijah in this story and what does this show about our attitudes and sympathies?

4. How does this story reveal how the Word of God works?

5. What does Elisha's call tell us about serving the Lord? How does this reflect or challenge our own attitudes?

6. How does the story teach us about Christ and His earthly ministry?

8

THE INESCAPABLE WORD
(1 KINGS 20)

Introduction

We seem to have left the atmosphere of chapters 17–19 and returned to the squabbles and intrigues of chapters 15 and 16. However, that would be to misunderstand what the author is doing in chapters 20–22. No less than chapters 17–19, the focus is on the inescapable Word of God and the responsibility of those who hear to obey. The central human character in these chapters is Ahab, and we are shown his repeated failure to obey that Word as it comes to him through Elijah and others. Chapters 17–19 have given both privately and publicly remarkable demonstrations of the power of that Word, but they repeat the themes of earlier chapters as prophets, named and unnamed, have brought that Word to kings, often facing opposition and persecution. So it is here, and as Ahab's story lurches to its sorry conclusion, it is punctuated at every stage by the prophetic voice. Ahab, by a mixture of

misplaced charity, ruthlessness and self-will forfeits his life
and dooms his dynasty to oblivion.

So, as we read this and the following chapters, we need
to be on the lookout for the persistence of God's Word and
the persistent failure of Ahab to obey. An important theme
is the continuing evidence of God's grace as the preaching
of judgment is a call to repent. The accepting of judgment
now avoids judgment *then*.

Listening to the text
Context and structure

The stories in these three chapters have a unifying theme,
but are not necessarily in chronological order. Often the
biblical writers group a number of incidents thematically
(e.g. Jer. 35–36 which are chronologically earlier than
chapters 30–33). Probably a brief historical note would be
useful here. This would not need to be part of our sermon
but could highlight the growing problem of Aram/Syria
which is to be the background of much of this story. The
general background is the growing power of the Assyrians
which is causing Aram to turn her attention south to try to
gobble up Israel, either by conquest or alliance, to form a
more powerful alliance against Assyria. Indeed, at the battle
of Qarqar on the river Orontes in 853 B.C., a coalition of
kings faced Shalmaneser III of Assyria. One of these was
'Ahab the Israelite' who supplied 2,000 chariots and 10,000
infantry. At that point, probably earlier than the events of
this chapter, Aram and Israel were in alliance. Shalmaneser
claims a victory, but this is doubtful because history tells us
he never returned to Syria.

In any case, the author's attention is elsewhere. We
already noticed in chapter 16 how the reign of Ahab's

formidable father Omri is dismissed in a few sentences, and the same principle operates here. He does not mention the battle of Qarqar, although it would plainly be a significant event in Ahab's reign. What matters is not the king's confrontation with Assyria but his defiance of Yahweh, shown in his persistent unwillingness to listen to the prophetic Word.

We can divide the chapter into four parts:

+ Shadow boxing (20:1-12)

+ Enter a prophet (20:13-22)

+ Where is God? (20:23-34)

+ The inescapable Word (20:35-43)

Working through the text
Shadow boxing (20:1-12)

Ben-Hadad is clearly out to impress and intimidate Ahab and takes his entire army along with thirty-two petty kings and their forces. His intention is to reduce Israel to a vassal state. At first Ahab agrees to his demands (v. 4) but Ben-Hadad, having picked a fight, is eager to continue it. With great bluster he threatens to reduce Samaria to dust, an unlikely claim because even the Assyrians were to take three years to subdue it (2 Kings 17:5). Ahab himself is not averse to a little bluster and uses a proverbial saying (v. 11), roughly equivalent to 'don't count your chickens before they are hatched'. He will need to do better than that if he is to drive the bully from his door. Yet Ben-Hadad is scarcely the terrifying figure he wants to appear. The little detail in verse 12 'he and the kings were drinking in their tents' illustrates this. Twice already the author has shown the silliness of would-be conquerors sitting drinking instead of preparing for battle: Adonijah as he faces Solomon (1:25) and Elah as he faces Zimri (16:9). There is stalemate here and the situation looks bleak, and Ben-Hadad is preparing to attack the city. No blows have yet been struck and the situation is full of suspense.

Enter a prophet (20:13-22)
At that moment the stalemate is broken, not by military action but by the unexpected appearance of a prophet. 'Meanwhile' (v. 13) does not really capture the nuance of surprise. Something like 'who should appear, but a prophet' might paraphrase the emphasis here. This unnamed prophet comes with something of the abruptness of Elijah himself (17:1). But amazingly this man is bringing good news of un-expected victory. Jehoshaphat was given a similar promise (2 Chron. 20:15) but he had asked Yahweh for help. No such concern is shown by Ahab here; this is entirely Yahweh's ini-tiative. This is grace, but it is also a challenge to Ahab to face reality. Why is Yahweh going to destroy the Syrian army? It is so that Ahab and the people may acknowledge Him as the true God (v. 13). This is a replay of chapter 18 and another demonstration of who the true God is. Ahab, characteristi-cally, is not prepared simply to accept the prophetic Word and has questions about the human agents (v. 14).

But the real catalyst here, as everywhere in Kings, is the prophetic Word. Notice the contrast with verses 2 and 5, ('this is what Ben-Hadad says') and verses 13 and 14, ('this is what Yahweh says'). It is Yahweh's Word which will determine the outcome of this battle, for it is his Word which has announced in advance what will happen. Pragmatically, two elements work in Ahab's favour: the element of surprise as the attack happens at noon, with

Ben-Hadad possibly mistaking them for a peace-seeking delegation; also the fact that the Syrian leadership was not not only drinking but drunk (v. 16). This leads, inevitably, to a sloppy and uncoordinated response from them and a resounding victory for Ahab, as Ben-Hadad makes his inglorious escape on horseback.

However, the last word in this section lies neither with Ahab nor Ben-Hadad but with Yahweh, who through His prophet. He warns Ahab that Ben-Hadad will return next spring and that preparation needs to be made. This is not advice, but revelation from Yahweh the Lord of history. God is giving Ahab another chance to return to Him and set the kingdom on a stable footing. The bookends of this section (vv. 13 and 22) tell us that victory and defeat alike are in the hands of Yahweh and that Ahab would do well to remember this. The challenge to king and people is whether they will return to Him and trust in His grace.

Where is God? (20:23-34)

The scene switches back to Aram and to preparations for the next attack on Israel. Doubtless, sobered by their defeat, Ben-Hadad's council plan their new strategy. That strategy is good: get rid of those petty kings, the ones whose idea of preparing for battle was getting drunk (v. 24) and replace them with real military men. Also mobilize a new army which would have more room to manoeuvre on the low ground. So far so good.

However, that sensible strategy is rendered null and void by their erroneous worldview. Yahweh, they assume, is a god of the hill country and thus ineffective on the plains. Once again the identity of the true God is in question. We have already seen Yahweh showing His power on hill country at

Mount Carmel in chapter 18 and in chapter 17 in the desert places and in a house of death. They are mistaken even though the opposition looks impressive ('the Arameans covered the countryside').

At this point we hear the third prophetic message of the chapter. It has three elements. First, the man of God emphasizes that Yahweh's writ runs everywhere. There is nowhere in heaven or earth that does not belong to Him. But second, this is not a message to Ahab; it is a message to Israel, 'so you will know that I am Yahweh' (v. 28). Essentially, paganism sees the world divided among territorial gods whose influence does not extend beyond their own spheres. We can mock this ancient worldview but how easily we slip into the same attitude. The Lord is fine in the world of church and conferences but not effective in the world of mortgages, humdrum routine and the frustrations of daily living. He is great on the mountain peaks of our experience but not so much stumbling through the valleys of difficulty and danger. Our theoretical theology often does not match our daily experience.

Battle is joined at Aphek (v. 26). The word simply means 'fortress' and is the name of several places. This one was probably a little to the east of the Sea of Galilee on the road from Damascus. The result, as foretold by the prophet, is complete disaster for the Arameans, as Aphek collapses around their ears. Ben-Hadad, recognizing realities, is quick to open negotiations with Ahab. His envoys wear sackcloth round their waists and ropes around their necks to show grovelling (and calculated) humility (v. 31). Ahab, for his part, although he has won, shows no sign of acknowledging that Yahweh gave him victory. Rather he is back at his old game of politicking, calling Ben-Hadad 'brother', a term from the world of treaties and alliances. It is not long before the Arameaen and Israelite kings are seated together in Ahab's chariot making agreements about carving up territory and economic arrangements. Plainly, if that were all that was at stake, the chapter could have ended here. However, there is more to come, and the final section of the chapter is to underline the dominant theme of the Word of God.

The inescapable Word (20:35-43)

Here we have what is in effect an acted parable illustrating the prophetic Word. The incident sounds strange but it is important to note that it takes place at the Word of Yahweh (v. 35) and is not a bizarre scenario dreamed up by the prophet himself. 'The sons of the prophets' are first mentioned here (see also 2 Kings 2:3-7, 15; 5:22; 6:1; 9:1). They appear to have been a group, perhaps attached to Elisha, who were possibly students or disciples.

The story has echoes of the lion incident in chapter 13 and again establishes the important principle that the prophet is not above the prophetic Word. The lion, here as there, is the instrument of God's judgment, and just as that judgment was a warning to Jeroboam, so here it is a warning to Ahab. What happened to the disobedient prophet is a parable of what will happen to the disobedient king. The very bizarre nature of the request to strike one of his companions with a weapon offends us; our natural reaction is to think that the prophet would thank his companion for his gentleness rather than condemn him for his disobedience. That would be a fair reaction if this was simply a silly game, but it is not; it is yet another way of Yahweh demonstrating how seriously His Word is to be taken and an object lesson to Ahab of how he will not escape if he continues to disobey.

The dramatic nature of the scene continues with the disguised prophet appearing to the king as a wounded soldier, doubtless assuming he would have more chance of gaining Ahab's attention as a military man rather than a prophet. There is irony here: the word 'disguised' – *hps* – is the same word used of Ahab (22:30) when he meets his death. Ahab is clearly annoyed at being consulted about such an apparently trivial incident of a guard failing to be sufficiently vigilant, and says that the soldier has effectively judged himself.

Then the truth dawns and Ahab realizes that a prophet stands before him who is effectively saying to him as Nathan said to David, 'you are the man' (2 Sam. 12:7). Ahab, by sparing Ben-Hadad, had effectively brought about death for himself and his people. He had failed as the hypothetical guard of verses 39-40 had failed. He also had been 'busy here and there' (v. 40) as he was fraternizing with Ben-Hadad. The comparison goes further: the wounding of the prophet is a sign that Ahab will be mortally wounded by the very Arameans he had spared. Some have argued that Ahab had no explicit command from God to kill Ben-Hadad. Yet Ben-Hadad was a ruthless and implacable enemy and letting him go free was not a diplomatic triumph but an action which would only lead to further bloodshed.

The prophet announces judgment on the king (v. 42) which is to be extended to the nation. Neither will happen immediately but the Word is sure. Ahab's reaction is significant. As he returns home, he is 'sullen and angry', and the recurrence of this phrase in 21:4 shows this to be no isolated incident. He is furious with the prophet, resentful of the Word of Yahweh and has no intention of changing,

From text to message

Getting the message clear: the theme

The theme (one which has run through the whole of 1 Kings) is that the Word of God is the decisive factor in both personal and national life. Here especially, it is the inescapable nature of that Word which, in every episode of the chapter, breaks into the deliberations of kings and the noise of battles. That Word can be ignored or defied, but it cannot finally be evaded and will destroy those who oppose it.

Getting the message clear: the aim

The aim here is to demonstrate the complete relevance of that Word in the very areas where it seems to have little effect. The captains and the kings, the politicians and the diplomats go their merry way, but the Word cannot be excluded from any part of national life.

A way in

It is easy to become completely discouraged as the growing tide of secularism seems to cover relentlessly the last vestiges of what was once a civilization based on Christian values. We need to remember the silent and mustard seed-like spread of the Word of God. There have indeed been times in our history when gospel values triumphed publicly for a time: the translation of the Bible into our own language; the work of Wilberforce; the Wesleys. More often, as in this chapter, the Word works in a hidden way but its ultimate triumph is not in doubt because it is the Word of the living God.

This also shows how the living Word Christ Jesus comes to people in His Word. He is persistent and keeps coming back until eventually rebellion and disobedience has gone so far that only judgment is left. It is not simply that the words are not believed but that the Word Himself is rejected. Christ for many has no beauty that they should desire Him (Isa. 53:2). Here in this chapter the totally discredited kingdom of the world is challenged by the kingdom of God and the longing for that kingdom increased. With Ben-Hadad and Ahab, we see how only King Jesus can sort out the problems of human kingdoms.

Ideas for application

+ The persistent way God sends His Word is an encouragement to keep on teaching and preaching it. People may ultimately refuse it, but that does not invalidate its power, which is the power to save and judge.

+ The universal range of the power of God is at the heart of the chapter, symbolized by the hills and the valleys. This means that wherever our ministry lies, whether the sweet and lovely suburbs, the thriving city-centre churches, the tough tower-block estates or pretty rural villages, the power of the Lord is present to heal.

+ We cannot presume to question God's judgments, strange as they may seem to us. We must avoid the trap of trying to be kinder than the Lord.

Suggestions for preaching

Sermon 1

This might concentrate on the prophetic words which punctuate the chapter with some such title as 'God speaks in many ways.'

Introduction – Whatever the tone or technique, the message is consistent: obedience leads to life; disobedience leads to death. This Word is persistent and the more often it is heard, the greater the responsibility of the hearer.

+ **The Word of encouragement** – centres on 20:13. God cares for His people and will defend them. He also cares for the honour of His name and wants His people to acknowledge that.

+ **The Word of warning** – especially 20:22. Victory must not lead to complacency, but depends wholly on who God is.

+ **The Word of judgment** – especially 20:35-43. The vivid acted parable demands attention and the story ends by the king condemning himself out of his own mouth.

Sermon 2

This could focus on the different responses to the Word with some such title as 'Be careful how you hear'.

+ **Glad acceptance – prophetic response.** This Word is announced to everyone: judgement as well as salvation, and the prophet is willing to risk ridicule for it.

+ **Narrow unbelief – Syrian attitude.** This limits the God of the Word and trusts in techniques and stratagems.

•   **Disobedient arrogance – Ahab's attitude.** He prefers
     diplomacy to obedience and appears angry and rebellious.

Suggestions for teaching
Questions to help understand the passage

1.   In what ways do verses 1-12 show the threat that is
     facing Ahab and Israel?

2.   Is there anything which somewhat diminishes that
     threat? Look at verse 12.

3.   What does the prophet say is the reason for Yahweh
     bringing about the defeat of the Syrians?

4.   How do we know the Syrians are to remain a threat
     even after they are defeated?

5.   What fatal mistake do the Syrians make even though
     their strategy is good?

6.   Why does Ahab treat Ben-Hadad so gently?

7.   How does the author show obedience to God's Word is
     so important in verses 35-36? You might like to reread
     chapter 13, especially verses 16-26.

8.   How does Ahab condemn himself as he condemns the
     prophet?

9.   How do we know Ahab rejected the Word of God?

Questions to help apply the passage

1.   In what ways does this chapter resemble chapter 18
     and how does this help us to see that it is about what
     kind of God we believe in and how that affects our
     attitudes and actions?

2. The warning of the prophet that the Syrians will come again (v. 22) is a reminder of the danger of complacency. What aspects of our church and personal life can easily lead to complacency?

3. Ahab decided not to destroy Ben-Hadad, but to form an alliance with him. What kind of dangerous alliances and accommodations can we be tempted by?

4. The incident in verses 35 and 36 seems bizarre. In what areas are we inclined to look for respectability rather than obey a clear Word from God?

5. 'Ahab was sullen and angry' (v. 43). What kinds of things provoke such a reaction in us?

9

MUCH ADO ABOUT NOTHING?
(1 KINGS 21)

Introduction

At first sight, it looks as if this incident is a lot of fuss about nothing much at all;: a stubborn and legalistic man refusing a generous offer. After all, initially at least, Ahab did not seize Naboth's vineyard but offered a generous compensation package: a trivial original dispute. But as we shall see, a passionate concern for God's justice is at the heart of this story, the concern which surfaces so regularly in the Bible of the God of justice and righteousness, nowhere more clearly expressed than by Jesus Himself when He said, 'will not God bring about justice for his chosen ones, who cry out to him day and night?' (Luke 18:7).

This will be our main concern in the exposition which follows, where Elijah again appears in a prominent role and where the Word of God again comes to Ahab. Here injustice as well as apostasy comes under God's judgment. Ahab's harsh injustice to a fellow countryman contrasts badly with his leniency to Ben-Hadad in the previous chapter.

Listening to the text
Context and structure
This is one of the three chapters (20–22) where Ahab is centre-stage and which culminate in his death. The opening phrase 'Some time later' is a common narrative device to move the plot along without specific notes of time. These three chapters, while moving in the world of politics and conflict, both national and international, have no less a concern with who God is and how His character is revealed than did chapters 17–19. He is Lord of heaven and earth, but cares about individuals and is concerned to bring about justice for His people.

The story unfolds in four movements:

+   Clash of king and subject (21:1-4)

+   Jezebel's plot (21:5-16)

+   Judgement on Ahab (21:17-26)

+   Ahab's repentance (21:27-29)

Working through the text
Clash of king and subject (21:1-4)
Jezreel was some twenty miles north east of Samaria, and Ahab had a palace there: Naboth's vineyard was adjacent to it. We need to see what is at stake here because Ahab's request seems reasonable and is presented as a generous offer. There is no threat of force at this point and no suggestion that Ahab had ulterior motives.

The key is the word 'inheritance' (v. 3) which is crucial to the way that the Old Testament understands the gift of land. This land ultimately belonged to Yahweh and the people who 'owned' it were tenants (Lev. 25:23), which is echoed in Josh. 13:1ff (especially v. 7) where Joshua allocates land to the tribes as their inheritance. There was not an absolute ban on ever selling land; the Year of Jubilee legislation (Lev. 25), says that in conditions of poverty an Israelite could sell land and services. Naboth was not in such conditions and thus honoured the Torah emphasis of land as an inheritance from Yahweh. Thus his refusal comes from faithfulness not stubbornness, and this is emphasized in verse 3 where his loyalty to Yahweh is what motivates him.

The attitude of Ahab shows his characteristic contempt for the Word of God. Again (as in 20:43) he is angry and resentful, and goes into a prolonged sulk. There may be deeper notes in the text. The vineyard is a metaphor for Israel itself (see Ps. 80:8-18; Isa. 5:1-7; 27:2-5). This image culminates in John 15:1-8 where Jesus Himself fulfils all that Israel failed to be, and thus the metaphor has powerful resonances. Ahab wanted to use the vineyard as a 'vegetable garden' (v. 2), a phrase which in Deuteronomy 11:10 is used of pagan Egypt. Without wanting to press this too far, Ahab wants to make Israel like Egypt. So often in biblical narrative, while the people, places and events are real, they throw windows open into deeper realities. In any case, the theme has now become familiar to us throughout Kings: attitudes to the Word of God. Here are two men, one of whom loves and honours it, and the other despises it.

Jezebel's plot (21:5-16)
Once again (as in chapter 19) Jezebel proves a more formidable antagonist than her husband, whom she castigates for being a wimp in imagining that the king needs to obey the law. Her dad, back in Sidon, had no doubt regarded himself as above the law. That was her idea of kingship. Ahab makes no mention of 'inheritance' here, it

is just a vineyard to him. Jezebel will have no truck with listening to subjects: 'I'll [emphatic in Hebrew] get you the vineyard.'

In case we have a sneaking sympathy for Ahab, his collusion in her action is underlined as official letters are sent out bearing his seal. So often tyranny and deceit are disguised under the language of piety ('cursed both God and the king') and if the reader wonders which 'god' is involved, then that is not specified. The establishment also falls in with Jezebel's wishes as this day of prayer takes place. The alert reader will remember how Baal's last day of prayer was a dismal failure (18:26-29). However, no fire from heaven falls; the false witnesses are believed and Naboth is stoned to death. This is often the stark reality in this world where the godless often triumph and evil reigns. Not only has a heartless establishment got rid of a good man, but spineless people have gone along with it.

Our thoughts inevitably turn to one greater than Naboth, who was also done to death on the testimony of false witnesses. Matthew's account of the trial of Jesus speaks of the two false witnesses who testified against Him, as our Lord suffered as Naboth did here. This is a powerful reminder that we have a great High Priest who walked the way of suffering and death, and calls His people to the way of the cross. Yet it is still a bleak story and we may ask where is the God of justice as the curtain falls on Naboth's life and Ahab now has the vineyard. Both Jezebel and Ahab probably feel the matter is closed; they have no regard for the law of God.

Judgment on Ahab (21:17-26)
But, with dramatic suddenness, the narrative changes course; the word of Jezebel is again challenged by the Word

of Yahweh. In verse 7, she had said to Ahab 'get up' but here it is Yahweh telling Elijah to 'get up' and deliver the Word which judges kings and overrules all other judgments. This consistent theme of Kings is at the forefront again, and as Elijah comes centre-stage once more we are reminded that the identity of the true God has been at the very heart of the narrative since his first dramatic appearance (17:1). This is underlined by the phrase 'Ahab king of Israel, who rules in Samaria'; Ahab may indeed rule in Samaria but Yahweh reigns in heaven and earth and the Word through his prophet 'sets up kings and deposes them' (Dan. 2:21). This Word uncovers all evasions and subterfuges, 'Have you not murdered a man and seized his property?'; Ahab is as guilty as Jezebel.

The confrontation between Ahab and Elijah recalls that earlier one, 'is that you, you troubler of Israel?' (18:17) and now, as then, judgment is announced. The immediate fulfilment of verse 19 is to happen in the next chapter (22:38) but the sentence extends to his whole house. 2 Kings 9 and 10 is going to tell the grim tale of how Jehu is to wipe out Ahab's dynasty and Jezebel is to meet the grisly end predicted here (2 Kings 9:30-37). Ahab's guilt is underlined as similar to that of Jeroboam who caused Israel to sin. In this connection, it is important to see the parenthetical verses 25-26 in case we might have some misplaced sympathy for Ahab. He is presented as uniquely bad, even by the abysmal standard of most of the Israelite kings. He didn't blunder weakly into sin, 'he sold himself to do evil'. He gave in to the deadly promptings of his wife. He reintroduced the massive idolatry of the pre-Conquest inhabitants of the land. This means he is ripe for judgment.

Ahab's repentance (21:27-29)

This story of twists and turns has yet another surprise for us, or rather two surprises. The first is Ahab's response of abject repentance; the other is Yahweh's response to Ahab. Was Ahab's repentance sincere? To that we can probably answer 'yes' and 'no'; yes, in the sense that in that moment he probably did feel the terrors of law and of God, but no, in the sense that it was not lasting, as we shall see in the next chapter.

What is more interesting is Yahweh's response, which comes in a further message to Elijah – a Word of mercy and patience. We need to notice that Yahweh does not withdraw judgment but postpones it. Ahab's evil has sealed the fate of his dynasty but Yahweh, who delights in mercy, responds to his repentance, however partial. After all, how many of us can honestly say that our moments of repentance are permanent? However, we must suppose that if Ahab's repentance had continued Yahweh would have shown further grace. This chapter shows vividly both God's stern judgment on the unrepentant and His patience with any repentant sinner, even one like Ahab.

From text to message

Getting the message clear: the theme

In the overall story of Kings, the power of the Word of God is at the centre. Here it is particularly that Word which brings justice and judgment. God is no indifferent spectator and cares passionately about justice. Ultimately there will be a new world in which righteousness reigns and the poor and needy will be safe.

Getting the message clear: the aim
God is a God who judges righteously but also loves mercy. Both aspects are prominent in this chapter and neither cancels out the other. The story is realistic; there is persecution and trouble in this world, and the prophetic Word is needed to make sense of this.

A way in
When people are in real trouble, what kind of God do they need to believe in? Obviously we need to know God's love in time of trial but that is not the emphasis of this passage. Yahweh is not a tame God. This is the God of Amos 1:2 who roars from Zion and confronts the giant evils of the world. This is the God whose Word overthrows kingdoms and tyrants.

Ideas for application

+ Although this seems to be a petty dispute, it is at heart about people's attitude to the promised land as the gift of Yahweh, which recalls Eden and looks forward to the new creation. As we anticipate that new heaven and earth, we need to remember that the land of Israel was a genuine anticipation of that, inevitably flawed but pointing forward to the kingdom where all injustice is banished.

+ Not all evil is done by malevolent people; much damage is done by those who let them get away with it.

+ God loves mercy and offers it even to those who seem to have gone beyond the limit.

+ God's servants often have to walk the way of false accusation and even death, as their Lord did.

Suggestions for preaching
Sermon 1
We could follow the narrative as it unfolds under the title 'The Word which brings justice'. Like chapters 17–20 we see here a concern about the kind of God Yahweh is: here the focus is justice.

+ **God seems to allow injustice to triumph** (21:1-16). Hearers need to understand what is at stake – the importance of inheritance and land belonging to Yahweh. This is a case of the establishment hitting back – again on the initiative of Jezebel but Ahab colludes –the triumph of a heartless regime. But …

+ **God judges injustice** (21:17-26). The Word judges Ahab and his dynasty and thus controls the future – even so, God is rich in mercy.

Sermon 2
It would also be possible to see this passage as responses to the Word of God with some such title as 'The Word which judges and saves'. An outline would be:

+ **The Word taken seriously** – Naboth's loyalty to the Torah.

+ **The Word trampled underfoot** – Jezebel supported by Ahab and an indifferent establishment.

+ **The Word bringing justice and mercy** – judgment inevitable but can be delayed by repentance.

Suggestions for teaching

Questions to help understand the passage

1. Why is Naboth unwilling even to discuss the sale of his vineyard?

2. What do verses 4 and 7 tell us about the character of Ahab and about his suitability to be king?

3. How does verse 9 show us that Jezebel is confident she will get her own way?

4. How do verses 14-16 show that neither Ahab nor Jezebel give a thought to the death of Naboth?

5. How does Elijah's confrontation with Ahab here remind us of earlier confrontations? (17:1; 18:16-19)

6. What do verses 25 and 26 add to the story?

7. How does God respond to Ahab's repentance?

Questions to help apply the passage

1. Naboth refuses to sell his vineyard because of his loyalty to the Word of God. What areas in our personal and communal lives show the extent of our loyalty to that Word?

2. Ahab and Jezebel are both examples of bad leadership. How do we recognize and guard against bad leadership?

3. This story shows that injustice often triumphs for a time. How does a robust doctrine of the new creation help us to deal with this?

4. Often cowards help bullies to get away with it. How do we deal with this in our fellowships?

5.   What do Elijah's words to Ahab reveal about the power of the Word of God in the future as well as the present?

6.   What can we learn from Ahab's repentance and God's response to it?

10

THE LIVING AND POWERFUL WORD
(1 KINGS 22)

Introduction

So far, the godless reign of Ahab has continued and seemed to survive all the prophetic warnings and denunciations. But the day of reckoning has come, and the Word Ahab has defied is about to destroy him. This is the third of this cluster of chapters (20–22) where Ahab has been challenged by an unknown prophet (20:35ff), by Elijah (21:17ff) and now Micaiah (22:17ff). Indeed, this has been the emphasis of the whole Ahab narrative since Elijah first confronted him (17:1). In fact, it has been the emphasis of the whole book since David's charge to Solomon to obey the words of Moses (2:2-4). Thereafter, a host of prophets, named and unnamed, have spoken to kings, calling them to faithfulness and obedience. Now the most evil of the kings so far is to be brought to book.

The chapter is a long and rich one; a fine example of narrative with suspense, deft characterization and powerful theological emphasis on the living and powerful Word of God.

Listening to the text

Context and structure

The immediate context is the continuing wars with Aram which have been interrupted by a three-year time of peace, probably as a result of the battle of Aphek (20:26ff); here, however, Ahab provokes the battle. He does not realize that Yahweh is providentially arranging this to bring about his long-predicted demise. Thus the themes of power politics and the Word of God come together again and dominate this story.

We shall look at the narrative as it develops in a number of scenes:

+ Reluctantly consulting the Word of Yahweh (22:1-8)

+ Different versions of the Word of Yahweh (22:9-23)

+ Who is Yahweh's true spokesman?(22:24-28)

+ Yahweh's Word cannot be broken (22:29-38)

+ Yahweh's Word puts down kings (22:39-40)

+ Yahweh's Word partially obeyed (22:41-50)

+ Yahweh's Word totally defied (22:51-53)

As we look at preaching the text we shall consider the links between the main narrative (22:1-40) and the 'footnotes' (22:41-53).

Working through the text

Reluctantly consulting the Word of Yahweh (22:1-8)

Ahab here is picking a fight; if Ramoth Gilead indeed belonged to him there is no particular reason why that exact moment was the time for military action. Ramoth Gilead was a strategic town controlling various trade routes on the south of the Golan Heights, so often a flashpoint in more recent conflicts. However, it is surely significant that this military venture was mooted during a state visit from Jehoshaphat king of Judah. We are to meet Jehoshaphat later in the chapter, but it is worth pausing here to comment on the relationship between him and Ahab, a relationship which nearly costs the king of Judah his life (vv. 32-34). His son Jehoram was to marry Athaliah, daughter of Ahab (2 Kings 8:18), who was herself to try to destroy the house of David following her own son's death (2 Kings 11:1). Indeed, in the Chronicles account, a seer called Jehu rebukes Jehoshaphat after the Ramoth Gilead episode: 'should you help the wicked and love those who hate Yahweh?' (2 Chron. 19:2). Jehoshaphat was essentially a good man, but he did not know how to say 'no' and avoid compromising entanglements.

Here Jehoshaphat immediately falls in with Ahab's plan to go against Ramoth Gilead in rather extravagant terms (v. 4). Yet he is uneasy and says they will need Yahweh's guidance. This is the wrong order; the guidance should have been asked for before the promise was made. This is the essential dilemma of Jehoshaphat: he wants to be liked and be seen as positive but he also wants to do the will of the Lord, and these are not always compatible.

The request was no problem to Ahab, whose court was awash with clergy ready to give advice. The four hundred prophets inevitably remind us of chapter 18 and the identical number of prophets of Baal. They are, however, at least in their own estimation, prophets of Yahweh. The probability is that they were centred at Bethel where Jeroboam had set up his religious stall (12:28-33). They represented civic religion and saw their task not as challenging but as buttressing the establishment, saying exactly what the king wanted to hear. The lack of integrity is vividly exposed here; Ahab has already made up his mind and they know that; and they also know where their loyalties lie.

Jehoshaphat, understandably, is uneasy; there has been no advice, simply a sycophantic approval of Ahab's course of action. He knows that genuine prophets of Yahweh do not behave in that way. Perhaps characteristically, he does not condemn the court prophets outright and his question, 'is there not a prophet of Yahweh here whom we can enquire of?' is ambiguous. Is the emphasis on 'another' (ESV), in which case the words of the four hundred simply need to be confirmed, or is it on 'of Yahweh' in which case their veracity is called into question?

Verse 8 is tragic. Ahab is condemning the one man whose words could have saved him from disaster. He hates what Micaiah says and prefers to castigate him as negative and judgmental. This is Ahab's final rejection of Yahweh's words and, like many another, he rejects the message because he detests the messenger.

Different versions of the Word of Yahweh (22:9-23)
There is tremendous irony in verses 10-12. This unpopular prophet is to be faced with the pomp and power of the establishment. 'Dressed in their royal robes' is meant both to impress and intimidate. Paul faced a similar situation when King Agrippa and Queen Bernice 'came with great pomp' (Acts 25:23). So the two kings, surrounded by every sign of authority, listen as the prophets babble on. More than that, Zedekiah has a visual aid to symbolize the spoken

Word, which is often the case with the genuine prophet (e.g. Isa. 20:2-3; Jer. 13:1-6; Ezek. 4:1-11). Zedekiah can claim some biblical authority for his iron horns. After all, 1 Samuel 2:10 speaks of Yahweh giving strength to His king 'and exalting the horn of his anointed'. Micaiah is facing formidable opposition.

The messenger, clearly a man with no ill-will towards Micaiah, urges him to toe the party line but the prophet is having none of this (vv. 15-16). For Ahab and the state prophets, Yahweh's Word is merely an echo of their own worldview to be manipulated and modified as suits them. For Micaiah, that Word is authoritative and binding. The message is non-negotiable and the prophet (and preacher) had better accept that. We are not prophets, but when we preach the message of the prophets and the apostles we have no liberty to alter the Word. Of course (and this is the point of this *Teaching* series) we will work hard to understand the text and be creative and imaginative in the ways we try to apply it. But the content is not to be altered or misrepresented.

At first, it seems as if we have been wrong in our expectations of Micaiah, for his answer in verse 15 simply parrots that of the court prophets. But it soon becomes plain that what we have here is the prophet's frustrated sarcasm at the habitual failure of Ahab to do what Yahweh says. Ahab has made up his mind. Yet, like many superstitious people, he wants to know the truth not in order to obey it, but with some notion that he may still manipulate it.

Then follows the vision given to Micaiah which reveals the inward reality of what is happening in Samaria that day. Outwardly there is the pomp and posturing of the establishment: human kings seated on royal thrones

surrounded by pliant advisers. Behind the scenes, Yahweh
of hosts is seated on His throne directing the affairs of the
world, including this part of it. Yahweh calls for a spirit to
go and deceive Ahab so that he will go to Ramoth Gilead
and to his death. Verse 23 is powerful and fits with what the
Bible reveals of Satan as the master of lies. The theology of
this is set out in Revelation 13:11-18 where Satan uses not
persecution, as in Revelation 13:1-10, but propaganda and
deception. Many have got alarmed here and argued that
Yahweh is setting Ahab up. The reverse is in fact the case;
Yahweh is revealing to Ahab the way he is being deceived by
his own prophets. But Ahab is now beyond hearing, for he
has disobeyed and disregarded the Word of Yahweh for so
long that he is no longer capable of taking it seriously.

Who is Yahweh's true spokesman? (22:24-28)

The official court prophet Zedekiah now shows his contempt
for Micaiah by slapping him on the face. His question about
which way the lying spirit went is cheap sarcasm, but there
is more to it than that. Implicit in Zedekiah's words is the
claim that he himself is a true prophet of Yahweh and that
since he had not seen the vision himself, it could not have
been genuine.

Micaiah does not enter a war of words, but warns
Zedekiah of judgment. Verse 25 probably means that
Zedekiah would flee into an inner room hiding from some
future disaster. We do not know how this would happen, but
the clear word is that the lying prophet (and his associates)
would be judged, as would the apostate king.

Micaiah himself is to be sent to prison and we know
nothing of his ultimate fate. Yet, as he disappears from the
scene, his final statement 'mark my words, all you people' is

a reminder that this Word is for everyone there (including the king of Judah). The prophet's words, like all of Scripture, were spoken to specific people in particular situations, but have a power beyond that to speak to all people at all times. Again we have a servant who points to his Lord and is prepared to suffer for Him. He is called to go the way of the cross and show himself a true disciple, and to do so without any certainty of what his future fate on earth will be. As so often, not only in Kings but throughout the OT, we see glimpses not only of the glorious coming but of the Servant who suffers on the way to that glory. Micaiah points to the Christ whose suffering and glory were inextricably linked. (Luke 24:26).

Yahweh's Word cannot be broken (22:29-38)

The prophets have spoken, and the kings depart for Ramoth Gilead – which was Ahab's intention from the beginning. Yet Ahab is clearly uneasy; if he believes the words of his prophets, why go in disguise? Does he still think he can cheat providence? This is not the first time this dodge has been tried in the book: Jeroboam's wife tried to deceive the prophet Ahijah, but, like Ahab here, she cannot evade the Word which brings judgment. Meanwhile the hapless Jehoshaphat goes into battle dressed in his royal robes; surely never were such garments worn less appropriately. Indeed this almost costs Jehoshaphat his life (vv. 32-33).

Yet it does seem to be going Ahab's way, because the king of Aram has told his commanders to ignore the rest of the army and hunt down the king of Israel. Now that they see Jehoshaphat is not that king, they are at a loss, seeing nothing but ordinary soldiers. This is where we see clearly once again one of the main themes of the book, the interplay of God's sovereignty and human freedom, as an unknown Syrian archer shoots an arrow intending to hit another ordinary soldier. Yet God guides that arrow unerringly, and while the Syrian archer sees only an ordinary Israelite soldier, it is Ahab who slumps mortally wounded. The battle continues all day without, apparently, either side winning. The call to disperse (v. 36) appears to have been from both sides.

All that remains is to record Ahab's death 'as the Word of Yahweh had declared'. This Word had in fact been delivered three times: by the unnamed prophet (20:42), by Elijah (21:19) and by Micaiah (22:17, 23). When we add to this the earlier warnings from Elijah, Ahab had been regularly confronted by the Word of God. Some have wondered if verse 38 truly fulfils 21:19: 'in the place where dogs licked up Naboth's blood, dogs will lick up your blood'. However, if we take 'place' as a general rather than specific designation, we can see that for both it was outside a city. The Word of Yahweh has come true in spite of opposition, evasion and unbelief. That Word has put down King Ahab.

Yahweh's Word puts down kings (22:39-40)
Ahab, like his father Omri, was a big player on the national and international stage, and verse 39 gives a concise summary of the events and achievements of his reign. The record of these was in 'the book of the annals of the kings of Israel', which undoubtedly speak of Ahab in glowing terms. But the one record which matters, the Word of the living God, sees him as idolatrous and disobedient. What comfort will these long-vanished royal records be when the books are opened at the great white throne (Rev. 20:11-15)? That Word not only judges Ahab but every human being who ever lived or will live.

Yahweh's Word partially obeyed (22:41-50)

This long chapter ends with two 'footnotes', one on Judah and one on Israel. While lacking the strong narrative drive of the first part of the chapter, they are important staging posts as we reach the end of 1 Kings and prepare to enter 2 Kings. It was pointed out in the Introduction that 1 and 2 Kings is a unified document, but only so much could be included in one scroll. These footnotes, in their different ways, comment on the ground covered so far, especially the reign of Ahab, and thus form a pause as we both look back and anticipate the future.

First, we return to Judah and, apart from Jehoshaphat's involvement in Ramoth Gilead, we have heard nothing of Judah since 15:24, where the death of the king's father Asa is recorded. Jehoshaphat is to reappear briefly in 2 Kings 3, but here only ten brief verses recount some significant events of his reign. This contrasts with the Chronicler's treatment, where four chapters (2 Chron. 17–20) treat his reign in much greater detail, including chapter 18 which parallels the earlier part of this chapter. But many significant issues emerge in this brief 'footnote'.

He has not succumbed to Baal worship and 'he did what was right in the eyes of Yahweh' (v. 43). Admittedly this is qualified in that he walked in the ways of *Asa* rather than *David*, and he failed to remove the notorious high places. The note that he was 'at peace with the king of Israel' (v. 44) is an ambivalent blessing, as we have already seen. However, he was a genuine reformer removing the cult prostitutes, and thus establishing true worship.

There is a glimpse of Jehoshaphat's commercial activities facilitated by the weakness of Edom, which was probably subordinate to Judah at that time. Thus Jehoshaphat could aspire to maritime adventures from Ezion Geber on the gulf of Aqaba. But unlike the commercial successes of Solomon (9:26-28), the fleet was wrecked and the venture came to nothing. The mention of Ahaziah is interesting, and the implication is that his involvement spelled doom for Jehoshaphat's enterprise. This is made explicit in 2 Chronicles 20:37 where a prophet called Eliezer tells Jehoshaphat that Yahweh would destroy the fleet because of the alliance with Ahaziah 'who was guilty of wickedness'. Probably here in verse 49, Ahaziah had offered further help, but Jehoshaphat probably had had enough.

This was Jehoshaphat's Achilles heel: he was fatally attracted to the house of Ahab. We have already seen his naive acceptance of what Ahab wants (vv. 1-33). Then his son Jehoram becomes the husband of Ahab's daughter (2 Kings 8:18). And Jehoram was to follow his father-in-law rather than his father. His wife Athaliah was nearly to succeed in destroying the Davidic line. Jehoshaphat was a decent man whose personal love for Yahweh was not in doubt, but his personal piety did not carry over into his public decisions.

However, having said that, it is important that we do not miss two significant facts that give us hope. The first is that, instead of the unstable political situation in Israel, Asa of Judah had reigned for forty-one years and while his reign was punctuated with wars, it was a stable kingdom he left to Jehoshaphat who was himself to reign for a quarter of a century.

The other is the reference to 'the city of David' (v. 50). The Davidic king reigns and David's city stands. Weak and fickle as he was, Jehoshaphat was a son of David and dimly and imperfectly pointed to the true King who was to come.

God had not abandoned David's line and from it would come David's Greater Son.

Yahweh's Word totally defied (22:51-53)

There is no such hope in Israel. Ahaziah, Ahab's son, is something special in wickedness. We are going to read about his end in 2 Kings 1, but here we have a brief summary of his truly dreadful reign, mercifully confined to a mere two years. He is presented as the peak of all the evil that had accumulated in Israel since the time of Jeroboam. This was deliberate; he did not slide into idolatry but vigorously practised it, as we are to see in 2 Kings 1. He 'provoked Yahweh to anger', defying Him to do anything about it.

From text to message

Getting the message clear: the theme

The Word of God, often disobeyed or mocked, outlasts kings and kingdoms, and carries out what it announces. It may take time – indeed it often does, to allow time for repentance – but it is unbreakable. In particular, here it destroys one of its most inveterate and determined opponents.

Getting the message clear: the aim

The aim is to show the reliability of God's Word and the need to tremble before it, both on the part of preachers and hearers. The words of Isaiah 66:2 are particularly applicable here, 'This is the one I esteem: he who is humble and contrite in spirit, and trembles at my word'. On my bookshelves I have a book called *Trembling at the Threshold of a Biblical Text* by James Crenshaw (Eerdmans 1994), which is a collection of sermons. Every time I start to prepare a sermon or lecture, or indeed write a book like this, that title is a sharp reminder of standing on holy ground. If a preacher or teacher is conscious of this, then the hearers are more likely to be so.

A way in

Some may remember the powerful 1966 film of Robert Bolt's play *A Man for All Seasons* where the role of Sir Thomas More was brilliantly played by the late Paul Scofield. During More's trial, his former protégé, now his accuser, Richard Rich, is sporting a chain of office as newly appointed attorney-general for Wales. More says 'Richard, it profits a man nothing to give his soul for the whole world. But for Wales?' It was often commented on how Scofield managed to say 'Wales' with a powerful mixture of pity and contempt. Ahab has sold his soul not for the world, but for the doomed throne of Israel.

Ultimately, this story is about how our choices affect eternity. Our only reliable guide is the Word of God in all its uncompromising condemnation of sin but also in all its unconditional grace to repentant sinners. Our attitude to God's Word is our attitude to God Himself and by this we stand or fall.

Ideas for application

+ In this chapter we have dramatized different responses to God's Word: defiance, compromise and humble acceptance. These remain today and the consequences are portrayed here.

+ Jehoshaphat and Micaiah both believe the Word of Yahweh. However Jehoshaphat wants to avoid confrontation, while Micaiah accepts the risk involved in faithfulness.

- ✦ Ahab in many ways is superstitious: he defies God's Word but still is vaguely fearful of it and wants to know it so that he can try to evade it. That attitude is still widely prevalent.

- ✦ Yahweh not only destroys His enemies, but preserves His servants, even when they are compromised; He is faithful to His promises.

- ✦ How we respond to the Word of God is ultimately about how we respond to the Word of God, Jesus.

Preaching Christ faithfully

The focus of these chapters is on a cluster of political and military issues and the fate of God's servants in a godless world. Here the prophetic condemnation of Ahab continues: from an unknown prophet (chapter 20); from Elijah himself (chapter 21); and from Micaiah (chapter 22). The fate of Naboth and of Micaiah points to the fate of the rejected Lord. However, the fate of Ahab himself points to the final Day of Judgment and the overthrow of godless powers. The prophetic voices are a call to repentance and a foreshadowing of the day when Christ will judge the world. In the midst of it all, the brief passage 22:41-50 is a sign that a Davidic king is reigning that the line continues and one day will rule the world.

Suggestions for preaching
Sermon 1

This would concentrate on hearing the Word of God with some such title as 'Hearing the Master's voice'. The preacher should start by putting the chapter in context, focusing on the many previous warnings to Ahab and then concentrating on the three voices:

+ **The lying voice.** The court prophets are nothing
more than the ministry for religious affairs. They
themselves are deceived by the lying spirit.

+ **The uncertain voice.** Jehoshaphat is a good man
but finds it hard to say 'no'. He thus fails to support
Micaiah.

+ **The authoritative voice.** Micaiah speaks from the
court of heaven, which marginalizes the court on
earth, and is prepared to risk his own safety.

We could conclude by showing how the uncertain and
defiant words continue in Judah and Israel.

Sermon 2

The passage could be split into two: 22:1-40 as a separate
sermon along the lines suggested above and a separate
sermon on 22:41-53, where the emphasis would be on
the aftermath in Judah and Israel, with some such title as
'Moderately good and totally evil'. The introduction would
place Jehoshaphat in context and outline contrast between
Israel and Judah.

+ **Moderately good** (22:41-50)

  + Real if qualified obedience of Jehoshaphat
  + Unwise alliances with Ahab's house and com-
  mercial disaster
  + God has not abandoned David's house or city

+ **Totally evil** (22:51 -53)

  + Culmination of all the sin of the northern kingdom
  + Dangerously provoking the Lord

Sermon 3
Alternatively, the preacher could concentrate on the main characters and their motivation:

- **Ahab's repeated defiance**
    - Ignores genuine prophets
    - Sets up alternative sources of revelation

- **Jehoshaphat's flawed obedience**
    - Personal piety and political naivety
    - Wants to hear true Word of God, but not always willing to risk unpopularity

- **Micaiah's brave stand**
    - Lone figure but uncowed
    - Speaks from revelation
    - Puts his life on the line

- **Ahaziah's dangerous defiance**
    - Idolater par excellence
    - Does not simply ignore Yahweh, but defies him

Suggestions for teaching
Questions to help understand the passage

1. Why does Ahab want to take Ramoth Gilead and why is he anxious for Jehoshaphat to accompany him?

2. How does the author show that Jehoshaphat is uneasy about the venture?

3. Why does Ahab hate Micaiah?

4. Why do you think the two kings dress in their royal robes? (v. 10)

5. Why does Micaiah seem to agree with the court prophets at first? (v. 15)

6. Why is Micaiah unimpressed by the kings on their thrones and the massed ranks of the court prophets? Compare verse 10 with verse 19.

7. What in verse 24 suggests that Zedekiah sees himself as a genuine prophet of Yahweh?

8. What is foolish about the battledress of both Ahab and Jehoshaphat? (vv. 29-33)

9. How does Yahweh overrule in order to bring about Ahab's death? (v. 34)

10. What does verse 39 tell us about the author's attitude to Ahab's reign?

11. How does the author show us in verses 41-50 that, although Jehoshaphat's obedience was flawed and his alliance with Ahab's house foolish, he is essentially a good king and that David's house is safe?

12. How does the author show in verses 51-53 that Ahab's house is doomed and has learned nothing?

Questions to help apply the passage
1. How do verses 1-7 show the danger of a good man compromising with evil? Also look at verses 41-50.

2. How do verses 10-13 show the power of the establishment to overawe and intimidate? Where can we find such attitudes today?

3. Verses 17-23 tell us a great deal about both true teaching and false teaching. In what way does that help us to discriminate between truth and error today?

4. How does Micaiah show courage and in what circumstances can we follow his brave stance today?

5. How does verse 30 show us that Ahab is superstitious and how do we recognize such an attitude today?

6. How does verse 34 show us the interplay between God's sovereignty and the freedom of people and their actions?

7. What does verse 39 tell us about how to value achievements in this life?

8. The brief summary of Jehoshaphat's reign (vv. 41-50) shows us that we only make it by grace. How will this conviction shape our lives and ministries?

9. What does the brief mention of Ahaziah (vv. 51-53) warn us about how we ought to regard the Word of God?

FURTHER READING

Kings is better served by commentaries in recent times than it often was in the past. Older commentaries tended to focus on the search for hypothetical sources and were marked by a rationalistic dislike of the supernatural. Such commentaries, while often helpful on matters of language, are virtually useless to the preacher. Recognize commentaries for what they are: resources to get us more deeply into the text, and different kinds will give different kinds of help. A heavyweight commentary will give guidance on language and background, and help us not to base sermons on mistranslations or inaccurate information. Commentaries written by preachers will seem more immediately relevant but we need to be careful not to copy other people's sermons.

Three commentaries have been particularly helpful in different ways .

Dale Ralph Davis, *1 Kings, The Wisdom and the Folly; 2 Kings, The Power and the Fury* (Fearn, Ross-shire, U.K.: Christian Focus, 2002). This is a sparkling commentary by a preacher who has also researched the background thoroughly.

Iain W Provan, *1 and 2 Kings NIBC* (Massachusetts, U.S.A.: Hendrickson, 1995) – a concise running commentary which takes text seriously and is concerned with NT application.

Donald J Wiseman, *1 and 2 Kings, Tyndale OT Commentaries* (Leicester, U.K.: IVP Books, 1993) – this is especially helpful on historical matters but does not neglect theology.

Other commentaries which I have not used as I complete 1 Kings, but will use for 2 Kings are:

Lissa M Wray Beal, *1 and 2 Kings* (Nottingham, U.K.: Apollos, 2014)

Walter Brueggemann, *1 and 2 Kings* (Macon, Georgia: Smyth & Helwys, 2000) is often very perceptive on individual stories; less so on the flow of the narrative.

John W Olley, *Bible Speaks Today, 1 and 2 Kings* (Nottingham, U.K.: IVP Books, 2011)

Those looking for a detailed engagement with the Hebrew text can find that in the two Word commentaries. Simon J DeVries, *1 Kings, Vol. 12* (Waco, Texas: Word Books, 1985) and Thomas R Hobbs, *2 Kings, Vol. 13* (Waco, Texas: Word Books, 1986). Both are useful on language and Hobbs very helpful on history; however, DeVries is unnecessarily sceptical.

Those looking for more on historical background (although Wiseman gives probably most that is needed) could consult Iain Provan, V Philips Long and Tremper Longman III, *A Biblical History of Israel* (Lousiville, Kentucky: Westminster John Knox, 2003), a cogent defence of the historicity of the Old Testament.

PT Resources

RESOURCES FOR PREACHERS AND BIBLE TEACHERS

PT Resources, a ministry of The Proclamation Trust, provides a range of multimedia resources for preachers and Bible teachers.

Teach the Bible Series (Christian Focus & PT Resources)
The Teaching the Bible Series, published jointly with Christian Focus Publications, is written by preachers, for preachers, and is specifically geared to the purpose of God's Word – its proclamation as living truth. Books in the series aim to help the reader move beyond simply understanding a text to communicating and applying it.

Current titles include: *Teaching Numbers, Teaching Isaiah, Teaching Amos, Teaching Matthew, Teaching John, Teaching Acts, Teaching Romans, Teaching Ephesians, Teaching 1 and 2 Thessalonians, Teaching 1 Timothy, Teaching 2 Timothy, Teaching 1 Peter, Teaching the Christian Hope.*

Practical Preacher series

PT Resources publish a number of books addressing practical issues for preachers. These include *The Priority of Preaching, Bible Delight, Hearing the Spirit, The Ministry Medical, Burning Hearts* and *Spirit of Truth*.

Online resources

We publish a large number of audio resources online, all of which are free to download. These are searchable through our website by speaker, date, topic and Bible book. The resources include:

- sermon series; examples of great preaching which not only demonstrate faithful principles, but which will refresh and encourage the heart of the preacher

- instructions; audio which helps the teacher or preacher understand, open up and teach individual books of the Bible by getting to grips with their central message and purpose

- conference recordings; audio from all our conferences including the annual Evangelical Ministry Assembly. These talks discuss ministry and preaching issues.

An increasing number of resources are also available in video download form.

Online DVD

PT Resources have recently published online our collection of instructional videos by David Jackman. This material has been taught over the past 20 years on our PT Cornhill training course and around the world. It gives step-by-step instructions on handling each genre of biblical literature.

There is also an online workbook. The videos are suitable for preachers and those teaching the Bible in a variety of different contexts. Access to all the videos is free of charge.

The Proclaimer

Visit the Proclaimer blog for regular updates on matters to do with preaching. This is a short, punchy blog refreshed daily, which is written by preachers and for preachers. It can be accessed via the PT website or through:

www.theproclaimer.org.uk.

About the Proclamation Trust

We exist to promote church-based expository Bible ministry and especially to equip and encourage biblical expository preachers because we recognize the primary role of preaching in God's sovereign purposes in the world through the local church.

Biblical (the message)
We believe the Bible is God's written Word and that, by the work of the Holy Spirit, as it is faithfully preached God's voice is truly heard.

Expository (the method)
Central to the preacher's task is correctly handling the Bible, seeking to discern the mind of the Spirit in the passage being expounded through prayerful study of the text in the light of its context in the biblical book and the Bible as a whole. This divine message must then be preached in dependence on the Holy Spirit to the minds, hearts and wills of the contemporary hearers.

Preachers (the messengers)
The public proclamation of God's Word by suitably gifted leaders is fundamental to a ministry that honours God, builds the church and reaches the world. God, in this task, uses weak jars of clay who need encouragement to persevere in their biblical convictions, ministry of God's Word and godly walk with Christ.

We achieve this through:

- PT Cornhill: a one-year full-time or two-year part-time, church-based training course.

- PT Conferences: offering practical encouragement for Bible preachers, teachers and ministers' wives.

- PT Resources: including books, online resources, the PT blog (www.theproclaimer.org.uk) and podcasts.

Christian Focus Publications

Our mission statement –

STAYING FAITHFUL

In dependence upon God we seek to impact the world through literature faithful to His infallible Word, the Bible. Our aim is to ensure that the Lord Jesus Christ is presented as the only hope to obtain forgiveness of sin, live a useful life and look forward to heaven with Him.

Our books are published in four imprints:

CHRISTIAN FOCUS

Popular works including bio-graphies, commentaries, basic doc-trine and Christian living.

CHRISTIAN HERITAGE

Books representing some of the best material from the rich heri-tage of the church.

MENTOR

Books written at a level suitable for Bible College and seminary students, pastors, and other seri-ous readers. The imprint includes commentaries, doctrinal studies, examination of current issues and church history.

CF4•K

Children's books for quality Bible teaching and for all age groups: Sunday school curriculum, puzzle and activity books; personal and fam-ily devotional titles, biographies and inspirational stories – because you are never too young to know Jesus!

Christian Focus Publications Ltd,
Geanies House, Fearn, Ross-shire,
IV20 1TW, Scotland, United Kingdom.
www.christianfocus.com